The British Film Industry in 25 Careers

The British Film Industry in 25 Careers

The Mavericks, Visionaries and Outsiders Who Shaped British Cinema

Geoffrey Macnab

BLOOMSBURY ACADEMIC
LONDON · NEW YORK · OXFORD · NEW DELHI · SYDNEY

BLOOMSBURY ACADEMIC
Bloomsbury Publishing Plc
50 Bedford Square, London, WC1B 3DP, UK
1385 Broadway, New York, NY 10018, USA

BLOOMSBURY, BLOOMSBURY ACADEMIC and the Diana logo are trademarks of
Bloomsbury Publishing Plc

First published in Great Britain 2021

Cover design: Charlotte Daniels

A catalogue record for this book is available from the British Library.

A catalog record for this book is available from the Library of Congress.

ISBN: HB: 978-1-3501-4069-1
         PB: 978-1-3501-4068-4
         ePDF: 978-1-3501-4071-4
         eBook: 978-1-3501-4072-1

Typeset by RefineCatch Limited, Bungay, Suffolk
Printed and bound in India

To find out more about our authors and books visit www.bloomsbury.com
and sign up for our newsletters.

Contents

Foreword

*T*he *British Film Industry in 25 Careers* is the third book that Geoffrey has written in collaboration with the Film Distributors' Association (FDA), following on from the previously well-received *Delivering Dreams: A Century of British Film Distribution* and *Stairways to Heaven: Rebuilding the British Film Industry*.

Whereas his two previous works concentrated on the wider UK film ecosystem and the often overlooked distribution sector respectively, this latest read takes a deeper, more personal look at some of the key individuals who have featured in UK cinema over the last century and more. The cast of characters is diverse and covers many different career paths in the industry, including writing, producing, acting, distributing and publicity, as well as directing, prop work and visual effects.

It is not an exaggeration to say that no two personalities featured in the book are alike. In fact, as the various journeys are uncovered, differences are often quite starkly contrasted. Certain characteristics though do appear consistently across the myriad players, such as energy, commitment, entrepreneurial spirit, versatility, resilience and a driving passion to make it in the film industry. It also becomes apparent that film is an arena where social mobility can fully thrive and being an outsider presents little limit to ambition.

Each of the twenty-five careers presented here is effectively self-made. The individuals featured all found their own way into the film business, and once in, went on to pinpoint their chosen specialist field of work for which they are now primarily recognized and acknowledged by the industry and their peers. Not all of the tales are ones of glory, and often failure has proven to be as important as success for our twenty-five featured professionals. Life's ups and downs are considered in equal measure, with fortune regularly playing a key hand.

What this book does so well is to provide insight and optimism for anyone considering a possible future career in the film industry. Equally, it is for individuals already at work in the arena, though yet to fully hit their career stride. In casting the net wide across 120 years of the seventh art's existence in the UK, whilst also focusing on specific personal journeys, it becomes apparent that anything and everything is possible for those prepared to embark on a filmic adventure.

Recent technological advances, commercial opportunities and cultural experience all lend themselves to the ongoing development and growth of a vibrant film sector. Geoffrey has chosen twenty-five remarkably interesting character studies for his latest book, and such is the wealth of industry talent that he could well have selected an alternative twenty-five, with equally rich lives and fascinating careers. There remains scarce doubt that further compelling figures will emerge and flourish over the coming years.

The mix of archival research and contemporary subject interviews makes *25 Careers* both an informative and a breezy read. This book should appeal to keen film students, anyone looking to enter the industry or those who just have an abiding interest in film and the human condition. Having occupied all of those positions over the years, I can heartily recommend picking up a copy. We wait with great interest to see where Geoffrey turns his gaze next.

Andy Leyshon, Chief Executive, Film Distributors' Association

Acknowledgements

I would like to thank former Film Distributors' Association Chief Executive Mark Batey who helped initiate the book and provided advice and encouragement throughout the research and writing period, just as he had done on my two previous collaborations with the FDA, *Delivering Dreams* (2015) and *Stairways to Heaven* (2018).

Thanks are due to current FDA Chief Executive Andy Leyshon, who very kindly provided a foreword for the book as well as support and advice, and to the rest of the FDA staff.

I must express my gratitude to my editor at Bloomsbury, Rebecca Barden, with whom I first worked over two decades ago on a book about J. Arthur Rank. Rebecca has been as helpful with this project as she was with the earlier one. Thanks, also, to Veidehi Hans at Bloomsbury for her invaluable assistance with sourcing photographs and putting the manuscript into shape.

The indefatigable FDA President Lord Puttnam, whose eightieth birthday in February 2021 roughly coincides with the publication date of the book, has been very generous with his time. I would like to thank him for the interview he gave me. I would also like to thank all the other subjects who agreed to talk to me in depth about their careers during the writing of the book.

I would like to acknowledge the help I have received from the staff in charge of Special Collections at the BFI Library and from many individuals who have facilitated my interviews, among them Neil Watson, Alex Deller at Framestore, producer Ben Pugh, Stefana Dragan at MUBI, Emily Hargreaves and Will Wood at Multitude Media, Haylie Read at Film London, Charles McDonald, Liz Parkinson at the BFI and Jessica Bullock at the Wylie Agency. Thanks, also, to those who shared their memories about some of the subjects in the book: Susan Day, who provided invaluable material about her grandfather 'Poppa' Day, Dennis Davidson, Guy Collins, Martin Myers and others.

Introduction

This book follows the unusual, uplifting and inspiring stories of a selection of unlikely people from different backgrounds, places and eras who have made significant, often long-lasting, contributions to the UK film industry.

It is a history of the UK film industry told from an unusual perspective – that of various mavericks, visionaries and outsiders from all over the country who've found their own way into that industry. Often against considerable odds, they've built enduring working relationships and reputations to become successful producers, distributors, writers, directors, technicians, stars and, sometimes, even moguls. Some are household names. Others are far less well known and generally overlooked in conventional histories of British cinema, which focus on stars and filmmakers. What they all have in common, though, is that they found their own pathways into the British film business.

The book combines archive research with original interviews. There is no claim that this is an exhaustive survey. Countless other figures could equally well have been chosen. However, the twenty-five men and women profiled in these pages are a representative cross-section of the talent that has shaped the British film industry over the 120 years of its existence to date. They come from a wide variety of backgrounds and from every part of the UK. They've worked in very different capacities – it is an industry requiring a huge range of creative and commercial skills. Some have been involved creatively, in front of or behind the camera. Others have distributed or exhibited films. A few have had multiple roles.

It is a timely moment for such a book. British film studios were busier than ever before in the years prior to the coronavirus outbreak in 2020. Thanks to the production in the UK of everything from Netflix and Amazon dramas to Marvel superhero movies, and Disney live-action remakes of animated classics, space was at a premium.

Several new initiatives were being hatched to make the industry more accessible and to 'skill up'. In 2017, the British Film Institute (BFI) launched a Future Film Skills initiative to improve 'entry level diversity' and to create 'professional pathways' into the industry. The aim was to 'make it easier for young people to pursue a career in the film and adjacent industries; to create opportunities specifically for those who are harder to reach and who would encounter additional obstacles; and to enable film businesses to recruit a skilled workforce that is representative of modern Britain'. Together with other partners, Working Title, one of Britain's most successful production companies, launched the London Screen Academy in September 2019, a new school intended to provide 16–19-year-olds with the 'background knowledge needed to join the screen industries'.

Adrian Wootton, a plasterer's son from the East Midlands who, in 2020, was the Chief Executive of both Film London and the British Film Commission, likes to say that when he was growing up he no more contemplated working in something as exotic and distant as the film industry than he did of going to outer space.

Many of the figures profiled and interviewed here have expressed a similar bewilderment at their own successful careers in British cinema and how far they have come.

'Film is an incredible industry to work in; but it is not always an easy industry to get into. Access to a career in film can often be dictated by connections and obscure pathways: visible and open to some, but notoriously not to all,' producer and actor Gemma Arterton, whose own career began with a role as the head girl in *St Trinian's* (2007), remarked at a BFI fundraising gala in October 2019 to 'raise money to ensure young people from all backgrounds can engage with, learn from and be inspired by film'.

This book explores those connections and obscure pathways. Its subjects have gone on circuitous journeys. They reached the very top of their professions and yet still talk about themselves as outsiders and pinch themselves at the thought of their own success. This book reveals, in their cases, how it happened.

The subjects' experiences reveal how insecure careers are in British cinema, even for the most established figures. That was a lesson drummed home again during the coronavirus pandemic, when studios and cinemas closed down overnight in the spring of 2020.

At the height of his fame and influence, Ealing boss Michael Balcon couldn't afford to remain at the studio which made his name. Britain's most prolific female producer of the 1950s, Betty Box, was all too aware that she was being paid less than her male counterparts. *Chariots of Fire* producer David, now Lord, Puttnam was barracked at the British Academy of Film and Television Arts (BAFTA) awards by an older generation of filmmakers simply because he came from advertising. Julian Fellowes (the creator of *Downton Abbey*) was told by a commissioning editor that there was no interest in the 'class-based period drama' he specialized in. Isaac Julien, the young, gay, black director from east London, remembers the harshness with which his film *Young Soul Rebels* was treated by critics – a harshness they rarely seemed to show to debut features by white directors. Liz Wrenn, the American single mother who set up one of Britain's most successful arthouse distribution companies of the 1990s, didn't even have legal residency in the UK when she came into the industry.

Self-evidently, as noted, this is a history told through the experiences of a tiny cross-section of its practitioners. If the selection of subjects seems haphazard, that reflects the industry they work in. There isn't necessarily much pattern or consistency to careers in the British film industry.

By 2020, in advance of the pandemic, the amount spent on 'high-end' TV and film production in the UK was over £3.1 billion a year. Activity was at fever pitch and the industry was desperate for new recruits. Without them, the production boom which the Office for National Statistics in October 2019 credited with rescuing the country from a 'pre-Brexit recession' and 'pushing the economy into the black' might soon come juddering to a halt.

Painstaking attempts were being made to ensure that UK cinema had a more diverse workforce. Sixth-form colleges and vocational apprenticeship schemes were being launched. Film distributors developed a sector-wide programme of paid internships which, for a high proportion of its participants, proved to be a successful springboard into full-time employment.

The stories told by the subjects here are likely to be found both daunting and inspiring by aspirants looking for careers in British cinema. Newcomers are entering an industry in which punishing hours are commonplace and both salaries and job security can be stubbornly low. Progression through the ranks is rarely straightforward. As with many industries, the business has traditionally been centred on London, the capital city. In certain sectors, nepotism is still obvious. Even those who, from the outside, seem successful and at the heart of the film establishment often feel themselves to be outsiders. However, the luck, passion, talent and sheer tenacity of those written about in the following twenty-five chapters have enabled most of them to flourish, and exert lasting influence, in a world which they may well have considered completely closed to them at the outset of their careers.

1

Michael Balcon

The public dismay which greeted Michael Balcon's decision to sell the freehold property and studios at Ealing to the BBC was obvious. No one had seen it coming. Britain's best-known and best-loved film company was vacating its long-term home and seemingly abandoning its identity.

'The news about Ealing Studios hit the Street like a blow in the face from Rocky Marciano. This was one of the best-kept secrets in a trade where little of consequence happens without whispers getting round,' wrote Bernard Charman, editor of the *Daily Film Renter*, in his 'Wardour Street' commentary column the day after the deal was announced.[1]

Balcon tried to reassure the public and industry alike that Ealing Studios would soon have a new home. This new home wasn't going to be at Ealing, though. The 'stronghold' at which films from *Whisky Galore* (1949) to *Kind Hearts and Coronets* (1949) had been made was about to be lost. Balcon and his business partner, Major Reginald Baker, had already agreed that the entire contents of the studios would be put up for sale by auction.

It is instructive to read the exhaustive press coverage about the sale. National newspapers and film trade magazines alike queued up to express their alarm and disappointment that Ealing's very particular type of British films would no longer be produced at their old home in this 'prim little suburb of West London'.[2] As *Tribune* put it, this was 'a national calamity'. What made the sale

---

[1] *Daiy Film Renter*, 20 October 1955.
[2] *Daily Express*, 21 October 1955.

Michael Balcon. Photo: © Hulton-Deutsch Collection/CORBIS/Corbis via Getty Images.

to the BBC all the more worrying was the fact that the BBC and ITV had already 'swallowed up film studios at Shepherd's Bush, Wembley, Elstree, Highbury, Manchester, Merton Park, Hammersmith and Barnes'.[3] It seemed as if the TV companies were taking over the entire British film industry.

Ealing was regarded as part of the fabric of British cultural life. British cinema-goers were always predisposed to give new Ealing productions the benefit of the doubt. 'At previews of its pictures, there is always an air of expectancy amounting to an attitude that many are apt to blame themselves and not the film if they do not like it. It is incredible, but when their efforts do

---

[3] *Tribune*, 29 October 1955.

not come up to scratch, everyone, even critics, seem genuinely sorry!' wrote Jock MacGregor, the London correspondent for New York-based film exhibitor trade paper *Showmen's Trade Review*.[4] The trust for the films made at Ealing also extended to the company's patrician boss. Balcon's name on the credits was seen as a mark of integrity.

The sale of Ealing came a decade after Clement Attlee's Labour Party had swept to power on a landslide in the 1945 election on its 'Let Us Face the Future' manifesto. To some pessimistic observers, Michael Balcon's decision to sell Ealing marked the end of that period of optimism and idealism that had characterized the early years of the Attlee government, when sweeping changes to health, welfare and housing were introduced. The politicians were blamed for Ealing's problems. As filmmaker Jill Craigie, the wife of prominent Labour politician Michael Foot, wrote in *Tribune*, 'the blunt fact is that Ealing Studios have been taxed out of existence. Far more goes to the state in tax than to the producing of the films.'[5]

'The last Labour Government was the only Government we have had that had some faint inkling – I suspect largely due to you – of the realities of the situation of the producer pure and simple; but in the long run the other branches of the industry succeeded in clouding the issue fairly effectively, the progress made still fell short of the progress desired,' producer Anthony Havelock-Allan (best known for his work with David Lean) wrote to Balcon.[6]

On learning of Balcon's decision to sell Ealing, trade union leader George Elvin, General Secretary of the Association of Cinematograph, Television and Allied Technicians (ACTT), had fired off a telegram begging Balcon to reconsider his decision:

URGE YOU ON BEHALF OF ACTT AND IN INTEREST OF BRITISH FILM FOR WHICH YOU HAVE DONE SO MUCH REOPEN NEGOTIATIONS WITH BBC TO OBTAIN RELEASE FROM CONTRACTS OF SALE STOP BRITISH FILM PRODUCTION CANNOT PROGRESS WITH DIMINISHING PRODUCTION FACILITIES STOP

---

[4]*Showmen's Trade Review*, 29 October 1955.
[5]*Tribune*.
[6]Letter from Havelock-Allan to Balcon, 27 October 1955, BFI Special Collections material on Michael Balcon.

PLEASE DON'T STRANGLE THE MAN [Elvin's characterization of the now mature British film industry] YOU HAVE BOTH MAGNIFICENTLY HELPED REAR FROM INFANCY STOP REQUEST YOU RECEIVE TRADE UNION DEPUTATION.[7]

Conservative elements within the film industry felt this telegram, which Elvin showed to the press, was in bad taste – a left-wing stunt. Balcon and Major Baker quickly came back to Elvin to tell him the arrangements they had made to dispose of Ealing were 'binding and irrevocable'.

Two final films – comedy *Who Done It* (1956), directed by Ealing veteran Basil Dearden and starring the young comedian Benny Hill in his screen debut as an ice-rink sweeper, and Charles Frend's crime thriller *The Long Arm* (1956), starring staunch British leading man Jack Hawkins – were to be completed at Ealing. Then, Balcon and his 400 staff vacated the premises, leaving it to its new owners.

In their letters and public pronouncements, Balcon and Baker repeated again and again that the team would soon be setting up shop elsewhere. They were already in discussions to lease space at the MGM Studios in Borehamwood. They mustered arguments intended to show that the deal with the BBC was a matter of common sense. It had always been a financial struggle to keep Ealing going. When Balcon took over at the studios in 1938, they had capital of £80,000 and debts of £300,000. Over the years, the debt had been paid off but Ealing's finances had been badly hit when one of their principal backers, the former chairman Stephen Courtauld, a philanthropist whose wealth came from his family's textile business, had withdrawn his backing from the studios in 1951 when he and his family moved abroad to live in Rhodesia.

By 1955, Balcon was in a continual struggle to keep Ealing going. He was borrowing money from the government-backed Film Finance Corporation and was relying on support from the Rank Organisation, which was itself retrenching. The studios, which had opened in 1931, were considered old fashioned; well suited for smaller films, they were no longer big enough to make the expensive movies that might be able to compete with the big

---

[7]Telegram to Balcon, BFI Special Collections.

Hollywood productions then being made to show up the majesty of cinema in a period when television was stealing away audiences.

Balcon wanted to believe that the famous Ealing spirit, its quiet professionalism and emphasis on teamwork, wasn't anything to do with bricks and mortar. If the same technicians were making films in Borehamwood, that spirit could be preserved. Balcon hoped he and his colleagues could continue making films 'in committee'.

'In retrospect there is a good deal to be said for the methods of Michael Balcon, the Knight of the Round Table ... is that Diana Dors? ... and Joan Collins? Yes. They were rare interlopers, for Ealing's world was largely peopled by strong, silent men,' former Ealing publicity man Monja Danischewsky wrote of Balcon's collective, masculine approach to the business of filmmaking.[8]

As it turned out, union leader Elvin was right and the shocked response from Fleet Street was justified. The moment Balcon took Ealing Studios away from its west London home, the magic surrounding its films began to dissipate. The 'fine team spirit'[9] which Balcon's old colleagues all talked about simply couldn't be replicated elsewhere.

There was a sense of 'all my sad captains' in the nostalgic and melancholic letters and telegrams Balcon's most trusted workers and associates sent to him after the sale was announced. Message after message from actors, cinematographers and members of the public came to Balcon, all expressing their regret that the Ealing spirit was threatened with extinction. Actor Derek Bond, who had played Nicholas Nickleby and Captain Oates in Ealing films, spoke of his 'deep affection for the studios and the folk who work here'.[10] There were similar sentiments in a telegram from cinematographer Douglas Slocombe, who had shot such many films at the studios. 'We both have very happy memories of Ealing, and always thought of it as a home of most that is worthwhile in films' wrote the Russian-born writer and producer Sergei

---

[8]Mona Danischewsky, 'The Ghosts of Ealing', *Daily Express*, 21 October 1955.
[9]Letter from Vernon Sanford, Bury Amateur Film Society, to Balcon, 20 October 1955, BFI Special Collections.
[10]Letter from actor Derek Bond to Balcon, 1 December 1955, BFI Special Collections.

Nolbandov,[11] who worked on many wartime Ealing films, among them *Convoy* (1940), *Ships with Wings* (1941) and *Undercover* (1943).

Vernon Sanford from the Bury Amateur Film Society sent a letter expressing his commiserations as 'a member of the public who sincerely appreciates the work you and your team have put into the job of putting British films on the map'.[12]

In 1955, Balcon, then aged fifty-nine, was Britain's best-known and most-respected film producer. To outsiders, he seemed a part of the filmmaking establishment. He had been knighted in 1948. He lobbied government and wrote letters to *The Times*. He was characterized as a benevolent headmaster type or as the equivalent of an editor of a national newspaper. There was nothing very humorous about his public persona. He was an earnest, strait-laced figure who had overseen the production of some of the most famous comedies in British cinema history. It's a measure of the precarious nature of careers in the British film industry that when Balcon was ostensibly at his peak, he was scrambling to keep Ealing Studios alive, horse trading with the BBC and MGM Borehamwood and preparing to sell off the cameras and props that had been used to make the classic films he produced, whether wartime classics like *Went the Day Well?* (1942) or the string of classic Ealing comedies that started with *Hue and Cry* (1947) and ended with *The Ladykillers* (1955).

Look a little closer at Balcon and you realize that very little in his career had come remotely easily. 'It happens that my adult life, having been devoted to the production of some 350 films, has run parallel with and is interwoven with a substantial and eventful part of British filmmaking,' he wrote in his autobiography *A Lifetime in Films*, with some understatement.[13] There was nothing in his background to suggest that he would make his living through cinema. Balcon was the youngest son of Louis Balcon (1858–1946), a tailor, and his wife, Laura Greenberg (1863–1934), Jewish immigrants from Eastern Europe who had met in England. He grew up in Birmingham. His family were respectable but in impecunious circumstances. 'My native Birmingham has

---

[11]Letter from Sergei Nolbandov to Balcon, 20 October 1955, BFI Special Collections.
[12]Sanford, BFI Special Collections.
[13]Michael Balcon, *A Lifetime in Film* (London: Hutchinson, 1969), Foreword.

one claim to a place in film history, for a Birmingham man, Alexander Parkes, was the co-inventor of celluloid . . . that was 1856,' Balcon (born in 1896) later observed of the Brummie metallurgist who had invented Parkesine, the first form of celluloid.[14]

Balcon used his autobiography to point out the precarious nature of the film business. One of the most distinguished figures in early British film history was William Friese-Greene (1855–1921), an inventor and photographer credited with designing some of the earliest working movie cameras. His career in films was ending at just the time Balcon's began. Friese-Greene (whose story was told in the 1951 film *The Magic Box*) was both an inspiration and his eventual fate a portent of the obstacles and hardship ahead. As Balcon noted, the celebrated inventor 'went to gaol for debt, and later, in 1921 . . . collapsed and died after eloquently addressing a meeting in London on the need to preserve British production and not surrender forever to the prevailing American domination of our cinemas. He was found to have in his pocket 1s 10d – his total worldly possessions.'[15] Balcon's financial situation when he died in 1977 was rather more comfortable than that of Friese-Greene fifty years before but nobody would mistake him for a Rockefeller.

If Balcon had been fitter and healthier, he might never have worked in cinema. He had left school at the age of thirteen because his family couldn't afford to keep him there. He worked briefly in the diamond business and was a second lieutenant in the Home Guard but his poor eyesight kept him out of the First World War. Instead, he ended up being employed by the Dunlop Rubber Company in Birmingham, in a department devoted to making solid rubber tyres.

Balcon's friend and fellow Brummie Victor Saville, born in 1895 and a year older than him, had been invalided out of the war after being injured during the Battle of Loos. Back in Britain, recovering from his war wounds, Saville had, in 1916, found a job with local entrepreneur Solomon ('Sol') Levy, a hustler cut, as Saville put it, from the 'same pattern as his contemporaries in America – Zukor,

---

[14]Ibid., 2.
[15]Balcon, ibid.

Mayer, Goldwyn, Cohn, Lasky, Warner'.[16] Unlike these early Hollywood studio bosses, Levy was a deeply religious man. He could buy and sell anything but found himself attracted to show business in general and to film in particular. He would eventually run sixteen cinemas but when he gave Victor Saville a job he had a distribution company called Sun Exclusives and a couple of movie theatres including the Star Cinema in Coventry. Levy hired Saville to help with his distribution operation. It was Saville's job to draw up contracts and check box-office takings. In other words, he entered the industry right at the bottom.

This was a Klondike era, though. There were opportunities for enterprising young executives in a business in which the rules were still being made. Sol Levy realized early on that audiences might be prepared to pay a premium to see 'super-films' rather than their usual cinema diet for the time of 'very middle-grade, harmless entertainment'. He invested heavily in order to secure the British rights for D. W. Griffith's blockbusters *Birth of a Nation* (1915) and *Intolerance* (1916). 'The gamble paid off; the gross from each of these films was tenfold the amount that the biggest [box-office] attraction [Mary Pickford] realized in the United Kingdom,' Saville remembered.[17]

Saville worked for various other film companies including Pathé, Gaumont and Stoll. As he learned more and more about the film world, he thought of his old friend, Mick Balcon. He was contemplating setting up his own distribution company.

To do so, Saville needed films. One of his former colleagues was an executive called Charlie Wilcox, who had worked with him in Leeds. Wilcox was also setting up on his own and brought his older brother Herbert (soon to become a celebrated producer-director and to make many hit films with his third wife Anna Neagle), just demobbed from the Royal Air Force (RAF), into his business. They were licensing distribution rights to product from the Mutual Company of America. As Saville explained in his autobiography, this meant they would pre-buy independent productions on the basis of their stars. Their investment would help the films get made and they could then license the films

---

[16]*Evergreen: Victor Saville in His Own Words*, ed. Roy Moseley (Carbondale, IL: Southern Illinois University Press, 2000).
[17]Ibid.

on in turn to the cinema owners. The Wilcox brothers suggested that Saville should do the same and pick up slates of films for the Midlands.

It's a strange quirk of British film history that Saville and Herbert Wilcox, two of the most prominent filmmakers of their era, were both ex-military and that both started their film careers as small-time salesmen and distributors in the provinces. There weren't then film schools or directing courses at the BBC at which they could learn their crafts. Their early experiences were as 'middlemen', acquiring rights. The Wilcox brothers licensed a package of twenty-four films from American Film Company including titles starring Mary Miles Minter, William Russell and Marguerite Fischer from Sol Levy. In 1921, Saville formed his own distribution outfit, Victory Motion Pictures ('a name in tune with the times'), and recruited Balcon to help him run it. Both men were in their mid-twenties. They had a third school friend from their childhood days in Birmingham, Oscar Deutsch (who came from a family of Birmingham metal merchants and was later to form Britain's leading exhibition chain, Odeon).

'Victor Saville persuaded Sol Levy to give us the distribution rights to some of the American films he had. Also at this time, in London, Charles M. Woolf, to whom Victor was related by marriage, had cut loose from his family wholesale fur business and set up in Frith Street, Soho, as a film distributor, with a partner named Freedman. Their company was called W&F Film Services . . . one of the acorns from which grew the mighty oak of the Gaumont-British Corporation, which in turn became an important part of the Rank Organisation,' Balcon remembered of how one of the biggest corporations in British film history actually began as a tiny, independent enterprise.[18]

The three young Jewish businessmen discovered quickly that distribution was one of the most perilous parts of the business. 'After scraping the cream off the top, there did not seem enough value in our product to make a satisfactory living,' Saville later lamented.[19] Nonetheless, they were making valuable contacts. Not only were they now connected with Woolf's distribution company in London. They had also met for the first time another entrepreneurial young figure working for Sol Levy in the Midlands, Graham Cutts.

---

[18]Balcon, *A Lifetime in Films*, 11.
[19]Saville, *Evergreen*.

Mr J. H. Graham-Cutts, as he was referred to in the trade press of the time, had started in the industry as the manager of a cinema in Sevenoaks, Kent, in 1911. His career as an exhibitor began to blossom. He had achieved a certain local celebrity as manager of one of Levy's cinemas, Scala Theatre, which opened in Birmingham in 1914 and was described as 'one of the largest, safest and most beautifully-appointed cinema houses in the Midlands'. The intention here was to show 'only the finest and most approved films on the market'.[20]

By one of those strange metamorphoses which seemed relatively commonplace in this period of British film history, the provincial cinema manager Cutts somehow turned himself into 'England's greatest director' in the space of just a few years.

Balcon and Saville left Birmingham and headed to London, hoping to achieve a similar transformation. The 'unknown young men from Birmingham' took tiny, drab offices in Leicester Square. They had decided that production might be a more lucrative field for them than distribution. Together with another friend, John Freedman, son of Charles Woolf's business partner in W&F Distribution, they formed a production company, Balcon, Freedman & Saville.

None of them had any practical experience of film production and this was a terrible period for British filmmaking anyway. The local industry had shrivelled up after the war. Cinemas were booming but they were showing precisely the type of American, star-driven films that Balcon and Saville had been distributing just a few years before. As Balcon summed it up: 'The war had virtually killed off British production, and the Americans, quite properly, had taken full advantage of this to provide all the films that British cinemas required.'[21]

Prospects for the new production company looked grim in the extreme. However, just as generations of British filmmakers after them would do, Balcon and Saville survived by making commercials and advertising films to be shown in cinemas. Their 'ally' who secured them a contract with the Anglo-American

---

[20] *Birmingham Gazette*, 4 May 1914.
[21] Balcon, *A Lifetime in Films*, 12.

Oil Company, to make a 'documentary on oil to advertise their product' (as Saville recalled), was another young Jewish businessman, Sidney Bernstein, then operating his cinema exhibition company, Granada, from a little office in Cecil Court, the street behind Leicester Square tube station on which many of the most prominent distribution companies were based. Saville and Balcon formed a separate company, Crane Paget & Co., for their advertising work.

'On a cold morning, I turned up with a camera crew at the Marquis of Granby pub on the Portsmouth Road to film a motor-car drive up to the first petrol pump in England and fill its tank. There was very little sex appeal in the scene, but at least I looked through a camera for the first time,' Saville, the future director of *Goodbye, Mr Chips* (1939) and *Kim* (1950), recalled of the extraordinarily humble and banal circumstances in which his filmmaking career began.[22]

The economic logic which determined British production in the early 1920s was precisely the same as it would be a century later. In order for bigger budgeted British films to have a chance of making a significant profit, they needed access to the American market. The easiest way to gain that access was to work with American talent – but US stars demanded very hefty salaries which the British producers could rarely afford to pay.

Balcon and Saville looked on in envy as their old colleague Herbert Wilcox made the leap into film production. Wilcox's distribution company, Astra Films, set up in 1919 in Leeds, had been conspicuously more successful than Victory. Wilcox began to think about making his own films. His production partner was none other than former cinema manager Graham Cutts. Full of ambition, they saw themselves as British equivalents to D. W. Griffith and his associates.

British production in this period was very much a cottage industry. Everyone knew everyone else. Careers overlapped in surprising ways. One of the first films produced by Graham–Wilcox Productions, the company set up by Wilcox and Cutts, was British love-triangle drama *The Wonderful Story* (1922), about a fiancée of a farmer who falls in love with his brother. It did only modest business at the box office. This prompted Wilcox and Cutts to take a

---

[22]Saville, *Evergreen.*

different tack and hire a big American star, Mae Marsh, who had appeared in several of the D. W. Griffith films they so admired, in the next of their features, *Flames of Passion* (1922).

As Saville noted, 'the star system had been born with attendant publicity and created a world demand for stars Hollywood-style. The English exhibitor bought his films at bargain-basement rates, slapped a few posters on the outside of his theatre, and went to the pub next door. The principal US producers became their own middlemen and set up distribution for their films worldwide.'[23]

Saville's analysis is fascinating. It suggests that creativity and entrepreneurialism went hand in hand. The most celebrated British filmmakers of the early 1920s first came into the industry as distributors and exhibitors. Producing and directing films themselves was a business decision – a way of being better able to tailor the films they released for the public and to hold on to the profits, if and when there were any.

The economic logic was daunting. Balcon and Saville realized that American films were sold and marketed on the back of their stars – but that the British in this period had very few bankable names of their own. They therefore decided to work with the US talent on the films they made. This was where the inflation set in. To secure that talent, they needed to pay very hefty salaries. The budgets of their films therefore shot up. As the budgets shot up, so did the necessity of finding markets beyond the UK in order to recoup their outlay.

At the start of his career, Balcon, the patrician British producer, was a gambler who took huge risks as he tried to establish himself. Not only did he leave Birmingham and head to London, trying to break into production with only £200 in capital. Together with Saville and Freedman, he hired the American film star Betty Compson for £1,000 a week (around £26,000 a week in today's currency) to star in their first film, *Woman to Woman* (1923) directed by Graham Cutts. This might not seem astronomical by Hollywood standards (Mary Pickford in her prime earned far, far more) but was a huge amount for two young British producers who had never made a film together before. Alfred Hitchcock (a grocer's son from Leytonstone) worked on the film in

---

[23]Saville, *Evergreen.*

various different capacities (including art director and assistant director) and had a hand in the script, based on a play by Michael Morton. He also met his future wife, Alma Reville (see Chapter 12), who was the editor. 'A general handyman ... little more than a boy', was how Balcon remembered Hitchcock at this stage of his career.[24]

Woman to Woman is a very heady, *Random Harvest*-style melodrama about a young English officer (Clive Brook) who falls in love with a French dancer, goes to the front, gets shell shock, forgets all about her as a result and marries somebody else. The dancer has his child. They meet again a few years later but, by the time he remembers her, it may be too late to salvage their relationship. The tyro filmmakers spared no expense. They hired the female chorus from the Casino de Paris, 'the home of large-scale revues', and built a special stage set in the studios on which they could appear between stage performances. The producers were obliged to hire 'a group of needlewomen', as Saville recalled, 'to fit the chorus with brassieres ... no French breast could be exposed on the screens of England or America'.[25]

'Very much above the average,' enthused *The Times* in its review, 'the photography is excellent throughout and the spectacular scenes are gorgeous without being oppressive.'[26] Others were even more enthusiastic. Balcon's debut was called 'England's greatest picture' by some provincial exhibitors. Even more important, it succeeded in the US market. The production cost of a reported £40,000, huge for the time, was soon recouped

At first, it seemed that Balcon and Saville's risk-taking had paid off. Balcon, however, promptly learned a very familiar lesson about the nature of British production – namely that the quickest route to failure is often success. He and Saville hadn't thought ahead or anticipated the familiar boom and bust syndrome which affected British filmmaking then and still does today.

'Engrossed in our first production, we had made no preparation for the second. Caught on the hop, we rushed into production with ... *The White Shadow*,' Balcon ruefully wrote in his autobiography.[27] Compson was still

---

[24]Balcon, *A Lifetime in Films*, 18.
[25]Saville, *Evergreen*.
[26]BFI Library cuttings.
[27]Balcon, *A Lifetime in Films*, 26.

being paid £1,000 a week but this second production was made on the hoof and conspicuously failed to replicate the success of its predecessor. It didn't help that their American distributors, Select Pictures Corporation, run by Lewis J. Selznick (father of legendary producer David O. Selznick), had run into trouble – and so the producers didn't see much of their American profits. Their business partner Freedman died young. Like their distribution company, the production company that Balcon and Saville had set up together soon hit the reefs. Nonetheless, by now, Balcon was firmly established. His network of contacts in every sector and region of the industry was vast.

Together with Cutts and C. M. Woolf, Balcon went on to form 'a 100 pound company called Gainsborough' which rented film studios from Famous Players in Islington on an ad hoc basis. He managed to secure backing from Reginald and Claude Bromhead, who ran the Gaumont Company which had studios at Lime Grove. Saville, meanwhile, stayed at the helm of the advertising business, Crane Paget & Co., and dreamed of directing his own films.

Balcon was nothing if not opportunistic. He was looking for potential new British stars (and found a couple in handsome young Welshman Ivor Novello, marketed as if he was the British Rudolph Valentino, and, in the early days of the talkies, brilliant dancer Jessie Matthews). He was targeting genres with mass appeal – crime thrillers and musicals. He was nurturing the young Hitchcock, producing several of his early films, among them *The Pleasure Garden* (1925), *The Mountain Eagle* (1926) and most successfully *The Lodger* (1927). He was looking abroad for inspiration and for partnership, co-producing with UFA Studios in Berlin. 'Years ago, when we were starting from scratch, I realised the need to introduce directors and technicians from abroad, not only to train our people but to cross-fertilise with our native talents,' he justified the joint ventures with foreign production companies.[28]

These weren't easy times. By 1930, Balcon was close to a nervous breakdown. He was a workaholic, so busy that he even had his hair cut at the studio while attending to business. Adding to the normal strains of running Gainsborough, he had to cope with a freak fire at the studios' premises in Poole Street, Islington.

---

[28]Ibid., 33.

A sound engineer called George Gunn had very nearly died in the blaze, jumping to his freedom down a lift shaft but severing his thumb in the process. The remains of his thumb stayed visible in that lift shaft for many years after, a grisly reminder of a night to forget.[29]

In February of that year, a wearied and battle-worn Balcon went to Madeira to convalesce, leaving the studio in the hands of his brother, S. Chandos Balcon. Leading trade paper *The Bioscope* wished him a 'quick recovery from the ill-effects of a series of business and domestic worries, in which family illness and personal nerve strain were followed by the heavy shock of the Islington fire'.[30]

He was soon back, though, and ready to fight on, both his drive and his personal popularity undimmed. *The Bioscope* described him as 'one of the young and the biggest men in British film production . . . a dynamic personality, quick of decision, a shrewd leader and delightful companion'.[31]

When Gaumont-British, as it had become, took over Gainsborough in 1931, Balcon was put in charge of production at both studios. In the space of less than a decade, he had established himself as Britain's most prolific and prominent producer. His prominence was underlined when the 1927 Cinematograph Act was passed, introducing quotas for British films, and the *London Evening News* illustrated the story with a picture of Balcon, as if he somehow embodied the British industry. The surprise, in hindsight, lay in the type of films he oversaw. A Balcon production at this stage in his career had no clear identity. As he acknowledged, the British were operating in a vacuum. 'Often, looking back, I am gravely concerned that the films which I produced at certain points of history reflected so little the society in which we lived,' Balcon later expressed his regret at his choices of subject matter.[32] He realized that British cinemas were still dominated by American product. Rather than

---

[29]Geoffrey Macnab, 'The Death-Trap London Studio that Time Forgot', *Independent*, 25 June 1999. https://www.independent.co.uk/arts-entertainment/film-the-death-trap-london-studio-that-time-forgot-1102265.html.

[30]*The Bioscope*, 26 February 1930.

[31]*The Bioscope*, 14 July 1927.

[32]Balcon, *A Lifetime in Films*, 25.

try to provide an alternative to this, he made British films in the vein of those from the US.

> I confess that for perhaps my first full decade as a producer I was solely intent on building an industry on a firm basis, giving employment, increasing the technical talent available, providing a profitable investment, including making a living for myself. It was only in the thirties that I began to give serious thought to the film's potential importance in the social and cultural life of the country. And it was only with the coming of the Second World War that I really appreciated and applied myself to putting into practice my beliefs in what the film could do on this level.[33]

Read any of the many interviews with Balcon in the consumer and trade press in the period before the Second World War and you can't help but be startled by the opinions he sometimes espoused or by the way he was characterized. One newspaper profile in the 1930s called him the 'Man Who Makes the stars,'[34] a considerable irony given that Ealing in its pomp was famous for its character actors and team ethos, its rejection of the conventional star system. Balcon talked about trying to capture the American market. He didn't make many comedies ('it's comedy stories that are hardest to find'[35]), again an irony given Ealing's later work in the genre, and he shunned period films. At the helm of Gaumont-British and Gainsborough, he oversaw a staff of 1,400 employees and had an annual budget of £1.25 million a year.

Hard though he strived, he didn't yet have a philosophy about the type of films he should be making. He was a mogul but no one could pinpoint what he stood for. The hits came – Jessie Matthews in *Evergreen* (1934), one of several successes directed by his business partner Saville, by then established as one of Britain's most reliable directors; *Rome Express* (1932), with imported German star Conrad Veidt; the J. B. Priestley adaptation *The Good Companions* (1933), again directed by Saville. Balcon was bringing talent into the industry, scouring 'the film societies of Oxbridge' for 'promising young men' and recruiting such

---

[33]Ibid., 27.
[34]Balcon, BFI Library microfiche cuttings.
[35]Ibid.

figures as Robert Stevenson, who would go on to make *Mary Poppins* (1964) for Disney, Frank Launder and Sidney Gilliat, soon to become a formidable writing and directing team, and editor-director-producer Ian Dalrymple.

For all Balcon's efforts, the scales were tilted against him. The fundamental problem remained that British cinemas much preferred to show American films and would discriminate against even the very best homegrown fare. Balcon later wrote of how British cinema bookers rejected Hitchcock's *The Man Who Knew Too Much* (1934) and only relented under fierce pressure from the powerful C. M. Woolf, a figure those bookers would have been loath to cross. 'They agreed to play the film, and then only at a modest fixed price instead of the standard participation in box-office receipts usually paid for what cinema men thought to be "good" films,' Balcon remembered.[36]

Partly on the basis of 'if you can't beat them, join them' and partly to support his friend Saville, Balcon left Gainsborough and Gaumont-British to work under Louis B. Mayer at MGM, running its British operations, overseeing films like *A Yank at Oxford* (1938), *The Citadel* (1938) and *Goodbye Mr Chips* (1939). However, he didn't get on with his overbearing Hollywood bosses and, according to his son Jonathan Balcon (*Independent*, 1 August 1993), was eventually 'sacked' by Louis B. Mayer in June 1938. The very next week, he announced plans to join with Reginald P. Baker, at A.T.P. Studios, Ealing. 'Large-scale popular box-office features will be the main product, and it is hoped that the new regime will turn Ealing into a major British studio,' *The Era* reported,[37] a surprising aspiration given that the studios under Balcon eventually became known for producing small-scale British films.

Jonathan Balcon wrote:

Basil Dean had made a series of the most awful loss-makers at Ealing, and Stephen Courtauld, main shareholder in Associated Talking Pictures, owners of the studios, asked Major Reginald Baker, the managing director, who could become production head. 'Balcon is the only person available,' said Baker. My father had been production head of Gaumont until late

---

[36]Balcon, *A Lifetime in Films*, 62.
[37]*The Era*, 7 July 1938.

1936. He was approached but insisted on coming to Ealing initially as an independent, with his own team. It was only when war seemed inevitable that he assumed the role of production head.[38]

Gradually, his long-term vision for British film became clear. He spoke of his 'growing conviction that a film, to be international, must be thoroughly national in the first instance, and that there was nothing wrong with a degree of cultural chauvinism'.[39] As his son noted, the way Balcon had been pushed around for so long by the likes of Louis B. Mayer, financiers and studio bosses was reflected in the films that made Ealing so famous. 'In fact the comedies very much reflect his fight of the small man against bureaucracy.'[40]

Cultural chauvinism was never carried off with more aplomb than at Ealing Studios in its glory years. This was the period when Balcon, the short-sighted Brummie businessman and failed film salesman, finally discovered a pathway not just for himself but for the British industry as a whole.

---

[38]*Independent*, 1 August 1993.
[39]Balcon, *A Lifetime in Films*, 61.
[40]*Independent*, 1 August 1993.

2

Richard Attenborough

One of Michael Balcon's most ambitious projects in the latter part of his career was Second World War epic *Dunkirk* (1958), starring the actor-producer who, two decades later, was to assume Balcon's role as the de facto leader of the British film industry. In *Dunkirk*, Richard Attenborough plays a civilian contractor who reluctantly joins the Armada of civilian boats which cross the Channel to rescue the stranded British soldiers from the beaches of France after the Dunkirk debacle in the early summer of 1940. Balcon encouraged Attenborough when the actor took his first steps into film production. There was a sense they recognized some of the same qualities in each other,

To outsiders, Attenborough (1923–2014), like Balcon, seemed the British film industry's ultimate insider. Late in his life, he was regarded by the British public as being akin to a secular saint, celebrated for his good cheer and tireless charity work and good deeds. There were few public film bodies that he wasn't associated intimately with. He had been the Chairman of Goldcrest Films, the Chairman of Channel 4 (at the time when it was first supporting British filmmaking, becoming Chair in 1984, just as Film Four International was established), the Chairman of the British Screen Advisory Council, the Chairman of the BFI and the President of BAFTA and of the National Film School. Prime ministers, whose ear he always had, knew him as Dickie. He was also President of the Royal Academy of Dramatic Art (RADA), where he studied, and chaired the UK industry-wide celebration of cinema's centenary in 1996. Many of the above bodies have Attenborough scholarships or bursaries in his name to this day, part of his enduring legacy.

Richard Attenborough. Photo: Central Press/Getty Images.

Attenborough, it was popularly assumed, had always been successful, both as a filmmaker and as a campaigner for social justice. He had been brought up to help others and cast light on injustice. As he would regularly tell interviewers, his parents had installed in him strong 'moral, social and political impulses'. 'They believed it was no use whatsoever offering sympathy; the point was to do something.'[1]

Writing in the *Guardian* just after Attenborough died, David Puttnam noted: 'We have lost someone utterly irreplaceable. Irreplaceable to his family, irreplaceable to the country he loved, irreplaceable to the industry to which he devoted his working life; certainly irreplaceable to me. In a world overused to hyperbole, "irreplaceable" may sound almost trite – but in the case of Richard Attenborough, it's a word hard-won, and all too accurate.'[2]

---

[1] Geoffrey Macnab, 'Eager Beaver: Richard Attenborough', *Sight & Sound*, 13, no. 9 (September 2003), 16–20.
[2] David Puttnam on Richard Attenborough, *Guardian*, 25 August 2014.

Few profiles of him neglected to mention that his father, Frederick, was a don, fellow of Emmanuel College, Cambridge, and later Principal of Leicester University, whose energy and steady patience enabled the then struggling university to flourish, or that his suffragette mother, Mary Attenborough, had helped found the National Marriage Guidance Council and marched against Franco in the 1930s. When he was growing up, his family took in two refugees fleeing Hitler in the Kindertransport. Frederick's academic specialization was Anglo-Saxon studies and his main form of recreation was (according to his obituary in *The Times*) the photography of buildings and landscapes.[3]

'It was an extraordinary background my brother Dave and I had,' Attenborough remembered, citing his younger brother David, the broadcaster and natural historian who, like Richard, became a household name in Britain. (The third brother, John, was successful enough in his own right as a senior executive in the UK car industry but next to Richard and David he was eclipsed.) 'My parents believed in the responsibility of one human being for another and in the idea that you had little right to experience the phenomenal joys of life unless you were aware of others who could be three feet or 3,000 miles away, facing difficulties you had no understanding of. They believed in the principle of putting something back. That, for them, was what life was about. And boy, they lived their life to the full.'[4]

Attenborough didn't just make films himself. He lobbied with huge energy on behalf of the rest of the industry. He was, as one of the many fulsome obituaries put it, 'a universally beloved figure.'[5]

Take a step back, though, and you realize that Attenborough's pathway into British cinema was far less straightforward than it appeared when he was at the height of his fame after winning his Oscars for *Gandhi* (1982) and ascending to the House of Lords (he was made a life peer in 1993). The patrician figure who called even relative strangers 'darling' may have looked authoritative and at ease but, even in his pomp, Attenborough didn't find it easy to secure financing for his films.

---

[3] *The Times*, 23 March 1973.
[4] Macnab, 'Eager Beaver'.
[5] Cited in BBC Online: https://www.bbc.co.uk/news/entertainment-arts-28923074.

In fact, nothing in his career had been straightforward. Pursuing a career as an actor, which was how he first came into British cinema, was a risky and surprising choice. His father ('the Governor' as he called him) didn't approve at all. His mother may have been president of the local amateur dramatics society in Leicester but that didn't mean the family thought this was a fitting profession for him. His father wanted him to go to university – and Attenborough wanted his father to take pride in whatever he did.

There is one reading of Attenborough's extraordinary career which sees that drive to succeed as being his way of trying to prove himself to his father. He wanted to show that filmmaking wasn't just about box office and superficial glamour but that it could inspire and educate audiences as well. He acknowledged as much when, in 1962, at the age of thirty-nine, he embarked on his twenty-year mission to make his film about the revered Indian leader Gandhi.

'I still desperately wanted to prove myself. I wanted the Governor . . . to take real pride in what I was doing. And, in addition, I knew that Mahatma Gandhi was someone he held in high esteem,' Attenborough noted in his informal autobiography *Entirely Up to You, Darling*, published in 2008.[6] By then, he was already well into his eighties but was still thinking about the father whose approval he wanted so badly. That drive and perseverance which sustained him through his career seemingly came from wanting the Governor to think well of him. He remembers his father as 'a forbidding figure' with very 'certain principles'. He believed fervently in 'community responsibility' and, by that token, the idea of a career as an actor or filmmaker must have seemed very selfish and superficial to him.

The young Attenborough failed to shine at school. He wasn't 'clever or assiduous' enough to scale the academic heights. His brother David excelled in the classroom but Richard looked as if he had little chance of being accepted at university. His prospects weren't helped by the amount of time he spent acting at the local amateur dramatics society.

It wasn't as if Attenborough was from a privileged background. His paternal grandfather, who came from a strict Methodist family, had been a baker in Nottingham. On his mother's side, his grandfather was Samuel Clegg, a

---

[6]Richard Attenborough, *Entirely Up to You, Darling* (London: Hutchinson, 2008).

renowned teacher and educationalist who shared his grandson's zeal for improving the lots of those around him and who had served as headmaster of the Long Eaton County School. In the Attenborough family, education and hard work were seen as the way to better yourself but Clegg, who had started teaching at the age of thirteen and whose father was a teacher too, wasn't wealthy.

Attenborough had had only one chance to make it as an actor. His father told him there weren't sufficient funds to pay for him to attend drama school and that if he didn't win the Leverhulme Scholarship at RADA, which came with living expenses included, he would be obliged to abandon his dream. At the age of seventeen, Attenborough won that scholarship, thereby providing himself with a gateway into the film industry. The way he remembered it later, Attenborough had had a single roll of the dice. If he hadn't been accepted by RADA, he would have had to look for another career. His father didn't have the will or the means to underwrite his apprenticeship as an actor. The Leverhulme Scholarship was RADA's only competitive award.

The fees were 15 guineas a term and his living allowance was £2.50 a week. Attenborough lived on the Edgware Road, in the 'basement of a house of questionable repute', as he later recalled.[7]

In this period, British theatre and cinema were at an arm's length from each other. 'People came up to you and said are you an actor or do you work in films? Films were beyond the pale as far as a trained actor was concerned,' he said of the low esteem in which cinema was then considered.[8] If serious actors did work in films, the assumption was always that they were doing so just trying to earn a little extra money, and would prefer for the subject not to be mentioned.

Attenborough started at RADA in 1940 and left the school in 1942. By then, his drive and talent were already apparent. In breaks from school, the young Attenborough already worked in rep, at the Intimate Theatre in north London, appearing in plays by Clifford Odets. During holidays from RADA, he had taken roles at the Arts Theatre, appearing in *Twelfth Night* and other classics.

---

[7]British Entertainment History Project (BEHP), interview with Richard Attenborough, conducted by Sidney Samuelson. https://historyproject.org.uk/interview/richard-attenborough.
[8]Ibid.

He had won the Bancroft Silver Medal and American agent Al Parker (who had seen him in a play at the Intimate Theatre) had secured him a role as the neurotic young stoker below decks in *In Which We Serve* (1942), directed by Noël Coward and David Lean. Coward at the time was looking for new faces. Attenborough had had to get special permission ('all against the rules') from the RADA principal, Sir Kenneth Barnes, to appear in the film. 'That's how I began, almost by chance, in the cinema rather than in the theatre,' Attenborough later recalled.[9]

Attenborough 'hero worshipped' Coward, who not only gave him his break but also gave his wife and fellow actor, Sheila Sim, whom he married in 1945, her first job in the theatre.

After RADA, Attenborough went into the air force to train to become a pilot. He expected to be sent to Canada. Then came the moment when he was summoned to see Flight Lieutenant John Boulting, who was stationed at Pinewood Studios and working as one of the directors at the RAF Film Unit. Boulting, who had seen *In Which We Serve*, was preparing *Journey Together* (1945) and wanted Attenborough to come out of the training programme to appear in his film. He co-starred opposite Edward G. Robinson, the legendary Hollywood veteran best known for playing the gangster anti-hero in *Little Caesar* (1931). The publicity was revealing. The two actors shared equal billing: 'A Great Star', the posters declared under an image of Robinson and 'A New Star' under that of Attenborough.[10]

During his subsequent time in the RAF, in which he abandoned any thoughts of becoming a pilot and trained as an air gunner instead, Attenborough began to learn about cameras. 'I was fascinated by film and by cameras,' he later remembered of his experiences in the RAF Film Unit. 'I was bewitched by the cinema. It was by going into the RAF Film Unit and using a camera instead of a gun that I became bewitched by movies. That shifted my focus from theatre into film really.'[11]

One of the paradoxes about Attenborough is that his highly successful career as a producer and director was built at least partly on his feelings of

---

[9]Ibid.
[10]*Kensington Post*, 24 November 1945.
[11]BEHP, interview with Richard Attenborough.

inferiority. He didn't have a degree or an Oxbridge education behind him. That made him too self-conscious to think about a career as a writer. He didn't feel he had the intellectual ballast to become a politician either, even if he did share his father's socialist beliefs. He therefore turned to film as the medium in which he was qualified to express himself.

'Because of this feeling of wanting to say something, either by advocacy or by opposition, I decided the way I might be able to do it was through producing and directing movies,' Attenborough told the BBC late in his life.[12] His career as a filmmaker was built on a sense of mission. That zeal sustained him even in periods when he was accruing rejection after rejection.

There is a revealing interview with Attenborough in *The Times*,[13] just after he has turned fifty, written by journalist and broadcaster Barry Norman, son of Leslie Norman, his director on *Dunkirk*. Whereas others might have been rueful about reaching middle age and worried that their best years were already behind them, Attenborough comes across in his quotes as that familiar ball of energy. 'I should like the good Lord to give me another six hours in every day and, please; not to let me have to cut down on my activity and become chair-ridden and crotchety but apart from that I haven't any fears about growing older,' he told Norman. By then, he was already President of RADA, Chancellor of Sussex University and heavily involved in the Arts Council. These were all roles that you would expect someone to take on when their career was winding down but Attenborough's really was only just beginning. He was in the middle stages of his epic quest to make *Gandhi* (although he had by then spent ten years on the project) and was working seventeen-hour days. Alongside his activities in education and culture, his acting and his filmmaking, he was also chairman of Capital Radio, a nakedly commercial venture. 'We're a capitalist company but we're terribly aware that we have an enormous responsibility not simply to make a profit but to contribute to the community. Unless we do that our position is untenable,' he told Norman. The journalist struggled at first to see just how Capital Radio, with its pop songs and nine minutes of commercials every hour, was a philanthropic endeavour. However,

---

[12]https://www.bbc.co.uk/sounds/play/b066gfbw.
[13]*The Times*, 1 September 1973.

Norman was won over by his sincerity, especially when Attenborough was discussing *Gandhi*. 'I feel that everything I have ever done, professionally or even privately, has been a sort of preparation for making this particular story, with all it has to say about tolerance, compassion and peace,' Attenborough continued. 'Coming from almost any other film maker this kind of remark would reduce an interviewer to quiet but helpless mirth but coming from Mr Attenborough it has a ring of conviction,' Norman noted.

The interview reveals Attenborough in all his guises: social campaigner and huckster, visionary and businessman. He may have been involved in many altruistic and charitable ventures but he was also hard headed enough to run a commercial radio station. His kindness was very well known but he wasn't a soft touch. He was part of the establishment but also frequently at odds with it.

'Dickie, who the hell do you think is interested in a little man dressed in a sheet and carrying a beanpole?' a big US producer famously dismissed Attenborough's appeal for financing for *Gandhi*.[14] At the end of his career, when he was in the House of Lords and was venerated as one of the leaders of the British film industry, financiers continued to turn him down. He had a project about eighteenth-century writer, political theorist and radical firebrand Thomas Paine, writer of *Rights of Man* (1791), which he spent twenty years after Gandhi trying and failing to get off the ground.

'The financiers aren't interested in the subjects I want to make,' Attenborough stated forlornly in an interview given to *Sight & Sound* to mark his eightieth birthday. 'Trevor Griffiths' script for Tom Paine is one of the best I've read but it needs $65 or $75 million. It's period, it's religion, it's politics, it's morality. They ignore the fact that there are some wonderful, evocative man-to-man battles involved. There's Washington, Robespierre, Danton and two great love affairs.'[15] Paine's was another story that Attenborough's father might have thought of as a sound subject for a biopic on screen.

Perhaps Attenborough saw a little of himself in Paine. Here was an Englishman who had been involved in the writing of the American Declaration

---

[14]Cited in the *Telegraph*: https://www.telegraph.co.uk/culture/film/film-news/11054681/Richard-Attenborough-interview-You-cant-outrun-your-grief.-You-have-to-confront-it.html.
[15]Macnab, 'Eager Beaver'.

of Independence and had visited France shortly after the Revolution. Paine was a radical who believed in free education and the emancipation of women. He also led an extraordinarily colourful private life, full of travel, tumult and controversy. It was a difficult life too.

As a young actor who became one of British cinema's most popular juvenile leads in the late 1940s, Attenborough had the status of a young pop star. 'Personal appearance of Mr Richard Attenborough Britain's famous film star dancing to Jack Hobbs & His Band,' ran an advertisement for a dance night at Kensington Town Hall in September 1947 which also offered a 'Beautiful Hair' competition.[16]

The clean-cut new matinee idol projected a surprising anxiety and unease. It would be far-fetched to compare him to later US Method actors like James Dean and Montgomery Clift, although Steve McQueen was a mentor and inspiration to him on *The Great Escape* (1963) and *The Sand Pebbles* (1966), but he had some of their restlessness and sense of inner torment. You could read the doubt and self-loathing in his face.

His most famous early role was the gangster, razor-wielding spiv in the Boulting brothers' screen adaptation of Graham Greene's *Brighton Rock* (1947). Pinkie, the character, is vicious but vulnerable. We read a sense of inner turmoil in his features and a shame about the callous way he treats the waitress (Carol Marsh) because she has seen a more sensitive side of him he would rather keep hidden. Attenborough had also tackled the role on stage. Instead of going to university and trying to change the world for the better, he was playing a sociopathic adolescent in a British gangster movie. There wasn't anything glamorous about playing 'Young Scarface', as the film was called when it was released in the US in the early 1950s. Some reviewers had been very hostile. 'Mr Attenborough's Pinkie is about as close to the real thing as Donald Duck is to Greta Garbo,' the *Daily Express* sneered.[17] However, Greene, who had co-scripted the film with Terence Rattigan, gave him a first edition copy of the novel in which the novelist wrote, 'to my perfect Pinkie'.[18]

---

[16]*Kensington Post*, 20 September 1947.
[17]Leonard Mosley, *Daily Express*, cited in Attenborough, *Entirely Up to You, Darling*, p. 144.
[18]BEHP, interview with Richard Attenborough.

Attenborough flourished in British cinema of the 1940s by taking roles as neurotic young outsiders. He was the cowardly youngster below decks in *In Which We Serve* (1942). He was the boy from the humble background who wins a scholarship to a public school and struggles to fit in among all the toffs and snobs in *The Guinea Pig* (1949). ('Attenborough does a nice job of showing native spunk and stocky resistance to snobbery,' the *New York Times*' Bosley Crowther wrote of his performance.[19]) One friend later commented, 'he uses his acting to express those parts of himself he simply daren't show in his private life.'[20]

Attenborough had begun his career at a time when British cinema was booming. Cinema admissions were at 1.64 billion in 1946 and were to stay at over 1.1 billion for the next decade. Not that this meant young screen actors were earning fortunes, being challenged creatively or setting up their own production companies so that they could pursue passion projects.

In the wartime years and their aftermath, films in which Attenborough appeared, like *In Which We Serve*, *Journey Together* (1945) – a wartime drama about the RAF bombers in which he played alongside legendary Hollywood gangster star Edward G. Robinson, who became a mentor and friend – and even *The Guinea Pig*, reflected British society of the time. Whether they were wartime propaganda or stories about the loosening of the class system in the Attlee era, they had an obvious relevance to their audience at a time when Britain was going through profound social change. By the mid-1950s, though, that relevance was ebbing away. Filmmakers were already beginning to look back in nostalgia at the world of only a few years before. Movies in which Attenborough starred in the mid to late 1950s like Ealing drama *The Ship That Died of Shame* (1955) depicted characters who had lost their sense of purpose after the war and couldn't adjust to the banality of civilian life. (*The Ship That Died of Shame* was a story of former wartime Navy officers drawn into smuggling and crime in the post-war era.)

The sense of drift in the industry was palpable. The great talents with whom Attenborough had worked in the 1940s had either started making films

---

[19]*New York Times*, 2 May 1949.
[20]*The Times*, 8 January 1968.

internationally (in the case of David Lean) or were working on constricted budgets (in the case of Powell and Pressburger) or had turned away from socially conscious drama to satire (in the case of the Boulting brothers). Attenborough, the young star of the 1940s, was frustrated by the roles he was being offered. He was turning into a very skilled character actor who developed a special knack for playing furtive and creepy types.

Attenborough was so chilling as the balding, bespectacled and very unctuous killer John Christie in *10 Rillington Place* (1971) that it was hard to believe the same actor would later play Santa Claus in John Hughes's version of *Miracle on 34th Street* (1994). Neither of these, one guesses, was a film which would much have impressed his father. Nor would Frederick Attenborough have seen much merit in his son's involvement as one of the original cast members in the West End stage production of Agatha Christie's whodunnit *The Mousetrap*, which opened in 1952 and is still on stage today after the longest run of a single production in theatre history.

As an actor, Attenborough was successful but frustrated. He felt typecast. His 'cherubic face' and 'short stature' counted against him as he told one journalist.[21] His move into producing was an expression of this frustration and also of his desire to control his own career. Together with his close friend actor-writer-director Bryan Forbes, he formed production company Beaver Films in 1958. The name, coined by their wives, reflected the work ethic both shared ('our two wives said we were idiots and always worked like beavers'[22]) and his home address, Beaver Lodge in Richmond Green.

'The need to have a professional partnership stemmed from a growing and shared dissatisfaction with the state of the film industry and our respective roles within the industry,' Forbes wrote in his autobiography.[23] Their first film was *The Angry Silence* (1960), directed by Guy Green. Attenborough played Tom Curtis, a worker in a factory who is ostracized ('sent to Coventry' in the slang of the day) by his old colleagues because he refuses to support an unofficial strike.

---

[21] *The Times*, 7 April 1969.
[22] Macnab, 'Eager Beaver'.
[23] Bryan Forbes, *A Divided Life: Memoirs* (London: Heinemann, 1992), 179.

A slice of hard-hitting social realism with trenchant points to make both about unions and bosses, *The Angry Silence* was a long way removed from the tasteful dramas and comedies made at British studios in the 1950s. Attenborough spent fourteen months raising the budget and refused to become crestfallen when his backers at British Lion agreed to finance it only for £100,000 rather than the £160,000 that he and Forbes had thought was the cheapest it would cost to make. Forbes later reminisced about Attenborough's enthusiasm and tenacity, suggesting they would have abandoned the project without his cajoling. When the actor originally cast pulled out of the production, Attenborough stepped in to take the lead role. For once, he wasn't playing a 'quivering psychopath'.

As a producer, Attenborough wasn't being paid. He was working full-time on completing the film, turning down acting work and depending on Forbes (who had some writing assignments) to ensure he could pay his bills. The film wasn't in any way an obvious commercial proposition but eventually it both provoked controversy and made money at the box office. As trade paper *Variety* noted in its review, this was a story told with 'passion, integrity and guts, but without false theatrical gimmicks'.[24]

It was telling that Attenborough identified so closely with Tom Curtis, the outsider shunned by his colleagues. Twenty-five years later, he had turned into the British film industry's quintessential insider but he always retained that underdog's mentality which enabled him to get *The Angry Silence* completed when other, less stubborn colleagues wanted to give up on it. His battle to finish the film seemed in hindsight like a rehearsal in microcosm for his twenty-year struggle to complete *Gandhi*.

Attenborough and Forbes went on to make *Whistle Down the Wind* (1961), *The L-Shaped Room* (1962) and *Séance on a Wet Afternoon* (1964). Attenborough, who was the producer, thrived on the job and hadn't even begun to think about directing. In order to make money, and to test himself, he also took roles in big films in the 1960s, among them *The Great Escape* (1963), *The Flight of the Phoenix* (1965) and *The Sand Pebbles* (1966). John Sturges cast him in *The Great Escape* after seeing him in *The Angry Silence*. It had only been when he

---

[24] *Variety*, 31 December 1959.

read about Gandhi that he began to think about directing. That, though, would take many years. Through John Mills, his near neighbour in Richmond, who showed him the screenplay, he was brought on to direct *Oh! What a Lovely War* (1969), based on the Joan Littlewood musical play about the First World War, which Len Deighton scripted and produced. There was no money to make it but Attenborough cajoled Charles Bluhdorn, the new boss at Paramount, into financing the film. Attenborough had lied to Bluhdorn about the big name actors already involved – most were his personal friends whom he then went and persuaded to appear in the movie.

In his later years, Attenborough was such a revered and familiar figure in British public life that it sometimes seemed his struggles had been forgotten about. He underwent an extraordinary metamorphosis. A well-regarded British film star and juvenile lead of the 1940s and character actor of the 1950s turned into an Oscar-winning producer and director. Attenborough attributed his leadership skills to his upbringing. 'It sounds cocky, but I have known ever since I became a Scout leader that I am good at being in charge,' he wrote late in his life. 'Maybe it's something to do with being the eldest son, but I am not afraid of responsibility. I'm happiest when I'm heading an enterprise, be it as a chairman or as a producer-director in sole charge of a film.'[25]

One of the ironies about his career is that although Attenborough was painfully conscious of his father's low opinions about the film industry and show business, his father's example sustained him in that industry.

Attenborough's close friend and collaborator Bryan Forbes wrote in an appreciation of Frederick Attenborough:

> It was impossible not to be infected with his enthusiasms or challenged by his humane opinions ... His conversations and his behaviour to the very end were those of somebody who believed there was something exciting around the corner. He scattered new ideas with the same recklessness as he smoked his pipe, and his listeners were scorched by both. I know his sons will forgive me if I say that their notable achievements stemmed entirely from the understanding he shared so generously.[26]

---

[25] Attenborough, *Entirely Up to You, Darling*, p. 47.
[26] *The Times*, 28 March 1973.

If his yearning to be worthy of his father drove him on throughout his career, he was also helped hugely by his wife Sheila, whom he met at RADA. They stayed together all his life; she was a bedrock at home but encouraged his career and interests throughout. Lady Attenborough died aged ninety-three, a little over a year after his death.

Attenborough didn't have an exaggerated sense of his own importance or qualities as a filmmaker. That meant he wasn't self-conscious about his work and was ready to accept the most varied of assignments whether rousing historical dramas like *Young Winston* (1972), musicals like *A Chorus Line* (1985), intimate dramas like *Shadowlands* (1993) or those epics like *A Bridge Too Far* (1977) and *Gandhi* (1982). He was famously good at taking charge of huge casts and crews. 'You have one operation, which is commanding a regiment, commanding an army. You either enjoy it or you don't. I do. I love organising and making all the logistics work,' he said of those set pieces he would shoot with multiple cameras and enormous crowds.[27] At the same time, he also acknowledged 'scenes played by one or two people who have lines are just as important, even set against that huge panorama'.[28]

Attenborough helped to re-establish the biopic as a genre of film drama in its own right. This was a form of filmmaking which had been popular in the 1930s, when Paul Muni was winning awards in Hollywood for films like *The Story of Louis Pasteur* (1936) and *The Life of Emile Zola* (1937) but had fallen out of fashion.

Attenborough was unashamedly an actor's director. 'I am not besotted by the technicalities of cinema. I am besotted by the subject matter to start with and therefore the telling of a story. I believe that the telling of that story is dependent on the skill of the actors. If an audience is prepared to suspend its disbelief and identify with the players, then you will win your audience, then you will tell your story, then you will make your points,' he explained his philosophy late in his career in an interview.[29] He always maintained that it was 'working with the actors that he loved more than anything else'. His pride

---

[27]Macnab, 'Eager Beaver'.
[28]Ibid.
[29]BEHP, interview with Richard Attenborough.

was in the performances he managed to elicit from actors as varied as Ben Kingsley in *Gandhi* (1982), Anthony Hopkins and Debra Winger in *Shadowlands* (1993), Simon Ward in *Young Winston* (1972) and Sandra Bullock in *Love and War* (1996).

The middle-aged British character actor of the early 1960s had two key traits which enabled him to keep on going in the face of continual rejection. He knew how to compartmentalize. Like Orson Welles, he would take acting jobs in big international movies to underwrite his own activities as a producer and director. When he was appearing in films like *The Great Escape* and *The Flight of the Phoenix* (both 1965) or singing and dancing in *Doctor Doolittle* (1967), he could concentrate on the work at hand, focus on the character he was playing (often very well) and forget about his ongoing struggles to finance films nobody else seemingly wanted to support or believed in.

Attenborough's other great trait, arguably the one which kept him afloat in the most difficult times, was his extraordinary Micawber-like optimism. In spite of the opposition and setbacks he encountered, he was always convinced that everything would turn out just as he wanted eventually. He didn't bear grudges or mope about missed opportunities. Instead, he started each new day as if it was a new beginning, full of possibility. He called himself a 'male Mary Poppins' whose glass was always half full. He was convinced that, sooner or later, he would successfully make the kind of film that would have made his father proud of him.

At the National Film and Television School gala launch of a Richard Attenborough fund for young filmmakers in 2013, a taped message was played from Steven Spielberg. He described Attenborough (who had appeared in his film *Jurassic Park*) as 'one of his favourite people on the planet'. Spielberg explained: 'He's made some of the best movies of all time – he made *Gandhi*! – and has made such a contribution to society, to cinema and to everyone whose hearts he has touched with his words, works, his leadership and that divine inspiration that radiates from that wonderful smile.'[30]

While pursuing his own career interests, Attenborough never lost sight of those of the British film industry as a whole. His role in lobbying the Margaret

---

[30]NFTS website.

Thatcher and John Major governments, ensuring public support for the industry and setting in motion the transformation of the UK into a hub for international filmmaking has been chronicled exhaustively elsewhere. At the famous Downing Street summit on the film industry in 1990, Attenborough had marched into meet the prime minister flanked by someone whose energy levels matched those of his own, the *Chariots of Fire* producer David Puttnam.

3

David Puttnam[1]

The wine-induced barracking took David Puttnam by surprise. The British film producer was at the BAFTA awards. His film *Chariots of Fire* (1981) was up for the main award. One of the other favoured nominees was Karel Reisz's *The French Lieutenant's Woman* (1981). Reisz was a respected, much-liked figure who had emerged as one of the new wave of British filmmakers in the 1960s alongside figures like Tony Richardson and John Schlesinger. These were Oxbridge-educated cineastes who wrote for film magazines as well as directing movies themselves.

Reisz's stable were in one part of the room. During what Puttnam remembers as 'an increasingly unpleasant evening' they made their disapproval obvious when *Chariots of Fire* won the Best Film BAFTA. 'When it was announced that we had won, they booed.' For Puttnam born in 1941, this was a reminder that he and his colleagues were still regarded as outsiders. They hadn't been to university let alone Oxbridge. They had come into the film business through advertising and were viewed as interlopers and even as 'thugs'. Winning BAFTAs and Oscars didn't necessarily change that perception.

It was just over a decade since he had decided to leave advertising. His rise through British cinema had been phenomenal but Puttnam still did not feel accepted or at ease. 'I was frustrated because having got quite good at what I was doing in advertising I was increasingly aware that I was engaged in selling other people's products. We had had no influence over the product itself,'

---

[1]Unless otherwise cited, material and quotes in this chapter are from the author's interview with Lord Puttnam, London, May 2019.

Lord David Puttnam. Photo: Ian Gavan/Getty Images for Film Distributors'
Association.

Puttnam recalls of his ten-year stint in the advertising business principally at
Collett Dickenson Pearce (one of the most influential agencies in the London
of the 1960s). 'If the product wasn't any good, it didn't matter how creative I
and my colleagues were. We had a problem.'

Matters came to a head when Puttnam was put to work on a campaign for
lingerie. His client was Pretty Polly Stockings, based in Nottingham. At a
meeting with its managing director he tried to point out that the campaign
wasn't clicking because women were switching to pantyhose, and away from
stockings. '[Film director] Alan Parker had done some very nice rather sexy
ads but the market was moving against us. I remember coming back on the
train and arguing with my boss that, "We are on a fool's errand here. We are
trying to sell something the market doesn't want."'

At around this time, Puttnam saw Mike Nichols's celebrated romantic
comedy *The Graduate* (1967), famous for its portrayal of the love affair between
a young man fresh out of college and a much older woman. 'I remember
thinking that [the movie] was a great product. I get that. There was this terrific
music [from Simon and Garfunkel], an attractive young man [Dustin Hoffman],
an interesting story and the whole thing was entirely identifiable to my age

group.' This was the moment Puttnam saw the light. 'The idea that I held the bridge of my nose and wanted to make great movies – it wasn't like that. It was actually the idea that there was a world out there you could market to and which was a bloody sight more interesting than selling stockings.'

His first move after quitting the ad agency in 1968 was to start up a photography agency, David Puttnam Associates, representing photographers like Brian Duffy and David Bailey.

Puttnam's father, Leonard 'Len' Puttnam, was a photographer who had served with distinction as a photojournalist during the Second World War. Len, who had started work at the age of twelve, had begun his career operating the lights at boxing matches and working as a messenger on Fleet Street.

The producer's beloved grandmother had been a charlady in Stoke Newington. 'She used to do people's steps . . . she had a very tough life.' She lived in humble circumstances close to White Hart Lane, the then Tottenham Hotspur football ground.

When David was growing up in north London, the idea that he would one day become an Oscar-winning film producer, let alone a senior figure in the House of Lords, would have seemed fantastical. 'When I got introduced into the House of Lords, the great brass doors opened, you've got all your robes on and right in front of you is the throne. I remember thinking that not in her wildest dreams could my grandmother have ever possibly imagined this would be happening to her grandson. I could almost see her watching from above the throne.'

He suggests that his success first in the film industry and later in politics 'speaks volumes for Britain in the twentieth century that those opportunities did become possible, that that degree of social mobility did occur'. Others from his school, Minchenden Grammar School in Southgate, were also able to carve themselves careers in science, the arts and industry. Fellow alumni, some of whom overlapped with Puttnam, include PR guru Lynne Franks, as well as NASA scientists, bishops, politicians, journalists and two fellow peers.

Puttnam began his career as a messenger at an advertising agency. He had grown up loving movies but without any specialist knowledge about them. 'I could walk to five cinemas. Actually, I could walk to four but it was only a short bus ride to the fifth,' he recalls of the easy access to new films in Southgate. As a kid, he went to Saturday morning cinema club at the local Odeon. 'It was mayhem. We used to see the western serials but the biggest thing was whether you could get up on the balcony and throw sweets at the people below. That was the principal object of the exercise.'

Many years later, when the Odeon Southgate was being demolished, the TV presenter and film journalist Barry Norman asked the builders to 'rescue' some bric-à-brac from the cinema for Puttnam. He ended up with an Odeon door handle, 'Sunday and all next week' sign and an electronic 'Exit' sign.

As he grew older, on Sunday nights Puttnam would search out the latest feature in Technicolor and then watch other Hollywood offerings throughout the week. He would only go to see British black-and-white films when all other options had been exhausted. Michael Balcon's Ealing Studios may have been in its pomp when Puttnam was a kid but he didn't search out their movies, like *The Man in the White Suit* (1951) or *The Ladykillers* (1953). He'd sometimes get to those at the end of the week, after he had seen the big western or the American screwball comedy or latest teen movie. 'I became obsessed with James Dean. I think I was in love with Susan Hayward. I was definitely mad about Montgomery Clift,' he says of his fascination with certain American stars.

Puttnam, though, was clearly curious about the British industry. During the holidays he would go on bike rides to Elstree Studios and linger by the gates, trying to catch glimpses of movie stars going in and out. His father was friendly with Robert Lennard, casting director at ABC, and Lennard's son was at the same school. The next-door neighbour was (Uncle) Charles Parkhouse, managing director of Kays Laboratories whose wife, Olive, had been a film editor.

Puttnam later met the young manager of the Odeon Southgate, Chris Hilton, who would go on to become manager of the Odeon Haymarket, during the time many of Puttnam's films (including *Midnight Express*, *Chariots of Fire* and *Local Hero*) were premiered there.

Working at the ad agency in London, Puttnam began to broaden his film-going habits. He'd go to the Academy Cinema on Oxford Street or to the National Film Theatre on the South Bank. The latter venue had the advantage of being next door to two of the best sunken tennis courts in central London. Puttnam was a fanatical tennis player. His aunt Kitty lived in a flat near the grounds in Wimbledon and he spent most of his summers in the mid-1950s staying with her during the Championships. If you lived locally and were therefore not a cost burden on the Lawn Tennis Association, it was no big deal to seek qualification for Junior Wimbledon. Puttnam entered, but after being humiliatingly knocked out in the first round by a younger opponent, he didn't pick up a racquet again for eighteen years! Prior to that he'd race out of work, have an hour of tennis and then watch the evening movie at the NFT.

By reading the credits, he worked out that the producer and director were probably the most important figures in the films . . . their acknowledgements coming last. However, most of the producers had names that ended with 'z', whereas he was an Englishman from the suburbs of north London.

After the epiphany of watching *The Graduate*, Puttnam began plotting a way to get into the industry. Thanks to his neighbour Uncle Charles, who was a senior member of the Association of Cinematograph, Television and Allied Technicians (ACTT), he was able to meet ACTT General Secretary George Elvin. They had tea together.

'Do you have a ticket?' Elvin asked.

'No,' Puttnam replied.

'Well, you can't join the union without a ticket – in fact you can't work without a ticket.'

Puttnam asked how to get a ticket. 'You have to find a way to work in the industry.'

The conversation went around in predictable circles. He eventually thanked Elvin for the tea and was leaving, with his hand on the doorknob, when Elvin called after him: 'You could always be a producer, you know. You don't need a ticket to be a producer because you're an employer.'

By then, Puttnam was in his late twenties and was well established as a photographers' agent. He may not then have known exactly what a producer did but he was a relentless networker. He knew Marit Allen, an editor at *Vogue*, and met her boyfriend, later her husband, Sandy Lieberson, the American agent and producer based in Britain. Lieberson had a company called Goodtimes Enterprises. Puttnam had his own company, David Puttnam Associates, so they joined forces at Goodtimes. 'Sandy provided an amazing address book and my job was the cash flow,' is how Puttnam characterizes the partnership.

Through his contacts in advertising and photography, he had got to know film industry figures like actor and producer David Hemmings, Hemmings's business partner at Hemdale John Daly, Island Records boss Chris Blackwell and music impresario Robert Stigwood. Puttnam asked Stigwood if he thought the Bee Gees would be interested in doing a musical score for a film. Stigwood came back and said they were busy but would allow some of their songs to be used in a movie.

Coming up with a viable script was the next challenge. Puttnam may have been well connected with photographers and pop stars but he didn't know many writers beyond his old colleagues from agency days, Charles Saatchi and Alan Parker. Saatchi wrote a script called *The Carpet Man* but that failed to get anywhere. Puttnam suggested to Parker that he write a screenplay about their childhoods and the jealousies and misunderstandings between boys and girls. Parker latched on to one of the Bee Gees' songs, 'First of May', as a particular inspiration as he set about writing what became *Melody*. 'There is a lyric in the song "The First of May" that goes, "When we were small, and Christmas trees were tall, we used to love while others used to play," and I framed the story around that thought, mixed in with memories of my own childhood growing up in North London, and a few memories from Puttnam,' Parker later told show-business trade magazine *Variety*.[2]

Puttnam and Parker knew so little about the film business that they had no idea how a film script was supposed to be laid out. Puttnam got a script from Sandy Lieberson to show to Parker. With their advertising backgrounds, they were as concerned as much with presentation as with content. They worked hard to make the script look as good as possible, providing a very glossy cover with elaborate graphics. Puttnam knew that Hemmings and Daly were looking for work for two young actors they represented, Mark Lester and Jack Wild, the young stars of Oscar-winning musical *Oliver!* (1968), but didn't have a project for them. However, Parker's script for *Melody* had roles that could suit them both.

Showing typical negotiating skills, Puttnam acknowledged to Hemdale that he couldn't afford to pay the young actors but that he would offer them a stake

---

[2]Alan Parker, quoted in *Variety*, 16 October 2015.

in the film instead. He had secured the Bee Gees' songs for a token fee and off the back of these two coups managed to raise the money to make the film, all in all a considerable achievement for someone with no track record.

At first, he had no intention of trying to produce *Melody* himself. He had approached Gavrik Losey, the son of director Joseph Losey, to take on the task. However, when he went to New York to meet his financiers Seagrams (the drinks company which was putting up two-thirds of the money), Seagrams' boss Edgar Bronfman was keen to trumpet his involvement to the media and brought in a journalist from *Variety*, Hy Hollinger, to make the announcement about his entering the movie business in earnest. Puttnam was invited to tell the journalist all about the film, which was to be directed by Waris Hussein. The journalist eventually asked, 'Who is going to produce it?' On the spur of the moment, Puttnam said, 'Me'. Chewing his pen, the journalist asked the follow-up question: 'How do you spell your name?' The following day *Variety* announced that Puttnam was a film producer. Nobody questioned what he knew about his job or whether he had ever actually done it before. Puttnam flew back to London to break the news to Gavrik Losey that he would now be the associate producer but cushioned the blow by boosting his salary.

Puttnam found himself startled by the level of nepotism and hostility towards outsiders he encountered in the film business. He came from advertising – a far more egalitarian environment. 'I found it quite weird and it became apparent that Alan [Parker] and I and later Ridley [Scott] had to gatecrash the British film industry. We were not invited in, in fact I'd say it was quite the opposite.'

Puttnam and his colleagues didn't have access to the very first rank of technicians. 'The first assistant directors who had worked for David Lean, John Huston, Billy Wilder or Fred Zinnemann were a fantastic elite and they were very, very good at their jobs – but they had little or no interest in us. Theirs was a different world.'

The producer still bristles at the way critics condescended to Ridley Scott, reminding their readers in reviews of his early films like *The Duellists* (1977) that he came from the world of advertising; that he had a strong visual sense but what, they would invariably ask, was he doing making feature films? 'I think it was because we came from advertising that we were always considered somewhat below the salt,' Puttnam remembers. He also points out that if you worked in film, you couldn't move sideways into television. The union regulations prevented that.

The resistance to Puttnam, Parker, Scott and co. wasn't principally based on their accents or their childhood backgrounds. If they had been working-class kids who had made it to Oxford or Cambridge and then written for the BFI's highbrow magazine *Sight & Sound*, they might have had the chance of being accepted. However, making adverts for Hovis and Bird's Eye didn't cut it. The old guard saw the industry in a very stratified way. There were the technicians whose families might have been in the business for generations; there were the writers who might have had their work put on at the Royal Court Theatre; and then there were the directors, many of whom came into features via documentary and saw themselves as social historians. 'There is nothing wrong with that but they could have been a lot more welcoming,' Puttnam says of the lack of warmth he and his colleagues encountered.

As he grew more successful, Puttnam enjoyed turning the condescension back against his detractors. He would try to infuriate them by telling them that he wasn't really a film producer at all but was 'an unreconstructed marketing man who happens to be making his own products'. He would also tell them that he thoroughly enjoyed making rock-and-roll films, and it was true that *Melody* (1971), *The Pied Piper* (1971), *That'll Be the Day* (1973) and *Stardust* (1974) were all music based. One early and important collaborator was Ray Connolly, the writer of *That'll Be the Day* and *Stardust* who had been at the London School of Economics at the same time as Mick Jagger and enjoyed a fair degree of fame as a journalist, specializing in interviewing pop stars. 'I wasn't working with anyone who was really of the industry,' Puttnam remembers.

One film which pulled him closer to the mainstream was Alan Parker's *Bugsy Malone* (1976), a gangster movie in which the main parts were all played by kids, with child star Jodie Foster in the lead role. The film played at the Cannes Film Festival. On the night it premiered, Puttnam and Parker attended an eightieth birthday dinner in honour of Ealing boss Michael Balcon, hosted by *Sunday Times* reviewer Dilys Powell and arranged by producer Michael

Relph. Balcon made a speech in which he went out of his way to praise *Bugsy Malone* and to credit it with reviving the hopes of a resurgent British film industry. Puttnam remembers this as the first piece of 'affirmation' he received from the industry establishment. 'It was almost as if, in a weird way, he anointed us.'

Bugsy had initially been shunned. The Cannes Film Festival hadn't wanted it but accepted it because there was no other British film available. It was programmed in a totally unfavourable slot, very late in the festival. After its wildly successful Cannes screening, Puttnam bumped into David Picker, a seasoned Hollywood studio executive who had just become President of Motion Pictures at Paramount. Picker said to him, 'Gee, that Parker, he's a very talented guy. Do you know any more like him? I'd love to meet them if you do.' Puttnam responded that, as a matter of fact, he did. He then went around asking for coins so that he could call Ridley Scott back in the UK and tell him to come straight down to Cannes. Scott quickly jumped on a flight and arrived in time for lunch on the Carlton beach with Picker and Puttnam the next day. Scott and Puttnam tried to sell Picker on one idea but the Paramount boss passed, saying it was too expensive. They then pitched him *The Duellists* instead. Picker asked how much they needed. Puttnam picked a figure out of thin air: '$1.4 million.' 'Ok, I'll do that one,' Picker replied. He didn't ask to see the script. He backed the project, which launched Scott's directorial career, entirely based on the conversation over the lunch table and Picker's admiration for Parker's work on *Bugsy Malone*.

During the mid-1970s, Puttnam was able to spend time with Michael Balcon. From a vantage point almost fifty years on, he can see parallels between his career and that of the Ealing boss. Just as Balcon had had a difficult time when employed by MGM and working within the Hollywood system (albeit based in Britain) in the late 1930s, Puttnam had been burned during his short stint as Chairman and Chief Executive Officer of Columbia Pictures (1986–1988). He learned how exhibitors had turned on Balcon after the Ealing boss broke the embargo on selling films to TV during the so-called FIDO (Film Industry Defence Organisation) years.

Balcon would tell Puttnam of his disappointment over *Tom Jones* (1963), the film the executive produced on behalf of Woodfall Films (the company set up Tony Richardson, John Osborne and Harry Saltzman). They just hadn't been able to raise quite enough money to finance the picture and had to turn to United Artists. When the movie won the Oscar and turned out to be a runaway success, UA were the ones who benefited most as Woodfall faltered. Balcon's career underlined the proposition that even the most successful and established British producers continually felt they were walking on quicksand.

Puttnam's time at Columbia remains a source of heated debate. He took a Balcon-like approach to running a Hollywood studio, stopping his executives from being picked up by stretch limousines at the airport or driving Rolls-Royces as he tried to foster a more collegiate atmosphere. He baulked at extravagance for its own sake, even refusing to green light a sequel to *Ghostbusters* on the grounds that the deal being proposed allowed no opportunity for the studio to make money. Warren Beatty was famously suspicious of him even though he went out of his way to keep his distance from Beatty's troubled production *Ishtar* (1987).

All the time, Puttnam was looking to enable other like-minded figures to enter the industry in a more straightforward way than he had himself. He may have been a Hollywood studio boss but he also served as chairman of his section of the trade union, the ACTT. This was during the apartheid era. Puttnam couldn't help but notice that at one packed union meeting, at which the union passed a motion in support of an anti-apartheid boycott, only one face in the room wasn't white – a sign that despite having its heart in the right place this had yet to become a diverse or inclusive industry.

'We were all of us in different ways trying to break the mould,' Puttnam says of colleagues who entered the industry around the same time as him. 'The deferential industry that existed was very much as it had been in the 1930s. From the beginning of sound film, that mould had not been altered very much. I'm in danger of making this sound too heroic. I don't mean it that way at all, but we simply had to find another way. The establishment of the film school [National Film School] proved to be that "other way".'

The then Managing Director of BBC Television, Alasdair Milne, had offered Puttnam the chance to become head of drama in 1979 but he didn't relish the prospect of giving up as a producer to become an executive at the BBC.

Distribution and exhibition were at that time as closed to outsiders as was production. The ABC and Odeon bookers, Bob Webster and George Pinches, operated as a de facto duopoly. They chose which films screened where, with little regard to concepts of free trade. Thanks to the support of Nat Cohen at Anglo-Amalgamated (owned by ABC), Puttnam was somewhat protected from Webster. He also eventually built a strong personal relationship with Pinches. Unlike many other British producers, he was able to ensure the films he produced were seen in both of the leading UK chains but he chafed against such obvious restraints to doing business in an open and fair way.

As an outsider, Puttnam quickly realized that to succeed he needed to get to know the industry inside out. Thanks to his marketing background, he knew how to sell movies to the public but he made it his business to understand exhibition and distribution as well. He would go 'night after night' to watch his own movies and to see how the public reacted to them. He quickly realized that when cinemas sold out a new release on a Friday night, the circuits would automatically re-book the films for the following week. He would therefore drive around and buy up any spare tickets to ensure his films stayed on screen. 'It's a bit like the charts. I got to know which of the cinemas triggered the decisions.'

His success and that of Parker paved the way for Ridley Scott and others to follow. He also mentored young producers like Iain Smith, who would go on to produce *Mad Max: Fury Road* (2013), Uberto Pasolini, producer of *The Full Monty* (1997), and Simon Bosanquet, producer of *Ripley's Game* (2002). Puttnam was also recruited early in his career to be a governor at the National Film School. He saw the School, founded in 1971, as an opportunity to counter the bad old habits of nepotism and special favours that had typified the British film industry when he had first encountered it.

Eventually, Puttnam's passion for producing would dissipate. He says that *Memphis Belle* (1990) was the last film into which he really threw himself, heart and soul. The second half of his career has been devoted to his political career in the House of Lords. Nonetheless, even during his years working for the Labour Party in the Lords, he has remained involved in the British film industry and film culture – and continued to use his influence to provide more straightforward pathways into the industry than had existed when he made his start as a producer.

'I've never stopped doing stuff on film. There has never been any time that I can think of when I wasn't advocating for cinema in the Lords,' Puttnam says. He stayed active as a teacher of Film Studies and is still regarded as one of the UK film industry's most influential spokespersons. Working closely with industry consultant and author Neil Watson, he has continued to intervene in every pressing debate. He has used his position as President of the Film Distributors' Association to make an annual address in which he provides an influential and very wide-ranging analysis of the way cinema is evolving. He sees his work there as 'a way of joining some of the dots together' and 'of giving voice to thoughts and feelings and beliefs that I've absolutely always had'.

At his home in Ireland, Puttnam has his own small cinema and watches around sixty to seventy films a year.

In the latter stage of his career, Puttnam had almost become the philosopher king of UK cinema. At the same time, as a politician in the Lords, he was heavily involved in debates about climate change, Brexit, education and the digital economy. As he said, it was impossible to combine film producing with a full-time career in politics. You can't work on a film unless you are fully committed to it. 'It's a bit like the tar baby – it sticks to you and you can't half do a movie.' However, the man who once felt shunned by the British film industry because he came from the dubious world of advertising finally became regarded as one of its most venerated and influential insiders.

4

Betty Box

Betty E. Box (1915–1999), the only female British producer in the immediate post-war British film industry, was a fixer extraordinaire. There was seemingly no problem that she couldn't solve. If a director wanted to shoot from a hot air balloon or to reconstruct the blood lust of the mobs around the guillotine during the French Revolution, she could sort it out. If an actor fell sick at the last moment, she would find a replacement. She charmed agents, exhibitors, Fleet Street editors and censors alike while balancing the books and making a series of films that were so successful journalists quickly nicknamed her 'Betty Box Office'.

Box was tiny, 5 feet 2 inches tall. She was a glamorous figure who liked fur coats and fast cars. 'Betty Box, vital young Englishwoman, has added much to the impressive record of achievement of eminent modern women,' enthused Australian newspaper *The Age*, in a February 1951 profile of her.[1]

The producer was also extraordinarily resilient and was involved in every aspect of the films she worked on. In the weeks they opened, she would drive up and down Oxford Street checking the posters. Crews loved her and would accompany her to the most far-flung locations while also working long hours for her at the studios.

Box once described herself as a 'girl Friday' who had only entered the British film industry to help her big brother in 1942. The Beckenham-born Betty had been working as a commercial artist. Sydney, seven years older, was a prolific

---

[1] *The Age*, 10 February 1951, 9.

Betty Box. Photo: Keystone Features/Hulton Archive/Getty Images.

writer and producer who had come into the business after working as a
journalist. They weren't from a wealthy background (their father was a market
gardener and florist). Sydney described the cottage they grew up in as 'a
cramped, inconvenient apology for a home, with a leaky slate roof and wooden
walls' and provided Dickensian descriptions of what he and his siblings
endured as kids. 'I still shudder at the memory of one period of two weeks

when our diet consisted solely of porridge, boiled sweets and cocoa.'[2] Both Betty and Sydney were relentlessly energetic figures. Betty, who had a twin sister Kitty, had had to leave school early after her father fell ill but didn't let her lack of qualifications hold her back.

Sydney set up his company Verity Films, together with Jay Gardner Lewis, at the start of the war and had hurled himself into producing propaganda and training films for the government. With many film industry employees away at war, Sydney was short-handed. He and his partner Lewis split up with each other after arguing over finances. That was why he recruited Betty, then in her late twenties, as 'dogsbody' to join him at Verity in 1942.

'I knew almost nothing about film production but I could answer telephones, add up accurately, type a little, make tea and sew on buttons,' Betty remembers her unlikely start in the film business in her autobiography. 'As even more of our colleagues went off to fight, there was no job I didn't do, except actually operate a movie camera or use the complicated editing equipment.'[3]

Between them, the brother and sister from Kent were credited with making over 200 short films during the war years. Betty had no film training whatsoever but, through common sense and very hard work, quickly transformed herself into one of the British film industry's most prolific and efficient producers, overseeing several filmmaking units at once.

Months after she started with Sydney, Box was already budgeting projects and cutting deals to get them made with (as she later listed them) the 'War Office, Admiralty, Ministry of Information (now the COI), the British Council and the Air Ministry'. She even did a 'Hitchcock', appearing in one of her own films, *Jigsaw* (1943), produced for the Admiralty and about how 'careless talk costs lives'.[4] The obvious irony is that Betty would never have had the chance to make such a rapid ascent if it hadn't been for the shortage in personnel caused by the war. She later told one journalist that she learned more in two years at Verity during the war than she would have done in a decade or more during peacetime.

---

[2] In Andrew Spicer, *Sydney Box* (Manchester: Manchester University Press, 2006), 8.
[3] Betty Box, *Lifting the Lid: The Autobiography of Film Producer Betty Box* (Lewes: Book Guild, 2000), 38.
[4] Ibid., 28.

'My sister Betty, who had never been in a film studio until 1940, never seen a production budget or handled a camera unit, had meanwhile blossomed in a matter of months into one of the best production managers the business has ever known, with a remarkable gift for persuading temperamental film technicians to give of their best,' Sydney marvelled at how quickly Box picked up the skills needed by a producer.[5]

Oscar-winning producer Jeremy Thomas, the son of Box's director partner Ralph Thomas, speaks of her 'drive to succeed in a male-dominated industry' and describes her as 'a powerhouse'. 'She is somebody who would be fully equipped in today's world to deal with everything that would be thrown at her. She is somebody who was very light footed and very, very delicate [but] persuasive and single minded,' Thomas says.[6]

Box graduated to producing features at Gainsborough Studios, where Sydney (who worked very closely with his writer-director wife Muriel Box) was put in charge of production by the Rank Organisation in 1946 after his runaway success with *The Seventh Veil* the year before. The young producer carried on much as before. She had experience at Verity Films of working with talented and sometimes difficult collaborators, among them writers Dylan Thomas and Laurie Lee and director Carol Reed. She knew how to stretch budgets, keep projects on schedule and placate crews. She produced ten feature films in under two years at Gainsborough's Islington base. (Sydney was markedly less prolific at Gainsborough's second home in Shepherd's Bush.)

Producing a film in 1940s Britain was an exhausting and mind-boggling task. 'In those immediate postwar years filmmakers worked long hours, six days a week and sometimes seven. And each year we had just two weeks' holiday; by tradition we closed the studios for the first fortnight in August, even if we happened to be halfway through a film,' she later recalled.[7]

On almost all her films, Box had to spend many hours corresponding both with the British Board of Film Censors and the Motion Picture Association of America (MPAA), which oversaw the Production Code, the list of strict and sometimes fussy and prudish regulations guiding films released in America.

---

[5]Spicer, *Sydney Box*.
[6]Jeremy Thomas, interviewed by the author, 10 June 2019.
[7]Box, *Lifting the Lid*, 43.

It is instructive to read the correspondence with the censors from one of her first projects at Islington, Arthur Crabtree's crime drama *Dear Murderer* (1947), starring Eric Portman and Greta Gynt. Box received a letter (7 May 1947) from Joseph Breen, head of the Production Code Administration (PCA), which went through the film in forensic detail, identifying moments which US audiences needed to be protected from. The film is about a jealous husband (Portman) who murders his unfaithful wife's lover. The script threw Breen and the American censors into a lather. They saw sex and violence, either real or implied, on almost every page.

The script (Breen wrote) could not be approved in its present state 'because of the number of details of crime which could easily be imitated and because of other unacceptable elements'. There were standard rules which the Production Code applied rigorously: it was (Breen reminded Box) 'mandatory that the intimate parts of the body – specifically, the breast of women – be fully covered at all times'. 'Open-mouthed or lustful kissing' was also strictly proscribed. Box would have known this already but Breen's letter went on to complain about a camera dissolve which 'seems to suggest a sex affair is taking place'. Even references to extra-marital affairs were considered out of order. 'The Inspector's line, "your brother had an affair with her," is unacceptably blunt, and could not be approved,' Breen warned. 'The Inspector's line, "and I'm sure nobody would have blamed you if you'd taken the law into your own hands," is unacceptable as a condonation of a proposed murder,' he added. Even scenes of someone wiping away fingerprints at the site of a crime were questioned on the grounds that they could inspire copycat crime among US audiences. 'The expression "to knock hell out of" is unacceptable,' was another warning.[8]

Box dealt with the American censor's recommendations as well as she could but her frustration was also apparent. Breen had fretted at the amount of drinking in the script and had advised that it be curtailed as much as possible. This rankled with Box who couldn't help but notice that two high-profile recent American successes, Billy Wilder's *The Lost Weekend* (1945) and Stuart Heisler's *A Woman Destroyed* (aka *Smash-up, The Story of a Woman*) (1947), both dramas about alcoholism, had been full of boozing. She also griped that

---

[8]*Dear Murderer* notes, June 1947, Betty Box, BFI Special Collections.

Breen was asking her to take out a conversation which he claimed was 'unacceptably sex-suggestive' but whose removal would leave a hole in the plot.

Eventually, Box won the Breen office's approval. When *Dear Murderer* was finally released in the US two years later as the supporting feature to the James Stewart and Joan Fontaine romantic comedy *You Gotta Stay Happy* (1948), it was warmly received. The voluminous correspondence over the censorship issues reveals one aspect of the producer's life invisible to the public at large. It must have been mind-numbing, distracting and exhausting to deal with letter after letter from Breen and his colleagues questioning every reference to sex, alcohol or God.

Betty was genial but decisive on set. There are hints of her ruthlessness in remarks she made to Sydney about the slow pace set by her cinematographer Bryan Langley on one of her next films, *When the Bough Breaks* (1947), about a young mother struggling to cope after giving up her child to foster parents. 'Our schedule is being thrown entirely out of gear. Yesterday although we had been on a set for two weeks he used up to 250 minutes out of the day's work for lighting,' Box complained early during production as Langley dithered.[9]

This was austerity-era Britain. Box was working on tight budgets and schedules and simply wouldn't accept any self-indulgence from her collaborators. By the time of her next film, *Miranda* (1948), it was telling that a new cinematographer, Ray Elton, was in place.

Miranda was about a mermaid (Glynis Johns) who gets up to high jinks in London. Again, Box showed her ruthlessness, replacing the two original co-directors with Ken Annakin, with whom she had worked at Verity Films, early in the production. 'If the two co-directors . . . completed it in the manner they had directed the first 10 days' work, the result would not have been capable of obtaining a major circuit release,' Box justified her behaviour. 'In my experience as a film producer it is generally accepted that a producer has the right to replace a director if he thinks the director's work is unsatisfactory.'[10]

The film provoked yet more interference from the Breen office. 'As to the scene of Miranda in the early part of the story, in which she is described as

---

[9]Letter to Sydney Box, 27 February 1947, BFI Special Collections.
[10]Betty Box, BFI Special Collections.

nude to the waist, with her hair the only covering for her breasts, it will be essential that some form of costuming be devised for her upper body. One suggestion which occurs to us would be to have her adequately covered with sea weed,' Breen suggested. The American censors were adamant 'no toilet should be shown in the bathroom scenes' and that any references to 'laughable effeminacy' and homosexuality should be deleted. Even the exclamations 'good Lord!' and 'good God!' were off limits (as, of course, was 'damn'). 'The showcasing of her Mer-baby could not be approved,' the American censor noted of the idea that the mermaid might actually give birth.[11]

As if dealing with the censors wasn't enough, Box also had to placate sports manufacturers Dunlop, who had furnished the mermaid with her rubber tail but felt their contribution wasn't fully acknowledged in the credits.

Box had a populist touch. In the late 1940s, she oversaw the production of the Huggett comedies, which can be seen as a forerunner both of the *Carry On* movies (they were co-written by Peter Rogers, Box's husband and later the producer behind the *Carry On* franchise) and of British TV soap operas. These were comedies about the everyday problems and dramas in the lives of a working-class British family. The films were aimed at audiences in the suburbs and the provinces – and were deliberately kept away from the carping London critics. They starred well-known British character actors (Jack Warner and Kathleen Harrison) as the parents and talented newcomers (among them Diana Dors, Susan Shaw and Petula Clark) as their kids.

On these films, as on all her other projects, Box as producer would be confronted with unlikely challenges and obstacles. A real life couple, Mr Vane Huggett and his wife Muriel, complained that the films were using their names and secured a £500 pay-off.

In today's British industry, producers will generally spend two to three years making a single film. Betty Box was turning out new films every couple of months as a producer or associate producer. *Dear Murderer, The Upturned Glass, When the Bough Breaks, Here Come the Huggetts, Daybreak, The Blind Goddess, Miranda, Vote for Huggett, It's Not Cricket, The Huggetts Abroad,*

---

[11]Ibid.

Marry Me, Christopher Columbus and *Don't Ever Leave Me* were all made over a two-year period between 1947 and 1949. Box was involved in everything to do with them. She had a reported annual budget of £500,000 to control and 250 staff under her – and so, just five years after coming into the industry, she was already a fully fledged mogul.

On *It's Not Cricket* (1949), Box and the publicity team tried to link up with the Australian national cricket team, in England for the 1948 Ashes under the leadership of the legendary batsman Don Bradman. 'Probably Bradman can be invited to the studios but this must be organised as soon as possible as they start their tour almost immediately,' Box and the publicists decided after a pre-production meeting in April 1948.[12]

At the same time, she was signing off on tie-up arrangements with Dolcis shoe stores and trying to ensure that the lead actress, Hazel Court, had half a dozen new outfits specially made for the production. This was a time of rationing, shortages and general post-war belt tightening and fatigue. Box realized it was her responsibility to provide British cinema goers with a taste of the glamour they didn't get elsewhere in their lives.

Box couldn't hide her frustration at the privileged treatment the Rank Organisation afforded to favoured filmmakers like David Lean and Michael Powell, who were allowed to spend fortunes and take mini-eternities in making films like *Great Expectations* (1946), *A Matter of Life and Death* (1946) and *Black Narcissus* (1947) at Pinewood or Denham Studios at the same time as she was working on a shoestring for Rank at Islington. British production in this period was a two-tiered system. Rank hoped that his extravagant, big-budget films would break into the all-important American market. (The UK on its own was too small to generate the size of profits Rank craved.) At the same time, the more modestly budgeted features made at Gainsborough Studios were expected to recoup their costs in British cinemas alone and perhaps to make a small profit.

For all the success of the Huggetts films, Box clearly craved to work on a grander scale. One of her first opportunities came with the period thriller *So Long at the Fair* (1950), co-directed by Terence Fisher (later to make the best

---

[12]Ibid.

known of the Hammer horror movies) and Anthony Darnborough, and starring Jean Simmons and Dirk Bogarde. The film, shot at Pinewood, was largely set in nineteenth-century Paris. A British brother and sister travel to the city for the World's Fair where sinister things begin to happen. A hot-air balloon bursts into flames. People go missing. There are hints that the plague may have returned.

Box only came on board as producer when Darnborough was held up on another film, *The Astonished Heart* (1950), but she hurled into the project with her usual enthusiasm. At first, she wanted to shoot in France. The unions in both countries baulked at that idea. The British were heavily in debt after the war and there were restrictions on spending sterling abroad. However, Box and her team were painstaking in their re-creation of late 1880s Paris and went to great lengths to ensure that the balloon sequence was as authentic as possible.

They consulted with Dr H. Roxbee Cox, the President of the Royal Aeronautical Society and Britain's leading authority on hot-air balloons. 'He [Roxbee-Cox] advised us it would be impossible to get what we want from home sources. It would, in fact, be necessary for us to design, manufacture and test etc our own balloon, which is an expensive and doubtful proposition, particularly with the time factor involved,' Box's assistant Vivian Cox noted of the decision to import the hot-air balloon from France.[13]

Box and her team had to provide the gas to inflate the balloon and to pay the expenses of Charles Dollfus and Pierre August Jacquet, the balloon pilots. They also needed to modify the shape of the balloon and to give it a 'pear-shaped silhouette' similar to balloons of the period. Getting the balloon was only the first step. Next, Box had to procure a 27-ton mobile electric crane from which to shoot the aerial sequences. This was considered 'hazardous and dangerous' by the union operator and so Box had to ensure that the technicians operating the crane had personal accident insurance.

All these details may seem banal but they reveal the reality of life as a producer in the British film industry in the 1940s. Outsiders had a preconception that movie producers were larger-than-life figures like Alexander Korda, smoking cigars, drinking champagne and enjoying long lunches. The job, at

---

[13]Ibid.

least as experienced by Betty Box, was a never-ending exercise in problem solving.

When Box set up her new independent production company, Carillon Films Ltd, in 1950, the problems intensified. She could no longer rely on the Rank Organisation to provide all the funding (although Rank continued to distribute the films) and had to rely on backing, which wasn't guaranteed, from The National Film Finance Corporation. Her brother Sydney had taken a one-year leave of absence from the industry and she was dealing with the financiers on her own. On *The Clouded Yellow* (1951), the first film through Carillon and also the first directed by Ralph Thomas (who had been in charge of directing trailers on some of her previous films), Box had to defer £3,500 of her £6,000 producer's fee in order to get the project made.

The National Film Finance Corporation refused to support two of her other projects, claiming that they did not know how well Box's previous features had performed because the distributors hadn't shared box-office information about them. 'I had managed to organise the distribution contract (without which it was unlikely that anyone would provide finance) and that meant that most banks would lend me 70 per cent of the budget. The remainder I persuaded Rank and The National Film Finance Corporation ... to put up fifty-fifty.'[14]

Then, late on, catastrophe struck: the NFFC pulled out. Rank wouldn't help make up the shortfall so she had to borrow heavily on her home.

The producer fretted over every pound spent on *The Clouded Yellow* but, true to form for Box's projects, it finished ahead of time. 'The sum of £152,835 represents the final cost, subject to audit and certification. It will be seen that shooting was completed 1½ days ahead of schedule and that, apart from the contingency allowance of £5000, production is £710 under budget,' the accountants reported, evidence of Box's drive and efficiency.[15]

When it came to casting, Box dealt directly with the agents and sometimes with the actors themselves. One of the strangest issues she had to deal with on *The Clouded Yellow* was foreign distributor apprehension about the allegedly blotchy and scarred skin of Trevor Howard, the star of *Brief Encounter* (1945)

---

[14]Ibid.
[15]Ibid.

and *The Third Man* (1949) and one of the leading actors in British cinema in this period. Howard was cast as the rugged ex-secret agent helping a wrongly accused woman (Jean Simmons) avoid arrest in *The Clouded Yellow*.

Rank's publicity boss Sydney Wynne wrote to Box confidentially passing on an extract from a letter from a senior British representative for Eagle-Lion Distributors (which released Rank films in most of Europe and the Middle East). 'It has been brought to my notice that Trevor Howard in *The Third Man* used a make-up which succeeded, photographically, in either deleting or making non conspicuous certain facial marks which, unfortunately, are visible in *Golden Salamander*,' the Eagle-Lion executive noted. 'Foreign exhibitors say that for their audiences the leading man must be as young and attractive as possible and they maintain that Trevor Howard could have been made more attractive in Golden Salamander by skilled make-up . . . as I believe that Trevor Howard will be the leading man in Clouded Yellow, you might perhaps convey this to Betty Box. I don't envy her the task as to how to explain this, however tactfully, to Trevor Howard.'[16]

There are no records of how or whether Box did break the news to Howard that continental audiences found him too swarthy and pock marked for their tastes. Howard appears to have had a gruelling time during shooting, though. Box's correspondence includes an item about the star on location in Southport when a crane driver panicked, 'hoisting him from floor to roof'.[17]

Rank's director of artistes Olive Dodds wrote to Box on behalf of Howard's co-star, Jean Simmons, asking if Box would pay for a course of massage during shooting. Box politely responded that she wasn't in a position to authorize such an expense. 'Every expenditure on The Clouded Yellow will be checked and counter-checked, not only by the Bank's auditors but also by National Film Finance Corporation, who would almost undoubtedly query an expenditure of this nature. The J Arthur Rank Organisation has much more reason for the expenditure than a small independent company like mine, which has only this one film to charge the cost against.'[18]

---

[16]Ibid.
[17]Ibid.
[18]BFI microfiche, Betty Box entry.

However, Box did ensure that Simmons was given a private suite (with private sitting room) at the Prince of Wales Hotel in Southport, a luxury not granted to any other members of the production.

The film premiered in late 1950 and was well received – regarded as a decent British attempt at a hardboiled noirish thriller. Its real significance was that it established a working relationship between Box and the avuncular director Ralph Thomas that would last for over twenty years.

'I'm a natural pessimist and he's a natural optimist. I'm always in the depths of despair and he is always full of joy. Good teams are often made of opposites . . . We do have awful, boring fights. Directing a film is not an easy job. For any man to stay sweet and gentle through eight weeks of purgatory is impossible,' is how Box later summed up their collaboration.[19]

In 1954, Box and Thomas had their first major success with their Richard Gordon adaptation *Doctor in the House*, about the comic misadventures of a group of young London-based medical students. Richard Gordon (who co-wrote the screenplay) was himself a surgeon as well as a novelist but, in preparation for shooting, Box, diligent as ever, dashed off letters to various doctors.

The Rank Organisation's hopes for the film were modest at best. Ealing boss (and Rank board member) Michael Balcon had offered his opinion about the screenplay. 'This subject is recommended, but nevertheless in my view, its appeal is largely for domestic markets (as indeed is that of most collegiate films), and I do not think we can anticipate large revenues overseas as the European and American audiences might have some difficulty in their appreciation of the characters, who are peculiarly and essentially British of a certain type.'[20]

Strangely, Balcon, famous for making films 'projecting Britain and the British character', appeared to be criticizing Box for trying to do exactly the same thing.

---

[19]Letter from Betty Box (credited also as Betty Rogers) to Olive Dodds, 15 June 1950, Betty Box, BFI Special Collections.

[20]Betty Box, BFI Special Collections, *Doctor in the House* file. Letter from Michael Balcon to Rank production chief, Earl St John, 11 August 1953.

There were casting problems. Box originally offered the part of the eminent surgeon Sir Lancelot Spratt to character actor Robert Morley but then discovered she couldn't afford him. The role went instead to James Robertson Justice. Dirk Bogarde was paid £5,000 for playing the leading role, young would-be doctor Simon Sparrow, but the Rank executives worried that he had little experience of comedy. As Bogarde's biographer John Coldstream noted, 'films about hospitals were considered to be toxic at the box office'.[21]

One up-and-coming comedian who was cast was Tommy Cooper, soon to become a household name but then at the start of his career. He was paid £50 for his efforts and then cut from the film. 'Dear Tommy Cooper, I'm writing to apologise to you because I've had to cut out from *Doctor in the House* the very nice sequence we made of you at Pinewood. Unfortunately, the picture went way over length and we had to make considerable cuts to conform to the distributors' requirements,' Box wrote to him not long after shooting on comedy *Doctor in the House* (1954) had finished. 'It was a very hard decision to make, particularly as we were all so very pleased with what you did for us.'[22]

The cast and crew evidently all enjoyed shooting *Doctor in the House* but, as Coldstream put it, 'no one was conscious of anything exceptional in the wind'. They were as startled as anyone that it went on to sell 17 million tickets in the UK alone and to become the most successful film of the year.[23]

Box had already optioned a second *Doctor* film (*Doctor at Sea*) from Richard Gordon's novels. As with the Huggetts a few years before, she had successfully launched a full-blown franchise. After her experiences as an independent producer on *The Clouded Yellow*, she and Thomas were happy to make their films directly for the Rank Organisation. Rank's managing-director Sir John Davis, a former accountant with a reputation as a hatchet man, savoured their success but kept them on a very tight leash. They came to an informal arrangement. As long as Box and Thomas served up a new *Doctor* film, they would be allowed to attempt something a little more ambitious between times.

---

[21]John Coldstream, *Dirk Bogarde: The Authorised Biography* (London: Weidenfeld & Nicolson, 2011), Chapter 9, 'You, what's the bleeding time?'

[22]Betty Box, BFI Special Collections, file on *Doctor in the House*.

[23]Coldstream, *Dirk Bogarde*.

Although Box was the most successful producer that the Rank Organisation then had, Davis paid her lower fees than he gave to the male producers working for the company. '"What do you need more money for? Another mink coat?" he asked. "You have a rich husband [fellow producer Peter Rogers]. You don't need a rise." I told him I'd have to tell my male colleagues I was being paid less than they, so no wonder I made more movies. My request was amicably granted,' Box remembers how she achieved parity with her male colleagues.[24]

It was a measure of Box and Thomas's fast-rising reputations that Katharine Hepburn approached them to direct her in *Not for Money* (later re-titled *The Iron Petticoat*) (1956), a comedy scripted by the legendary Hollywood screenwriter Ben Hecht, whose earlier credits included such gilt-edged classics as *The Front Page* (1931), *Scarface* (1932) and *Notorious* (1946). The film, which has shades of the Greta Garbo vehicle *Ninotchka*, is about a female Soviet pilot (Hepburn) who succumbs to the luxuries and temptations of the capitalist West. Bob Hope plays the US officer she eventually falls in love with.

As Box's records confirm, this was a famously troubled production. Hecht and Harry Saltzman (later to produce the James Bond movies with Cubby Broccoli) had formed a new company, Benhar, to make it. It was financed by MGM and Romulus Films, the British company which had worked with Hepburn on *The African Queen* (1951) a few years before. Rank gave Box and Thomas permission to make it – and to rent space and facilities at Pinewood Studios.

Hecht and Saltzman had hoped to cast Van Johnson, Glenn Ford or Van Heflin as the male lead but Bob Hope learned about the project and lobbied hard for the role. Box had been used to paying British stars like Bogarde and Kenneth More between £4,000 and £6,000 a film. Hepburn received $150,000 and 10 per cent of the net profits while Bob Hope was on $200,000 – astronomical amounts by comparison with what British actors received.

'I am a little worried about your future. Both you and Ralph are so nice that I hate to think what may happen to you as a result of contact with Hollywood picture making. The house swank – the cretinism and smugness of this

---

[24]Box, *Lifting the Lid*, 215.

dingleberry of a town continue to disturb me more than ever did communism,' Hecht wrote to Betty Box.[25]

He was right. Box and Thomas were caught between the film's two stars, both of whom felt their parts should be prioritized, and between two filmmaking cultures.

The screenplay was rewritten to bump up Hope's role but Hepburn hated the changes. She fretted to Box that the original had been 'rearranged' into 'something ordinary and cold' out of something 'delicious and warm and provocative' and suggested it would be 'suicide' to shoot the new version. 'I do not think that the additions and shifts make his a good part. Quite the contrary. I am sure I am correct about the removal of the emotional warmth in the script. And I am certain that this is largely because Hope has been made a cheap fortune hunter. There can be nothing funny about a middle aged man marrying for money, unless the story is about this. This one is not,' she wrote to Box.

> I shall undoubtedly go to my grave carping, but for Chuck to be going to London to marry a millionairess is so revolting and every comment he makes about it is so hard that you would have to be a charmer of 20 or Peter Townsend to get away with it. He revolts me at the start instead of arousing my sympathy. I think Hope will be hard put to it to be funny, for initially he's in a rotten position and would have no modesty or pathos. Make him an American goon – sweet and gullible and he's most likeable. Make him a sharp mutt marrying for money and the pathos of his character evaporates and so when he gets drunk he is vulgar and awful.[26]

Box was working with a Hollywood legend – and Hepburn was determined to have a say in everything from script to costumes.

The producer and her team went about their producing duties in their usual diligent fashion. Part of the film is set in Moscow Airport and so they approached Sovietexport Film to see if they could shoot there. (They received a polite but curt 'no'.) They approached the US Air Force with more success.

---

[25]Undated letter from Ben Hecht to Betty Box, included in *The Iron Petticoat* file, Betty Box BFI Special Collections.

[26]Telegram from Katharine Hepburn to Betty Box, 24 October 1955, Betty Box BFI Special Collections.

As the production went on, Hecht and Saltzman, Hope and Hepburn, Hecht and Hope all managed to fall out with each other. The film ended up being chosen for the Berlin Film Festival. In the rush to finish it on time, Box left Romulus and Saltzman's name off the credits. Saltzman, already irked at being marginalized, turned up in Berlin for the premiere, complained bitterly about the treatment he received from the festival and left without paying his hotel bill.

To complicate matters further, the British press threatened an embargo on the film because of notorious remarks Hecht had made in a 'letter to the Terrorists of Palestine' published as a full page ad in the *New York Post* in 1947: 'Every time you blow up a British arsenal, or wreck a British jail, or send a British railroad sky high, or rob a British bank, or let go with your guns and bombs at the British betrayers and invaders of your homeland, the Jews of America make a little holiday in their hearts,' Hecht wrote.[27] Hecht, though, was devoted to Box and Ralph Thomas. 'I miss you and Betty and the daily crises,' Hecht wrote to Thomas after the production finished.[28]

Bob Hope liked them too. 'MISS YOU ALREADY HOW ABOUT RETAKES IN PALM SPRINGS STOP BEST TO BETTY AND THE GANG REGARDS BOB HOPE,' he telegrammed the British director in familiar jocular fashion.[29]

Following their turbulent experiences on *The Iron Petticoat*, it was understandable that Box and Thomas preferred to stay making films in Britain rather than trying their luck in Hollywood. On films like their Charles Dickens adaptation *A Tale of Two Cities* (1958) and their remake of *The 39 Steps* (1959), there were plenty of problems but they were familiar British ones.

For the former, partly shot in France, Box gathered together hundreds of extras for the guillotine scenes. 'We had to call on the American airforce to augment our French soldiers for the big day, and when the 700 French crowd were bellowing out "Mort aux aristocrats," my astonished ears picked up the American contingent shouting "Hang the Bums!"'[30]

---

[27]*New York Post*, 14 May 1947.

[28]Letter from Ben Hecht to Ralph Thomas, 2 May 1956, Betty Box BFI Special Collections.

[29]Telegram from Bob Hope to Ralph Thomas, 9 March 1956, Betty Box BFI Special Collections.

[30]Letter from Betty Box to Miss Vyvyenne Newcombe, Newnes & Pearsons (chief features editor of *Woman's Own*), who had been on set, 6 August 1957, Betty Box BFI Special Collections.

On *The 39 Steps*, Box had to negotiate both with British Rail and the Scottish summertime weather in the Trossachs: 'rain every day and it is very cold'.[31]

Box and Thomas turned into arguably the most successful producer–director team of their era. They were British filmmaking royalty. However, by the early 1970s, they were reduced to making sex comedies like *Percy* (1971) and *Anyone for Sex* (1973). As Jeremy Thomas noted, they struggled when the old studio system ended and when they had to hustle for financing. 'They were having difficulty with the new reality of independent movies.'[32]

Whatever her struggles in the 1970s, Box was a trailblazer: one of Britain's first female producers, she excelled in a male-dominated business and outperformed almost all her male colleagues at the box office.

---

[31]Letter to Earl St John, 25 September 1958, Betty Box BFI Special Collections.
[32]Jeremy Thomas, interview.

5

John Maxwell

The Cautious Scottish Visionary

John Maxwell's obituary in *The Times* in October 1940 hints at one of the most unlikely transformations in the history of the British film industry. In his early twenties, Maxwell had been a small-time solicitor in Glasgow with a 'steady family clientele'.[1] By the time of his death aged sixty-three, forty years later, he was a full-blown movie mogul in charge of a corporation which had assets of over £50 million and controlled a circuit of cinemas which, *The Times* told its readers, was the second largest in the world.

The story of how Yorkshire flour magnate J. Arthur Rank came into the British film industry in the early 1930s to find suitable material to screen in Sunday schools is relatively familiar. Rank ended up at the helm of a company as big as MGM. Maxwell's metamorphosis was almost equally spectacular but is far less well chronicled. He is a shadowy presence. We know very little about his childhood and private life. The British Film Institute keeps no cuttings on him in its archives. However, as the British film industry made the transition to sound in the late 1920s, Maxwell (whom the trade press liked to call the 'dour Scot'[2]) became probably its single most influential figure, both in production and distribution.

Maxwell didn't speak much to the press. When he did, he sometimes put his foot in his mouth. 'I am not the Mussolini of British film, by which title I have

---

[1] *The Times*, 4 October 1940.
[2] See, for example, *The Bioscope*, 4 December 1929.

John Maxwell. Photo: David Savill/Topical Press Agency/Getty Images.

been described. I am a businessman and a Scotsman, and although I have a certain admiration for Benito Mussolini, I think that I do not talk quite so much,' he declared in late 1928.[3]

Maxwell founded ABC Cinemas in 1927 and folded it within British International Pictures (renamed Associated British Picture Corporation in 1933) having taken over British National Studios in Elstree the year before. In one fell swoop, he created a vertically integrated British studio complete with production, distribution and exhibition.

Historians are very grudging about Maxwell. He is called 'the thrifty Scot' or the 'old man'. According to Rachael Low, he had 'little of the impresario's personality', he lacked 'artistic sympathy', he was 'a notoriously quarrelsome man' and he took a 'brusque and commercial approach' to the film industry.[4] Patricia Warren writes that he was never seen 'without a hat' and that he was a 'stern' and very private figure who frowned on levity and would never be seen with money or matches in his pockets.[5] *The Times'* obituary called him 'conservative and prudent', and suggested he was always more interested in exhibition than production. This, though, was the man who paid a fortune to put Alfred Hitchcock under contract and produced his first talkie, *Blackmail* (1929), and who invested in some of the most extravagant movies of the late 1920s and 1930s. Beneath his dour exterior, he was a gambler and a quiet visionary.

Some accounts suggest that Maxwell entered the industry by accident. 'A cautious gentleman, he had been surprised to discover from his accountant in 1912 that he had interests in the "cinema theatre business"', one historian writes.[6] Other sources suggest he acquired his first cinema, seating 400, in Shawlands in Glasgow's South Side, in 1910.[7]

Maxwell gradually expanded his cinema holdings in the Glasgow area, buying cinemas in Govan and Springburn, while continuing to work in the legal business as leading partner at his company, Maxwell Waddell, based in Hope Street, Glasgow. He later recalled:

[3]*Fife Free Press, & Kirkcaldy Guardian*, 24 December 1928.
[4]Rachael Low, *Film Making in 1930s Britain* (London: HarperCollins, 1985), 122.
[5]Patricia Warren, *Elstree: The British Hollywood* (London: Elm Tree Books, 1983), 80.
[6]Ibid., 20.
[7]*The Scotsman*, 4 October 1940.

Originally I had no intention of being interested in film production companies. I was articled to a firm of Scottish lawyers – Writers to the Signet we call them. Later I became a Writer myself, and it was in my professional capacity that I first had to do with a Scottish company which owned picture houses, and began to take slight interest in them. This interest grew. By this time I had made up my mind that the law did not interest me as much as I had originally thought. It has its limitations, and, although I was glad of the basic knowledge which it gave me and the reasoning qualities through the legal training, I found myself attracted to journalism.[8]

The journalism, though, didn't stretch him enough. He wanted to make more use of the formidable organizational abilities that he already knew he possessed.

By the end of the First World War, Maxwell 'controlled' over twenty cinemas in Scotland through his Scottish Cinemas & Variety Theatres chain, among them the Princes Cinema in Springburn. He had also moved into distribution. His company, Waverley Films (named after the Walter Scott novels), founded in 1918 and run by Arthur Dent, was handling the Scottish releases of London-based Wardour Films Ltd, a company he later took over. Maxwell moved from Glasgow to London in 1925 and took over Elstree Studios a year later. Waverley merged with Wardour which eventually merged with British National Films, becoming British International Pictures, and thus, in 1927, one of the UK's first major, vertically integrated companies was born.

Maxwell had been brought up in Cambuslang on the south-eastern outskirts of Glasgow. In the years before the First World War he had been entering a business still in its infancy but he immediately saw a very strong commercial opportunity. Although the historians called him thrifty and cautious, he was rapidly building up his stake in both distribution and exhibition. In his self-effacing way, Maxwell was very ambitious. As a qualified professional, he was also far more practical than others entering British cinema from music hall and travelling fairgrounds. There are references to major Scottish banks supporting his companies. In the few photographs of him that survive, he looks an eminently sensible and practical man: a balding figure with horn-rimmed spectacles who wore heavy suits and was far more likely to be pictured

---

[8]*Fife Free Press, & Kirkcaldy Guardian*, 24 November 1928.

at his desk with piles of paper in front of him than at premieres with starlets on his arms, If you didn't know better, you would think he was a provincial bank manager. He is an example of someone applying skills learned in another field to the film business and of building himself a substantial career as he did so.

Although he was characterized as a dour and self-effacing Scot, Maxwell was always ready to throw himself into public debates about how the British film industry should best evolve. If he needed to spend money to find an audience, he would do so.

The passing of the Cinematograph Films Act 1927, which obliged British cinemas to show a quota of home-produced films, gave Maxwell his platform. The government hoped its intervention would lead to the emergence of big integrated British companies which, like the Hollywood studios, would have production, distribution and exhibition arms. It was envisaged that these companies would make films with a similar international appeal to those being turned out by the US majors. That was certainly Maxwell's intention. He had been on a fact-finding mission to Hollywood to see just how the US studios operated and he was the first UK mogul to try to ensure the same continuity of production – and of employment.

'British films at that time were moribund,' Maxwell commented in the late 1920s of the UK industry after the war. 'They had no chance in those days. America, who had speeded up production, bought the best brains and captured the world market during the war years (and why not?); and had got everyone else well beaten. Incidentally, I believe that it was this fact which decided thoughts. I like a fight, and, in those days, it was fight.'[9]

Maxwell realized that what he called 'hole in the corner' production, done in the old makeshift fashion and on the cheap, wasn't good enough. British films had to be big and brassy, with top production values and the best British and international talent behind them. He would do anything to find a market for his movies and startled some observers by striking deals with Soviet Russia to have them shown there. 'Here is a great country, a great potential market for our goods,' he enthused.[10] He also sold films to Hungary, Japan and France.[11]

---

[9]Ibid.
[10]Ibid.
[11]*The Bioscope*, 12 December 1928.

Prior to the 1927 Act, as Maxwell wrote in a lengthy article in *The Times*, British production had been 'spasmodic' in character. 'There was not an adequate volume of capital behind producers to enable them to maintain a continuous output of pictures,' he lamented. 'As a result many producers had to wait until the capital which they had sunk in one picture was recovered by its exhibition, usually 12 months later, before they could start upon their next film.'[12] There was no risk capital. Filmmakers faced frequent hiatuses between projects. That meant they couldn't hold on to actors or technicians. It also meant those actors and technicians struggled to acquire the experience that would make them better (and more efficient) at their jobs. Now, though, the opportunity was there to make more British films.

Maxwell claimed that the boost in British production levels was already capturing the attention of foreign distributors. 'They have come to realise quickly that an important producing industry has grown up almost in a night in England, and they have sent their agents and buyers here to acquire British pictures . . . as a result, British pictures are circulating today all over the world. We have customers, either agents or purchasers, handling our pictures in every civilised country.'[13]

For the first fifteen years of his involvement in the British film industry, from 1912 onward, Maxwell worked patiently behind the scenes in exhibition and distribution. Once he felt he had the chance to be successful as a producer through British International Pictures, and had access to his own studio (Elstree, then the largest in the country) at which to make films, he hurled himself into that side of the business.

Maxwell spent lavishly. The 28-year-old wunderkind Alfred Hitchcock was hired on a three-year, twelve-picture contract at the then princely sum of £13,000 a year – which made him the highest paid director in Britain.

As he continued his expansion drive, the canny Scottish mogul also looked to the continent for top talent, investing a fortune in two heady melodramas, *Moulin Rouge* (1928) and *Piccadilly* (1929) from German film industry pioneer E. A. Dupont. He imported stars both from Europe and from the US, Tallulah

---

[12] *The Times*, 19 March 1929.
[13] Ibid.

Bankhead, Lionel Barrymore, Anna May Wong and Olga Chekhova among them. He took control of a leading German film production outfit, buying 90 per cent of the shares in the Sud Film Company in February 1928. He even hatched a venture, Worldwide Pictures Corporation, to release British films in the US. Showing that he was open to documentary as well as fiction film, Maxwell had taken over control of Pathé newsreels.

Initially sceptical about sound movies (dismissing them according to Rachael Low as 'a costly fad'[14]), Maxwell quickly began to invest in sound equipment. The trade press reported that 'the energetic and enterprising John Maxwell will undertake the production of synchronised films on the de Forest Phonofilm system' in December 1928.[15]

A year later, Maxwell was the producer of Hitchcock's *Blackmail* (1929), although it is a moot point whether he expected the film to be a full talkie. According to some sources, Maxwell had intended the sound to be used just towards the end of the movie in order to give audiences a surprise – and to provide distributors Wardour Films with a marketing hook. He was reportedly startled to discover that Hitchcock had added sound the whole way through.

'From the presentation of *The White Sheik* in 1927 to the introduction of talkies, Maxwell had produced or invested in twenty-four feature films at Elstree – no mean achievement,' Warren writes.[16]

Of course, Maxwell's relentless optimism in his article in *The Times* belied the real situation for UK production. The 1927 Act didn't help the industry in the way he expected. It precipitated the birth of the so-called 'quota quickies', British films shot cheaply by his rivals and with scant regard to quality simply to fulfil the letter (but not the spirit) of the law. These films would be shown in graveyard slots where nobody would watch them apart from the cinema cleaners – and the best screening times would still be reserved for the big Hollywood titles.

It wasn't at all clear, either, that Maxwell's theory about British films finding big new audiences abroad was correct. He believed that a growing export

[14]Rachael Low, *The History of the British Film, Vol. IV: 1918–1929* (London: Routledge, 1997), 207.
[15]*The Bioscope*, 5 December 1928.
[16]Warren, *Elstree*, 40.

market would enable producers to increase their budgets because they wouldn't just be relying on British cinema-goers to help recoup their costs. His prediction that the film business would provide 'useful and lucrative employment' to some of 'the million or more unemployed' in Britain at the time proved too optimistic.[17]

Nonetheless, many of his remarks anticipate rhetoric still being heard from producers and public film bodies eighty years later, when film was still being flagged up as a key part of the creative industries and seen as a driver of inward investment. 'On the export side, [cinema] will create one of the new trades which it is desired to call into existence to take the place of those export trades that have fallen on evil times and are not likely to recover the full volume of their pre-war strength,' he predicted.[18]

There is an obvious contradiction in the way Maxwell has been written about by film historians and Hitchcock biographers. They portray him as a cautious figure who was happy with contracts and budgets but didn't understand artists. The influential Rachael Low is especially withering about him. She characterizes him as 'less a producer than a manufacturer' and suggests he left production decisions to his apparatchik Walter Mycroft, a former journalist and critic. Low calls Mycroft 'a bitter man with Fascist views who ... operated a policy of cut-price window dressing, trying to make cheap films which looked like expensive ones'. 'If [Michael] Balcon was an artist's businessman and Wilcox a showman's businessman, Maxwell was a businessman's businessman,' Low wrote.[19] This verdict has generally been allowed to stand unchallenged and is recycled in many subsequent studies of British cinema between the wars. Donald Spoto repeats it in *Dark Genius*, his biography of Hitchcock. He calls Maxwell 'coolly efficient' and doesn't mean it as a compliment.[20]

There is plenty of evidence Maxwell was a much richer character than the gloomy Scottish miser that his detractors picture him to be. He had a flair for

---

[17] *The Times*, 19 March 1929.
[18] Ibid.
[19] Low, *The History of the British Film*, 194.
[20] Donald Spoto, *The Dark Side of Genius* (New York: Da Capo Press, 1999), 100.

marketing that hasn't been properly acknowledged. In the 1930s, he was the Chairman of Madame Tussauds, not a post you associate with a dour Glaswegian whose critics seemed to think he was made of wax anyway. In 1931, he set up a film festival. This was a year before the creation of the Venice Film Festival, generally credited as the oldest festival in the world. His event, which was held in Malvern over three weeks in August, was a festival of British talking films. It opened with Hitchcock's *The Skin Game* (1931), adapted from the John Galsworthy play. In 1933 Maxwell brought ABC, BIP and Wardour Films together in a new company, the Associated British Picture Corporation (ABPC)

Maxwell was also fervently patriotic. In 1935, he commissioned *Royal Cavalcade*, a film specially made to celebrate the Silver Jubilee of King George V. 'The time available is short, but the need was there – the need was a duty, so that the British millions who throng the cinema could find expression for their loyalty and devotion to the king ... Every patriotic Briton will want to see this picture – every wise exhibitor will want to book it,' he wrote in *Kine Weekly*[21] when he first announced the project, which was rushed into production.

Another trait of the Scotsman's personality was his extreme competitiveness. At the same time that BIP/Associated British Picture Company was growing into a British studio to rival the Hollywood majors, so was Gaumont-British. Maxwell always wanted to have more cinemas, to make more films and to hire bigger stars than his rivals. In 1937, he launched a bid to take over Gaumont-British, ostensibly to prevent it falling under foreign control but really because it was his biggest competition and he yearned to put one over on Gaumont-British's then owners, the Ostrer brothers. In the event, he was out-manoeuvred; the Ostrers brought in Fox instead and lawsuits followed. However, as historian Jeffrey Richards noted, he consoled himself 'by gobbling the financially ailing Union circuit of 136 cinemas, thus giving ABPC a total of 431 cinemas to GB's 345'.[22]

Rachael Low is disparaging about the production Maxwell oversaw at Elstree. 'Hitchcock was the only first class British director to work at BIP at this time and most of his films there were a disappointment,' Low claimed.

---

[21] *Kine Weekly*, 14 March 1935.
[22] Jeffrey Richards, *The Age of the Dream Palace* (London: Routledge, 1984), 38.

BIP came more and more to resemble its ideal, Hollywood. Aiming at sophistication and glossy, opulent production, they were ready to spend money on talent which had proved itself elsewhere, but lacked the artistic sympathy to encourage any development of the medium in their own studio ... what they did was to create in a wealthier and more sophisticated form the mass production of sausage-machine filmmaking of the early Stoll and Ideal days.[23]

Low's remarks are belied by the brilliance of some of the work Maxwell commissioned, for example Hitchcock's *Blackmail*, not only historically important but still reckoned a classic thriller, and Dupont's *Piccadilly*, which has been re-evaluated in recent years and is now regarded as one of the greatest silent films made in the UK in the late 1920s. The Scotsman is an example of a white-collar professional who entered the business sideways but whose drive and common sense built up a formidable empire. He died aged only sixty-three in 1940 at a time when the Rank Organisation was growing and Hungarian emigré Alexander Korda fixed ideas in the public mind of how producers should behave. Just as he had been undervalued in his lifetime, few other than his obituarist in *The Times* seemed to have noticed just what an enormous film empire he had left behind him. He had groomed another Scot in a similar mould to succeed him. Robert Clark had been an office boy at Maxwell Waddell and had gone on to qualify as a solicitor. Two years after Maxwell's death, he had become a director of ABPC. The company that Maxwell had started was finally sold to EMI in 1969 for £63 million. One analyst calculates that would be between £1 billion and £2 billion in today's currency – quite a legacy given that Maxwell had begun his career in 1910 almost on a whim. Quickly, though, filmmaking became 'not only his business but his hobby,' as his obituary in *The Scotsman* put it.[24] He was a key figure in the development of the British film industry, one whose contribution is yet fully to be acknowledged.

---

[23]Low, *The History of the British Film*, 194.
[24]*The Scotsman*, 4 October 1940.

6

Muriel Box

Visitors to the 2018 San Sebastian Festival were surprised that one of the centrepieces of the festival was a comprehensive retrospective of the films of British filmmaker Muriel Box (1905–91). There were twenty-eight titles including the ones she had scripted as well as the ones she directed. Most of the San Sebastian attendees had never heard of her. Even students of British cinema were unlikely to know much of her work beyond a few titles that were still in circulation in film studies departments or broadcast on obscure satellite channels. Among them were comedy-drama *The Beachcomber* (1954), shot in Ceylon; *Simon and Laura* (1955), revived frequently primarily because it captured perfectly the paranoia and disdain the film industry of the 1950s had for its new rival, TV; and *The Truth about Women* (1957), which had a swaggering star performance from Laurence Harvey.

Muriel Box, the San Sebastian Festival programme informed its visitors, was a filmmaker who 'tackled complex, taboo subjects including prostitution, child abuse, abortion, illegitimate children or adolescent sex'. She had 'an extremely clairvoyant and brave approach given the social and political context in which said films were made. Her contribution in relation to those subjects played a fundamental role in the British cinema of the 1950s and first half of the 1960s, at which time she was the most adventurous female filmmaker working in Britain.'[1]

'Muriel was a curious mixture: easily disheartened yet doggedly ambitious,' Rachel Cooke wrote of the filmmaker in *Her Brilliant Career* (2013), her book

---

[1] https://www.sansebastianfestival.com/2018/news/1/7267/in.

Muriel Box (right), Great Britain 1958. Photo: ullstein bild/ullstein bild via Getty Images.

about British career women in the 1950s.[2] Box was a late starter. Her debut feature as director came in 1949 when she was already middle aged. Opportunities presented to younger male directors with half of her talent hadn't been given to her. She had won an Oscar for Best Original Screenplay for *The Seventh Veil* (1946) and her husband, Sydney Box, was one of the most prolific producers in British cinema of the 1940s and 1950s, but that didn't make her attempts to establish herself as a director any easier.

Box was born in New Malden, a nondescript suburb of south London associated in later years with the popular British sitcom *The Fall and Rise of Reginald Perrin* (1976–9), about a commuter who goes AWOL. 'Twenty-two minutes late, badger ate a junction box at New Malden,' was one of the most famous lines written by Reggie Perrin's creator, David Nobbs. It seemed to sum up perfectly the absurdism and despair of the office worker's life, condemned

---

[2]Rachel Cooke, *Her Brilliant Career: Ten Extraordinary Women of the 1950s* (London: Virago, 2013), Chapter 5, 'The Brontës of Shepherd's Bush'.

to repeat the same journey every day, subject to delay and humiliation both en route and once he or she actually arrived.

Violette Muriel Baker, as she was christened, wasn't from a particularly well-to-do family. Late in life, after she married her second husband, the prominent Labour peer and former Lord Chancellor Gerald Austin Gardiner, in 1970, she was to become Lady Gardiner. However, her father was a railway clerk, working at Waterloo. Her family had no professional connection with the world of British cinema or the arts, although her parents were cultured. Her father was a violinist in a local amateur orchestra. Her mother was a Fabian who revered George Bernard Shaw and took her daughter to hear the great man speak at the Kingsway Hall in Holborn. Muriel shared her mother's admiration for GBS, describing the writer as 'her first object of hero worship'. She later characterized her family background as being 'respectable poor' and described in excruciating detail in her memoirs the social embarrassment of shopping for food. 'If a local trader overcharged by so much as a ha'penny, we children were blamed for not being sharp enough to notice or having courage enough to bring it to his attention.'[3] The family pawned its jewellery, scrimped and saved, walked miles to source the cheapest fruit and vegetables, and tried to get refunds of anything they could.

Despite their very modest circumstances, her mother fought hard to give her an education and she was, for three years, a boarder at the Holy Cross Convent School in Wimbledon.

The young Muriel was determined to break free from her south London background. She hated school and felt she got nothing out of it. An autodidact, she claimed to learn far more from reading books on her own than from listening to her authoritarian teachers at her schools in Kingston and Wimbledon. 'My life, on looking back, appears to have been influenced more by what I have read than by anything else,' she wrote in her autobiography, reminiscing about becoming hooked as a young child on the novels of Alexandre Dumas and Victor Hugo.[4]

[3]Muriel Box, *Odd Woman Out: An Autobiography by Muriel Box* (London: Frewin, 1974), 34.
[4]Ibid.

Muriel was female, from a humble background and without academic accomplishments. That didn't give her an obvious pathway into the film industry. She liked movies, though. 'The highlights of our lives were occasional visits to the cinema,' she later wrote.[5] They would walk two miles to Kingston and sit in discomfort on 'low wooden benches' at the local Classic, opposite the railway station, lapping up with glee whatever was being shown, whether slapstick comedies or newsreels.

Once, in a bizarre chance encounter which seems vaguely sinister in hindsight, she met a friendly stranger on a train to Southsea who gave her his card and said she should come down to see a film being made. This was Joseph Grossman of Stoll Picture Productions Ltd. She took him up on the offer and visited the studios at Cricklewood on a few occasions. During these visits, she was sometimes even given work as an extra. Even so, she was still a bystander, with no prospect of building any sort of career. Back home, she studied dancing, singing and briefly entertained the possibility she could break through as an actress or even a professional ballet dancer. She was passionate about the work of silent film pioneer D. W. Griffith and once gave a lecture to the local literary society about the brilliance of Griffith movies like *Intolerance* (1916) and *Broken Blossoms* (1919). She may not have had any practical experience of filmmaking but she had already studied Griffith's use of close-ups and all his other 'clever innovations'.[6]

Her real break came in unlikely fashion via her stint as a shorthand typist in Welwyn Garden City, where she had gone to live after leaving home in her early twenties following furious rows with her mother. She had had an affair with a friend of her father's who was much older than she was and her parents didn't approve at all. Rather than put up with their criticism, she left home for the model town founded by Ebenezer Howard in 1920. One of her jobs was as a secretary at Barcley Corsets, whose art deco factory contained a glazed central staircase and pink and black tiling. She also joined the local amateur dramatics society, the Folk Players, before eventually finding a new job in 1929 at British Instructional Films, which ran the Welwyn Studios.

---

[5] Ibid., 43.
[6] Ibid.

This was the period in which British cinema was converting to sound, 'an operation fraught with anxiety and many pitfalls'.[7] As a typist, Muriel was occasionally able to make suggestions about how dialogue in the scripts she was busy typing on behalf of directors and writers could be improved. Eventually, she was set to work reading unsolicited stories and plays. She was also press-ganged occasionally to fill in as an extra.

British Instructional Films built Welwyn Film Studios in 1928. It operated until 1950, producing educational films and some features such as Alfred Hitchcock's version of *The 39 Steps* (1935), with Robert Donat and Madeleine Carroll, and the Boulting brothers' adaptation of *Brighton Rock* (1948), starring Richard Attenborough in his career breakthrough role as Pinkie Brown, but made long after Muriel had moved on.

'Not only did I see how films were written but also how they were made, for any odd person around the studio was hauled in by the director if an extra artist was required in a hurry when a "pro" could not be sent down from London in time,' she recalled the haphazard way films were sometimes crewed, cast and made.[8] One of her stranger roles was as a nurse in a documentary about the perils of venereal disease.

Her chance for promotion arrived, though, when she was asked to help out with the continuity of Anthony Asquith's early talkie *Tell England* (1931), when the continuity girl (today known as script supervisor) fell ill with flu. She told her bosses that she didn't know anything about continuity but they responded that she was not to worry and that they would teach her. 'They were awfully decent. They helped me with everything and so I began to learn about it,' Muriel recalled in an interview she gave late in her life to editor Sid Cole, famous for his work at Ealing Studios and for his part in the formation of the film workers' union, ACTT.[9] Box relished the experience and picked up the job very quickly but was intensely frustrated when the sick colleague came back and she was relegated to her old role as a secretary. Even worse, soon afterwards,

---

[7] Ibid., 98.
[8] Ibid.
[9] Muriel Box interview, 1991, British Entertainment History Project. https://historyproject.org.uk/interview/muriel-box-gardiner-nee-baker.

she was laid off altogether. The studio was struggling to adjust to the formal and financial challenges of the talkie era and couldn't afford to keep her.

Asquith agreed to write her a letter of recommendation. With this letter as a reference, she set about trying to get a proper start in the industry as a 'continuity girl'. She approached Joe Grossman, the man she had met on the train and by now the studio manager at British Instructional Pictures (BIP) at Elstree. Grossman promptly hired her. She was paid a pittance, £3 a week, but she didn't grumble. She was excited to be cheek by jowl with Hitchcock (on whose *Number Seventeen* (1932) she was later to work at the end of her time at the studio).

One of Muriel's first assignments was overseeing the continuity on *How He Lied to Her Husband* (1931), a short film based on George Bernard Shaw's one-act play of the same name and starring Edmund Gwenn. Muriel met Shaw several times and was even photographed alongside him. There is a wonderful picture of her standing behind Shaw on the set of the film. He is dressed in a tweed suit and is watching events on set. She is holding the script and seems almost as amused as he is. She approached him for an autograph, which he wrote on a folder of her poems that was being used as a prop. Her delight at having the great man's signature was tempered when the prop man took the folder away and wouldn't let her have it back.

'I was not so exceedingly naive at this time as to imagine success in films came to anyone without the necessary talent and accomplishment in some direction. Having none, I began to thrash about in all directions in the hope of developing any I possessed,' she later wrote. As a young woman, she was resourceful and ambitious but had no focused or practical idea how to break into the industry. She wanted to learn continuity but, as she lamented in her memoirs many years later, there were 'no books on the subject, no schools to teach its rules'.[10]

The job at Elstree was only on a temporary basis. Nonetheless, Muriel found an agent willing to take her on. This agent began to put up for jobs in continuity. She picked up 'bits and pieces' of work at studios like Walton Studios. She

---

[10]Box, *Odd Woman Out*, 65.

eventually landed a slightly longer-term job with aspiring young director Michael Powell, who was then making low-budget quota quickies. (Muriel served as secretary not only to him but to his American producer, Jerry Jackson.) She worked at Gaumont-British as a continuity girl on the permanent staff, overseeing such films as the Will Hay comedy *Boys Will Be Boys* (1935). She had also flirted again with an acting career, auditioning unsuccessfully for RADA. Her nerve failed her at the crucial moment and her audition speech came out as a feeble croak. She dried up and fled the theatre, convinced she had 'muffed' her last chance of any kind of theatre career.

Muriel's route into the industry was remarkably similar to that followed by Alma Reville (see Chapter 12). She came in sideways, as a typist and continuity girl. Like Reville, she married an up-and-coming figure in the industry. Unlike Reville, however, she retained her identity as a writer and filmmaker in her own right. She also encountered far more setbacks than Reville. However, almost unconsciously, she had been honing her craft. During her time at Welwyn and Elstree, she not only became expert in continuity and script construction. She also began to understand how film sets worked. She picked up the rudiments of editing. Losing jobs was ultimately to her benefit. It meant she had to find something else – and that something else would always add to her store of experience.

Muriel had met Sydney Box, a freelance journalist and aspiring playwright from Kent, at an amateur dramatics festival in Welwyn Garden City. She thought him a 'very original thinker' and was clearly attracted to him, later describing him in her autobiography as 'this broad-shouldered amiable journalist of twenty-five who looks thirty-five (his fair hair already thinning above the temples) bursting with ideas like a coruscating catherine wheel and impatient of the follow-through'.[11]

Box was married but that didn't prevent them from starting a relationship. She too was writing plays. They were able to compare each other's work. They also wrote film scripts together including crime drama *Alibi Inn* (1935), directed by Walter Tennyson and starring Wilfrid Hyde-White. This was a

---

[11] Ibid.

potboiler about a young man wrongfully imprisoned for a murder he did not commit. Their union was much more one of equals than that between Hitchcock and Alma.

Muriel and Sydney collaborated on one-act plays together. Sydney was both enterprising and idealistic, one reason why he and Muriel set to work writing half a dozen one-act plays with all-women casts. They weren't only doing this in the name of gender equality. They realized there was a huge demand for such material among amateur dramatics societies. They were eventually able to find a publisher willing to pay for the dramas.

'No West End producer would have known either of their names, but Muriel and Sydney Box were soon the most performed playwrights in Britain,' Cooke claims of the couple.[12] One of the plays was attacked in a newspaper as blasphemous. Sydney wanted to sue but his case would have been undermined if it had been discovered he was living 'in sin' with Muriel. They therefore quickly married, in 1935. Muriel had a daughter, Leonora, the following year.

Muriel gave up her continuity work on the grounds it would get in the way of her writing and because she wanted a family. Sydney was also thriving by the late 1930s, writing advertising and documentary films for a commercial company, Publicity Films.

Early in the Second World War, Sydney formed Verity Films through which he and (later) Muriel wrote and produced publicity and training films for clients like the Ministry of Information and the Ministry of Food. They were joined at Verity by Sydney's enterprising younger sister, Betty Box (see Chapter 4). Verity had been formed under duress. Thanks to the war, amateur dramatics societies were closing down and there was no demand for the couple's plays. Sydney had lost his job at Publicity Films and Muriel didn't have full-time work either. They had secured the funding for the new company by writing a compendium for wartime readers called *The Black-out Book: 500 Family Games and Puzzles for Wartime Entertainment*. Published in 1939, this fitted the mood of the times perfectly and was a big popular success.

---

[12]Cooke, *Her Brilliant Career*.

Verity Films produced over 100 training films in a little over two years. At last, in her mid-thirties, Muriel was given the chance to direct some of them. By then, she had been in the business, in one capacity or another, for fifteen years and was infinitely more experienced than most of the men around her.

'Women have always found it difficult to break into this particular branch of filmmaking, even more to become a director of full-length films with an international distribution,' she later recalled. 'The obstacles in my case seemed almost insurmountable. My chance to direct in the documentary field would not have come but for the scarcity of male directors in wartime.'[13]

Sydney was eventually approached to executive produce a more mainstream film, *On Approval* (1944), starring Clive Brook, one of British cinema's biggest stars from the previous decade.

Sydney could turn his hand to just about everything. He started making films at Riverside Studios, starting off with low-budget romantic comedy *29 Acacia Avenue* (1944), which Muriel co-scripted. Starring Jimmy Hanley and Dinah Sheridan, this touched on pre-marital sex and was considered very risqué by a disapproving J. Arthur Rank. Nonetheless, it was successful and well received. Sydney therefore embarked on another production, *The Seventh Veil* (1945), which Muriel wrote. This starred James Mason as a sadistic musician and Ann Todd as the highly strung woman he has trained to become a top pianist. It was heady, melodramatic stuff. The film was a huge hit at the British box office. Sydney and Muriel had staked everything on the movie. At one stage, it looked as if the funding had fallen through and that the project would have to be abandoned. Producer William MacQuitty agreed to underwrite the project. Its runaway success led to Rank appointing Sydney and Muriel to run Gainsborough Studios, Shepherd's Bush.

The more Muriel wrote and the longer she stayed in the business, the more experienced she became. By the mid-1940s, she was an expert script doctor. She was efficient and pragmatic. Rank wanted her and Sydney to make ten to twelve films a year from a standing start. Amazingly, they just about managed it. Not all the films were very distinguished. There were melodramas like *Jassy*

---

[13]Box, *Odd Woman Out*.

(1947) and popular comedies like *Holiday Camp* (1947), which introduced the Huggett family. They adapted Graham Greene's novel *The Man Within* (1947).

By the early 1950s, Muriel had served an apprenticeship which had lasted half her lifetime and still hadn't been given the chance to make her own features. At Gainsborough, she would work as a dialogue director and sometimes reshoot scenes but wasn't credited as a director in her own right. She was credited as a co-director alongside Bernard Knowles on one Gainsborough film, the drama *The Lost People*, but that was only because she had done so much work on the project that it would have been indecent not to acknowledge her. Her full directing debut came three years later on comedy *The Happy Family* (1952), starring Stanley Holloway and George Cole, and set during the Festival of Britain. She told Sid Cole that she had been 'terrified'[14] when she walked on set on the first day but, by then, she was a seasoned executive who knew the production process inside out. Thus, finally, was launched the directorial career of the most adventurous female filmmaker of her era.

Not that things were getting any easier. As Sydney Box's biographer Andrew Spicer notes, Independent Film Distributors, the company set up by the Woolf brothers, John and James, had initially pledged £50,000 towards the production but withdrew their backing a week before production began partly because 'they were nervous about a woman directing'.[15]

Her challenge was to prove that she could 'bring in a film on a reasonably low budget with a measure of success'. The film was shot in twenty-three days, under considerable financial pressure. It eventually made a 'handsome' profit, although Muriel was dismayed to have discovered that the distributors used the proceeds to buy 'B pictures from the US' that had ended up being failures. This meant there was little upside for her and Sydney.

By then, though, she had completed a second feature as director, *Street Corner* (1953), a documentary-style drama about a policewoman in Chelsea. This was distributed through Rank's General Film Distributors and did strong business. After that, she had 'no difficulty in being accepted as a director by

---

[14]Box, British Entertainment History Project.
[15]Spicer, *Sydney Box* (Manchester: Manchester University Press, 2006).

artists and producers in this country', but no US producers would consider hiring her. 'The mere mention of my sex was sufficient to damn any prospects out of hand.'[16]

Street Corner epitomised what Muriel Box was about. It was a lowish-budget drama which seemed conventional enough on the surface until you realized that it was a movie made by a woman about women, and that it covered subject matter rarely seen before in British movies. All those years of continuity and script work had made her into a formidably concise and effective director. She had a brisk matter-of-fact style which blinded some critics and audiences to how daring her films often were.

Not that her career became very much easier. 'If a film for some inexplicable reason runs smoothly one is inclined to be nervous or highly suspicious, usually with just cause,' she wrote, as she detailed the financial problems, run-ins with temperamental or drunken stars, censorship issues and other assorted challenges she faced during her ground-breaking career.[17] Her films were diverse. There were poignant adult-themed dramas like *Rattle of a Simple Man* (1964), starring Harry Corbett as a repressed middle-aged man courting a beautiful woman (Diane Cilento), little aware that she's a prostitute, and comedies like *The Passionate Stranger* (1957), starring Margaret Leighton as a respectable middle-class housewife who writes bodice-ripping novels secretly in her spare time.

'Women ... have a raw deal from the very beginning. You can't cite any profession where women don't come second, that's what I have to say as I have found it's true,' Muriel reflected late in her career. 'Why they can't give women a chance, they haven't any confidence at all in them, they never say to women let us try and see what she's done. Right into my last film, which is interesting, they didn't want a woman director on that last one ...'[18]

Given the opposition she had to overcome at every step of the way, Box's achievements seem all the more remarkable. Her sheer determination to progress, and her range of talents, enabled her to keep going when other less

---

[16]Box, British Entertainment History Project.
[17]Box, *Odd Woman Out*, 218.
[18]Box, British Entertainment History Project.

tenacious filmmakers would certainly have quit. She was also giving opportunities to other women. For example, on *Street Corner*, Anne Crawford had one of the leading roles as the female police officer, WPC Susan, a part that would have gone to a male actor in a more conventional police drama. That film had a female editor, Jean Barker, a female casting director, Nora Roberts, a female script and continuity executive, Phyllis Croker, and a female wardrobe head, Irma Birch.

Muriel herself received at least some support along the way from men like Joseph Grossman, Asquith, Rank and, of course, Sydney Box, but she did her best to provide opportunities for women to work alongside her. After she died in 1991, obituarists belatedly realized what a ground-breaking figure she had been. 'She was a role model for young women. Her chequered career illustrates the difficulties for a woman working in the film industry, and also its volatility, particularly in the 1950s and 60s when she and her husband struggled to retain a measure of independence and integrity,' wrote the British Film Institute in its summation of her career. 'If Muriel Box never directed a masterpiece, her oeuvre remains the most significant achievement of a woman director in the British film industry.'[19]

---

[19]http://www.screenonline.org.uk/people/id/479374/.

7

Efe Cakarel[1]

There weren't any other figures in the British film industry of 2020 who had backgrounds which matched that of the Turkish-British entrepreneur Efe Cakarel who founded arthouse streaming platform MUBI.

A maths prodigy as a child, Cakarel used to compete in high-level mathematics Olympiads. Born in 1976, he grew up in the Mediterranean port town of Izmir, in Anatolia. His father ran a successful electrical engineering company and expected Cakarel to join it and, one day, to take it over. His mother was an executive at Turkish Airlines. The idea that he might one day have offices off Carnaby Street in London and be releasing films online and in British cinemas seemed very far-fetched indeed.

Cakarel had an idyllic childhood. He didn't even learn to read until he was eight years old, instead spending much of his time 'out in nature', as he puts it. The family was cultured and Cakarel was a creative child but he was left in no doubt that he was being groomed to take over his father's engineering business. His parents didn't want him studying anything which would get in the way of this long-term goal.

The parents noticed and encouraged Cakarel's mathematical ability. The boy liked structured thinking and had a near genius with numbers. After passing many exams, Cakarel, then fifteen, was chosen for the Turkish national team. He had a transformative moment which indirectly changed his life while away with his teammates, preparing for the European Mathematical Olympiad

---

[1] This chapter is based on the author's interview with Efe Cakarel, 8 August 2019.

Efe Cakarel. Courtesy of MUBI.

at a summer maths camp in the northern part of Turkey. It was a hothouse where young mathematicians like himself would be studying and solving puzzles in the company of the country's most distinguished professors. They spent their summer holidays solving equations between fourteen and sixteen hours a day. It was gruelling but Cakarel relished the experience.

Every evening the professors would give the young boffins a puzzle to solve overnight. On one occasion, the riddle they set was to 'find the formula for the nth prime number'. It seemed straightforward enough for a maths specialist like Cakarel. He stayed up all night and filled fifty sheets of paper but couldn't find the solution. Nor could any other members of the team. The next morning, they went to their professors and told them, shamefacedly, that they had failed. 'Don't worry about it. This problem hasn't been solved by anyone yet. Nobel laureates in maths are worrying about this problem,' the young maths hotshots were told.

Rather than feel dismayed, Cakarel was exhilarated. He realized he had been working on a problem that the finest minds in the world hadn't yet solved. This gave him confidence. He began to think that, if he put his mind to it, he could do anything. His father wanted him to study electrical engineering. Cakarel, whose own passion was to become an architect, decided that if he was going to do so, he would study at the very best school. This was the Massachusetts Institute of Technology in Cambridge, Massachusetts, USA. If he couldn't go there, he wouldn't go anywhere else. He was a Turkish adolescent growing up in Anatolia. He had no contacts at MIT and no idea of the enrolment process but that didn't put him off in the slightest. For Cakarel, career hurdles had become like knotty maths problems. He had the inner conviction that, if he worked hard enough, he could always find the answer.

At the European Mathematical Olympiad in Geneva in 1994, Cakarel won third prize. On the day he phoned his parents to tell them of his triumph, they revealed to him that, back home in Izmir, he had just received a package from MIT. These were his acceptance papers. 'It was the best day of my life. I was at the time seventeen. I wrote to the President of MIT and explained what had happened over the weekend [at the Olympiad]. He responded and gave me a full scholarship. It was a wonderful journey to go from this little town to MIT. It opened up the world for me.'

Cinema was already a passion. Growing up in Turkey, Cakarel went regularly to the movies from an early age. Izmir had a series of small but welcoming arthouse cinemas where he was able to see films like *Cinema Paradiso*, *Casablanca*, *Dr. Strangelove*, *Vertigo* and *The Godfather Part II*. Sadly, these movie theatres would soon close. In Izmir today, the chances for youngsters to see foreign-language cinema are very limited. That is a gap that Cakarel is seeking to plug through his online company MUBI.

His parents may not have allowed him to pursue his original dream of becoming an architect but his older sister studied architecture. As a teenager, in breaks from his maths study, he would stay up late at night helping her with her drawings. He was a capable draughtsman.

Cakarel started his course in electrical engineering at MIT in the autumn of 1994. He arrived at the time that Netscape Navigator, one of the first popular internet browsers, was being launched after the success of the Mosaic browser. The World Wide Web was being spun and the online revolution was gathering pace. 'That was the beginning of the internet, the fall of 1994 when I landed at MIT. That same year, Amazon was founded and the rest is history,' Cakarel recalled. He was so fascinated by this new phenomenon that he quickly enrolled in a new course in computer science.

'While I was there [at MIT], I decided to follow my own path. I didn't know what that was but I decided not to go back to Turkey and join my family. I sort of rebelled.' Predictably, his father was very angry to learn Efe wouldn't be taking over the family business and for several years they were estranged.

Cakarel may not have had a precise career path planned, or any particular desire at this stage to work in the film business, but he showed the extent of his ambition by joining the blue chip investment bank and financial services company Goldman Sachs. 'At the time, 1997/1998, Goldman Sachs and McKinsey were the two most difficult places to get in. Those were the two companies in the world that everybody wanted to work for.'

Cakarel decided immediately that he would work for Goldman Sachs and for nobody else. During his freshman summer at MIT, he wrote to the company. He didn't even get a reply. He therefore went home to Turkey and spent the whole summer windsurfing. The following year, his sophomore summer, he wrote again. This time, they replied and gave him an interview but didn't hire him. Cakarel reacted by ignoring everybody's advice (conventional wisdom had it that your sophomore summer was crucial for finding a career-defining job) and spending another summer windsurfing. 'If I am not working for Goldman, I am not working for anybody else,' he declared.

By the following year, the young Turk had a new fascination – trading. At the time, Chicago was the global centre of commodity and foreign exchange trading through the Chicago Mercantile Exchange. The best firm for trading foreign exchange was SBC Warburg – and so naturally Cakarel went there. Instead of windsurfing, he spent the summer trading foreign exchange – and quickly became very proficient. 'It's maths, it's quick thinking and it was something I felt very comfortable with. I was fascinated by the finance world. So that was a great summer.'

After his fourth year at MIT, Goldman finally gave Cakarel a chance. That year, they hired only two people from MIT and Cakarel was one of them. In taking up a job at Goldman, Cakarel wasn't primarily motivated by money or the desire to be a Tom Wolfe-like 'master of the universe'. Instead, he was following advice from older mentors who told him that whatever he later did in business, whether he was launching companies, buying or selling them, a stint with Goldman Sachs would provide a useful grounding. He saw his time there as a continuation of his education. He spent four years with the company, working on cross-border mergers and acquisitions. When two companies in two different countries merged, he would be part of the team working on tax, legal and accounting structures of the merger. For example, when German industrial company Mannesmann was acquired by British mobile operator Vodafone in 2000, Cakarel worked behind the scenes making sure the deal went through.

Cakarel realized that in business, there are three basic roles. Either you are an advisor (as he then was) or you are an operator/manager or you are an investor. 'It is very important in your twenties to experience these three things – to see where you feel comfortable in your skillset. In your thirties is when you start building experience in your chosen field and in your forties is when you start creating real value,' Cakarel says of the way in which a business career is expected to evolve.

There was a five-month period, working for Goldman Sachs in New York, when Cakarel didn't take a single day off. On weekends, the only concession was that he would get to the office at 11 a.m. instead of 8.30 a.m. The culture was one of very intense hard work. The company philosophy was 'nothing happens unless you work twice as hard as anyone else'. Not that the young executive felt abused or exhausted. 'You are working with some of the smartest people in that business, working on some of the biggest and most interesting deals. As a result, it is really exciting as a young professional. On day one, as someone right out of college, you are with the winners. For the right personality, it is an amazing place to be.'

These were Cakarel's formative years. He was happy at Goldman but decided that taking an MBA would enable him to take a step back and determine what he really wanted to do with his life. He had already discovered that he worked best as an operator/manager.

At Stanford Graduate School of Business, where he took his MBA, Cakarel had further formative experiences. One key encounter was with Shai Agassi, the head of products and technology at giant software corporation SAP, who had come to give a lecture. He ingratiated himself with the SAP boss and began working for the company at the same time he was doing his studies, which were in computer science. After he left Stanford, SAP recruited Cakarel to run its new team overseeing a web-based enterprise resource planning (ERP) system for small businesses. This was where Cakarel cut his teeth in building 'scaleable, web-based internet applications working with some of the best developers in the world'. He was considered a prodigy.

It was while at SAP that Cakarel had the idea which would bring him into the film business. He had always remained a movie lover. 'It is just the most wonderful art for me.' Although he was working gruelling hours, he still made time to go to the cinema.

At one stage, Cakarel aspired to become a movie director but he quickly discovered he was no Stanley Kubrick. During his time at Stanford, the would-be auteur took time off his studies to go to Paris and write a script. He would sit in cafes, drinking cup after cup of coffee and waiting for inspiration to come. When he finally managed to finish the script, he came back to America to make the film. The producer-director didn't skimp on the expense. He hired himself a full crew, the very best equipment and lights, a professional editor and the most talented actors he could find. There was a premiere at Stanford with his classmates in the audience. Cakarel watched his own movie with a gradual sinking feeling. He realized that it just wasn't very good. The film (a Guy Ritchie-style thriller about three entrepreneurs who find a formula for a genetically modified piece of fruit but then fall foul of venture capitalists and gangsters) was called *Lemon* – and a lemon was what it turned out to be.

'There is a huge premium between being the best and the second best. For the best restaurant, you would drive for two hours and pay £500 per person. When you get sick, you want the best doctor and you do not care how much it costs ... I wanted to be the best in whatever I do in life, the best in the world, and I realized when I saw that film that I could never be the best, no matter how much I tried. I just didn't have it ...' his voice tails off.

Being the best at whatever he did had always been Cakarel's goal. When he realized he was only a mediocre director, he abandoned any plans to continue in that field. However, he also trusted his own instincts. He might not have been able to make a good film but he knew instantly when he saw one. 'I know when I am in the presence of greatness.'

In 2006, when Cakarel had the idea for what was eventually to become MUBI, it was sparked by his desire to watch as many 'great films as possible'. He was in Tokyo at Christmas and he wanted to watch Wong Kar-wai's *In the Mood for Love* (2000) on his brand new Apple laptop in a cafe in Roppongi Hills. At the time, Tokyo had the fastest average broadband speed in the world. The Japanese were very device-savvy. Even so, the film simply wasn't available.

By his own admission, Cakarel at this stage had no idea how the film industry worked or what process of rights management and licensing would be needed for him to be allowed to watch the movie in a cafe in Tokyo. This was a question which nagged away at him as he flew back to San Francisco, where he was then living. It prompted him to write a proposal for an online platform which he called 'The Auteurs' and which would show all the films he loved. Two months later, he quit his job at SAP and set about trying to launch the platform.

Backers weren't interested in investing in what was then simply an idea. Cakarel was therefore dipping into his savings. He recruited a pair of computer engineers. They worked from Coupa Cafe in Palo Alto, Silicon Valley. Eventually, after a few weeks, they came up with a prototype for what he later called 'a Netflix for independent film'. The idea seemed robust enough apart from the fact that he didn't have money to pay for licensing the films. Nor could he persuade rights holders to sell him work on a revenue-sharing basis – there wasn't yet any revenue to share.

In February 2007, Cakarel launched The Auteurs (later to be re-christened MUBI). In May, he set off to the Cannes Film Festival in search of movies and contacts. The picture he paints of himself in this period is of a Dick Whittington-like outsider. He didn't know anyone. He wrote a letter to the festival director, Gilles Jacob, asking him how he should go about getting an accreditation to the festival and also telling him that if Cannes, then about to celebrate its sixtieth anniversary, wanted to stay relevant for another sixty years, it should embrace bold new companies like his one. Perhaps impressed by his chutzpah, Jacob indulged him. He was given accreditation.

On arriving in Cannes, Cakarel was so intimidated by the sheer scale of the event that it took him two hours even to summon up the courage to enter the

Palais du Cinema, where the market was based. He had never spoken to either a sales agent or a producer. No one would take meetings with him. Eventually, Hengameh Panahi, the Iranian-born boss of the Paris-based sales and production company Celluloid Dreams, picked up his brochure, which he had left at her office. She gave him a call. By then, though, Cakarel had already left the festival.

One of the doyennes of the independent arthouse market, Panahi sold, financed and marketed films from directors like Alexander Sokurov, Takeshi Kitano and Jacques Audiard, all 'auteurs' whose work might have fitted on Cakarel's new platform. He flew to Paris to meet her. In his mind, she was the indie film world's answer to his old bosses at Goldman Sachs, one of the top dogs in the business. She had 'incredible taste'. He had a proposition for her. He wasn't in the position to buy rights to release films in the major territories but maybe she could let him have those films for the territories she couldn't sell. Even Celluloid Dreams' most beloved films didn't get released everywhere. For example, Marjane Satrapi's *Persepolis* (2007) was never distributed in cinemas in Colombia. Cakarel's idea was that he could come in and take the rights for the unsold countries and make the films available online on a revenue-sharing basis. 'I would say, Hengameh, *Persepolis* is sold in fifty-four countries. Can you give me the other 140 and I can immediately start monetizing it for you, from Jamaica to Vietnam.'

It was a smart business manoeuvre but Cakarel soon discovered that the revenues the films generated were still tiny. It was hard to attract subscribers to the new service. Nonetheless, he persevered. The films picked up were curated. There was always editorial to explain their background, put them in context and to enhance viewers' experience. People liked the service but there weren't enough of them to make it profitable.

In 2010, The Auteurs rebranded as MUBI. 'I approached the brand very systematically. I wanted the name of my company to be a CVCV name – consonant–vowel–consonant–vowel. They are the easiest names that can be pronounced across different languages, and can become global brands ... Coke, Visa, Muji, etc.' One of Cakarel's friends, who is the creative director of Dentsu, a Japanese advertising agency, came up with the name.

Cakarel describes the unlikely circumstances in which his business secured its name and domain site:

Of course, we needed MUBI.com – it was taken by someone in Pakistan back in 1994 as it represented the initials of his name and it became the name of his company which is a repair shop for broken appliances in Karachi. I couldn't explain to him that I wanted to buy just the domain from him, so I ended up buying his shop [which came with the MUBI.com domain] for $14,000. And I immediately gifted him back his shop. He couldn't believe it. I can't make this up! That's the story of MUBI.

Cakarel realized that he needed to appeal to a much wider consumer base. The best way to do that was to strike deals with the US studios for their movies. Of course, he couldn't afford such movies on the open market. (In the first thirteen years of its existence, the company raised only $25 million, a reasonable amount from one perspective but a tiny figure from another – roughly the budget of two or three episodes of a big HBO series like *Game of Thrones* (2011–19). Investors in MUBI included friends and family as well as high-profile industry figures, among them Working Title Co-Chairman Eric Fellner, former CEO of Apple Europe Pascal Cagni, former Co-President of Goldman Sachs Jon Winkelried and Brazilian computer scientist Hugo Barra, who had been with Cakarel at MIT and whose jobs have included running Facebook's Oculus VR brand.

The ever ingenious Cakarel came up with a way of persuading the major studios to work with him. 'If we can't show everything, why don't we show a much smaller, limited selection of films that we refresh fairly often?' He had the idea of one film a day. Each film would stay on the platform for thirty days so there would always be a selection of films on the site. It was the digital equivalent to the staff's pick at your favourite video store. He would license big studio movies from directors like Francis Ford Coppola and the Coen Brothers – but only for thirty days.

The company had started in Paolo Alto but Cakarel noticed that the service was far more popular in Europe than the US. He decided to relocate to London (where he had worked briefly during his time at Goldman Sachs). 'It's a great place to be, close to everywhere I want to spend my time . . . it was close to a lot of the key markets where we wanted to grow MUBI including Germany, France, Italy, Scandinavia and the Netherlands, and it's in between our future growth markets, Asia and Latin America.'

Gradually, the company that Cakarel had launched in Silicon Valley became part of the British film industry, albeit still a subscription VOD company with a global reach. It began to release some films theatrically in the British marketplace. Cakarel was recruited to sit on British film industry panels, for example the British Film Institute's 2018 Commission on UK Independent Film. In 2015, Paul Thomas Anderson, the Oscar-winning director of *Boogie Nights* (1997) and *There Will Be Blood* (2007), gave MUBI the premiere of his short film, *Junun*, on the grounds that the VOD platform would connect him with precisely the kind of discerning viewers he wanted the film to be seen by. With no marketing behind it, *Junun* reached a huge audience.

'That really opened our eyes to what really moves the needle in this business which is new films exclusively available on your platform and that you show in an earlier window,' Cakarel noted of what his collaboration with Paul Thomas Anderson taught him. There were two ways of getting those films, either licensing them or producing them yourself.

MUBI was beginning to pick up all rights to bigger films for the UK market, giving theatrical releases to *Suspiria* (2018) and *Under the Silver Lake* (2018). These had big stars like Andrew Garfield and Dakota Johnson but had an indie sensibility and were expensive to market.

'The difference between us and a regular distributor is that I don't need to make money on the theatrical distribution,' Cakarel says of such acquisitions. On one level, making sure these films were seen on the big screen simply reflected his passion for cinema. They were, he felt, movies that were best seen in cinemas. 'The theatrical experience is infinitely better if you are lucky enough to have access to it. We are very committed to doing as wide a theatrical release as possible for all our films,' he declares, an intriguing perspective for the owner and operator of an online company. Nonetheless, he discovered films which were released theatrically would go on to boost subscriptions to the site when they finally surfaced on it.

By now, MUBI was investing directly in production. Its first project, transgender love story *Port Authority* (2019), screened in official selection in the 2019 Cannes Film Festival. It was a small budget film, at around $2 million, but Cakarel aspired to make bigger projects, in the $15–$20 million budget range. Yes, he acknowledged, being involved in production is risky for a distribution company. 'But it is existential. We have to figure it out ... we have to be in this game.'

Ask Cakarel if he was welcomed into the British film industry and he suggests that when his company was 'purely' in the subscription video on demand business, it wasn't really part of that industry. 'We were around it. Our interaction with the industry was as buyers, as people who licensed content from [UK distributors] like Curzon, Altitude, StudioCanal and so on. That is a very different relationship than production. Production is when you are really coming across the industry.'

Paul Thomas Anderson changed Cakarel's approach by giving him the premiere of *Junun*. The MUBI boss was also heartened by the fact that so many prominent independent filmmakers, figures like Wes Anderson for example, were MUBI subscribers. 'All these people they are actually on MUBI ... we are like the restaurant that chefs go to. The industry actually respects what we are doing. We are really committed to championing great cinema.'

The teenage mathematician from Izmir had metamorphosed into an important 'player' in British cinema. Cakarel has also learned to adapt in a period when traditional releasing models began to creak – and remain highly precarious. 'If I was a pure distributor relying on theatrical and on somebody like Sky or Netflix licensing my content – my God that is a very difficult business.'

What about his father's electrical engineering business back home in Turkey that he was once supposed to take over? With his father's retirement, the company was wound down.

The way my father built it, it needed to be run by family. He didn't institutionalize it. I want MUBI to be different. I want MUBI to still be here in 100 years so I need to take certain steps to make sure we have enough of a talent pool to take the leadership down the line ... I want it to survive without me. My father's company couldn't survive without him. He made all the decisions himself. He found it very hard to delegate. A company like that cannot maintain really good people because they get frustrated very, very quickly. At MUBI, I get overruled a lot. I try to bring on people who are smarter than I am!

8

Mickey Pugh[1]
King of Props

Mickey Pugh has worked with many of the top names in the film business – Stanley Kubrick, Steven Spielberg, Michael Mann, Guillermo del Toro and David Lean among them – on features including *Eyes Wide Shut* (1999), *Empire of the Sun* (1987), *A Passage to India* (1984), *Hellboy* (2004), *The Last of the Mohicans* (1992), *Braveheart* (1995), *Saving Private Ryan* (1998) and *Ali* (2001). He is a props master and he came into the industry in an unlikely and roundabout way.

Pugh still lives in Borehamwood, where he grew up. He was born in 1944 in Norfolk, where his father was then stationed in the RAF, but his family originally came from Islington. They moved out to Borehamwood in Hertfordshire in 1952 when Mickey was eight. He had no particular interest in the film business but, as a kid, used to gaze up in awe at the castle built for *Ivanhoe* at the nearby MGM Studios in Borehamwood. His father's civilian job after being demobbed was as a sheet metal worker. He wanted Mickey to get an apprenticeship in a proper industry as soon as possible. Mickey did well at the local secondary modern school but left at the age of fifteen. His prospects weren't bright. The idea that he would one day be working in Hollywood seemed impossibly far-fetched. His main desire was simply to ensure that he didn't land up in a factory job that he couldn't escape.

---

[1]This chapter is based on the author's interview with Mickey Pugh in Borehamwood, 3 April 2019.

Mickey Pugh was chargehand dresser for The Italian Job *(1969) and appeared briefly in the film too. Photo: Paramount/Getty Images.*

Employment, though, was easy enough to come by. He worked as a labourer in engineering shops. When one job finished, he walked into another. 'I started working on building sites because you got fairly good money. I told them I was older than I was. I was still only sixteen and you had to be eighteen so I told them I was eighteen. I was getting men's wages.'

One job was concreting the car park at the ABPC Studios in Elstree. 'It was summer. Being young, I had a pair of shorts on all the time. We were working outside the Pathé labs. One of the guys came out at his lunchtime. He always used to talk to me. He said you look so fit and healthy and he was very friendly with me,' Pugh remembers. This man gave him a phone number for MGM, which was looking for stagehands. Pugh was taken on.

The British film industry wasn't considered especially glamorous to work in behind the scenes. Pugh was in a labouring stagehand job where his main task was 'pulling nails out of timber' and helping out the carpenters. He was presentable and had suppressed his cockney accent. He dressed well. This was a period of (very slight) sartorial change in the film industry. A few years before, everyone, even those doing heavy manual labour, had worn a shirt and tie. Now, as long as you were clean and smart, you could get away without the tie – but you still had to be smart. A casual racism was also commonplace. Pugh remembers that the chargehand/prop man's nickname was a racially tinged epithet. That was because he never stopped working and was needed all the time.

Pugh wasn't anywhere near the filming. He liked to boast to friends that he worked for MGM but didn't tell them that his job was mainly about salvaging old timber. Still, it wasn't nearly as arduous as being on the building sites – and it was better paid.

Once Pugh had been in the job for a month, he was invited to join the union, the National Association of Theatrical Television and Kine Employees (NATTKE). When the studio was busy, so was he. When work dried up, he was promptly laid off.

In the early 1960s, the film industry was in one of its periodic slumps. NATTKE had Pugh's name on its books but when no work came up, he took a driving job instead. He'd ring from time to time to see if any more film work was available. 'Not as a stagehand but they want props at Pinewood Studios.' Pugh replied that he didn't know anything about props. Not a problem, they reassured him. He'd be taught once he got there. Then his career began in earnest.

One of the biggest challenges was getting to Pinewood Studios on time. He didn't have a car and it was a twenty-three-mile journey with unreliable public transport. By chance, another prop hand, Tommy Bacon, lived nearby with his wife and seven children. Bacon had an old minibus and agreed to give Mickey a lift.

At first, Pugh wasn't very popular. He was a teenager and therefore considered as trouble. He didn't know the job, so wasn't much practical use. He was working on films like *Lancelot and Guinevere* (1963), *Call Me Bwana* (1963) and *The Mouse on the Moon* (1963), dressing the sets and providing an extra pair of hands for the more experienced technicians. Georgie Ball, a senior props man and chargehand, took him in hand. 'Run and get this, sweep that up' were the instructions that tended to be barked out at him but Ball took the time to teach him the ropes. 'I learnt a lot from Georgie Ball,' he remembers. A crucial piece of advice was to pay attention at all times. If you were distracted, you would forget what went where.

'The continuity was something I always found a speciality in,' Pugh says. 'Most prop men didn't take much notice of continuity because you had a script girl, a continuity girl and they relied on them. But I saw it was just as important for me to know that there was half a biscuit on that plate and that when the camera came around, you had to put it back exactly the same.'

Props men couldn't rely on photos taken on cell phones or Polaroids. They would do rough drawings to remind them of the positioning of the props. Pugh was lucky in that he had a photographic memory. If he studied the set for a few moments, he had a near perfect recall of where everything was. He could strip a room and then reconstruct it.

Again, Pugh worked on a few films and was then laid off as work dried up. As a newcomer, he was at the bottom of the union list to be employed. During one lengthy lay-off in 1964, he took a job delivering and installing fruit machines – and learning how to repair them. Just when he was thinking about staying in the fruit-machine business for good, another film job came up.

Gradually, Pugh overcame his nerves. He was sometimes put on 'standby' and called on set during shooting. In the UK, props technicians were regarded as labourers. Pugh began to challenge that perception. As he became more established in the business, he became one of the first not only to read the script but to read between the lines and realize there was a lot more needed than what was written in the script. That was a skill in itself.

'I could read between the lines which a lot of people can't do. It's easy to say a cup of tea or a cup of coffee but actually to produce that on set, which seems the easiest prop in the world, you need about sixteen things.' He lists some of them: kettle, water and electricity (on Danny Boyle's *The Beach*, he brought his own paraffin heaters). Perhaps the actors won't like tea or milk so you have to provide substitute versions that look convincing on camera. 'And the actor is quite liable to break the cup so you've got to have more than one cup!'

Pugh would liaise with the set decorators and art directors. He would also talk to the actors and see if they wanted specific props. On one production shooting on the Yorkshire moors, Bernard Cribbins asked for a bugle (even though there was no mention of one in the script). Pugh got him one by knocking on doors of local farmhouses. Directors like Anthony Asquith, on whose productions *The VIPS* (1963) and *The Yellow Rolls-Royce* (1965) he worked, were 'too grand' to speak to crew members below a certain level. There was a strict hierarchy. 'I didn't like being treated like that and I never treated anybody like that,' Pugh says of the high-handed behaviour he sometimes encountered. Not that 'Puffin' Asquith, an aristocrat who was also a union leader and was generally very popular with his crews, was any kind of tyrant.

MGM had its own storehouse full of props. Later, when Pugh became affiliated to the prop-making department, he was allowed to make props too. Sometimes, he bought them. Prop masters used to be regarded as the equivalent of factory managers but Pugh treated the job as a craft – something that went beyond the logistics of sourcing, fetching and carrying.

There were still hiccups. When Pugh fractured his arm, he didn't like the way he was treated by his boss, who removed him from *Operation Crossbow* (1965) because he wasn't able to work for a week. He took exception to such treatment and threatened to quit.

As he gained more experience, Pugh was able to assess which directors were the most talented. Director Sidney Lumet, with whom he worked on *The Hill* (1965), was an intense figure but one with obvious flair and ability. He didn't 'lord it over people' in the way that some more insecure filmmakers did. Pugh was able to show off his ingenuity, for example building an ice cave out of candle wax for *The Double Man* (1967) and the snow effects for Roman Polanski's *The Fearless Vampire Killers* (1967). 'He [Polanski] was another man who shouted a lot,' Pugh recalls.

Pugh was learning all the time. He was also meeting some big names. On Bette Davis vehicle *The Anniversary* (1968), the legendary star had to wear a watch with a difficult, fiddly clasp on it. No one else could put it on for her properly. Pugh was therefore assigned to do the job. 'I was the only one allowed to do it. So many people messed it up, she got irritated,' Pugh remembered.

'She liked me. Being a young guy as well ... older women like well-mannered young men.'

The young prop master to be was no longer confined to the studios. He went on location. He was in Bath with the Dave Clark Five ('as big as the Beatles') on John Boorman's debut feature *Catch Us If You Can* (1965), and in Estoril in Portugal on Diana Dors vehicle *Hammerhead* (1968), which was considered a prestigious project at the time but sank without trace at the box office.

'Most people who went on foreign locations were established people who had been doing it for years,' Pugh says. It was a sign of his growing status in the industry that he was allowed to travel abroad.

As a chargehand dresser on *The Italian Job* (1969), Pugh worked in Turin. 'We were generally dressing the streets with all football regalia because the robbery took place during a football match,' he remembers of the classic caper movie starring Michael Caine. Pugh and his colleagues were putting England flags up at roundabouts and on the roadside. 'Oh, they [the Italians] didn't like that!' he remembers. The locals came out, swearing at them and charged at them. 'We were doing it on the fly. We had a certain amount of permission. When we were putting them [the flags] up in the streets, we had ladders and we had to knock on the doors of apartments and ask if we could attach them on the balconies ... Sometimes we just attached the flags and bunting without permission.' Pugh even had a small part in the film. You can see him on screen opening the doors for the minis (used to commit the robbery) to come through.

At the start of his career, Pugh had been employed by the studios. Eventually, he began to go freelance. Fewer films were being shot in studios. There were also 'too many old regulars who were used to doing nothing,' as Pugh puts it. Producers wanted younger, more enterprising technicians. 'That's one of the reasons I became quite good at it. The old regulars, apart from one or two like Tommy Welsh and Tom Ibbotson, weren't interested in bettering themselves. They did as little as possible ... but enough. They would disappear half the time and I would be left on set to run the floor on my own.'

There was a strong drinking culture. The camera crews were very professional but every lunchtime they would all go to the pub. The operator, the focus puller and everyone else had the traditional three pints at lunchtime. (They wouldn't drink shorts until the evening.) Pugh managed to avoid this particular ritual, joking that he would have become an alcoholic if he hadn't. 'Seventy per cent of the crew would drink at lunchtime.' The studios had their own bars and there were also pubs nearby. Sometimes, stars like Robert Mitchum would join them.

Working hours didn't fit comfortably with family life. On Michael Caine film *Pulp* (1972), Pugh had to travel to Malta. He had been out of work for a while. He was paying both the deposit on a new flat and the living expenses of his girlfriend, who was a law student. Therefore, when the call came through, he took the job immediately, flying out on the same day without telling his partner first. He needed the money. 'That was when it [the relationship] started to go downhill. She wasn't too pleased that I just went and took the job.'

One moment Pugh was out of work, wondering when his next cheque might come from. The next, he was flying first class to Malta, 'champagne all the way'. ('I travelled club class all over the world – now they put you on EasyJet!' the veteran props man reflects on the way the industry has changed since the rise of low-cost airlines.)

His work would take him further and further afield. On Bob Rafelson's *Mountains of the Moon* (1990), he spent the entire production living 'under canvas' in remote parts of Kenya.

Pugh did his share of period films, among them Ridley Scott's debut feature *The Duellists* (1977). Securing the money to get hold of the necessary props on British films was sometimes a struggle. On British productions back then prop masters were not given much respect. They were regarded as just 'workmen in the studios'.

The set decorators controlled the purse strings and spent lavishly on their own work. They were so busy with the planning of the sets and acquiring the props for the sets that action props generally took a back seat and it was often a struggle at the last minute to get them organized. Pugh, though, was eventually able to convince them that his job was crucial too. 'I saw that this was a really important job, like it was looked on in America. You worked closely with the actors. You had to service them with all the action props they needed and it had to be spot on. It couldn't be messed around with.'

Over the years, Pugh collected his own war chest of props: guns, snuff boxes, period matchboxes and cigarette lighters, ornaments, armour, binoculars, daggers and opera glasses that he has bought from the films on which he was employed. This meant he could earn more by renting these props to later productions he was working on. In his home in Borehamwood, he keeps many of them in a cabinet, among them a tomahawk from Michael Mann's *The Last of the Mohicans* (1992) which doubles as a peace pipe.

When Pugh finally went to America, he was amazed at the respect he was treated with – respect then in short supply for props masters in Britain.

Pugh's credits include films with arch perfectionists Stanley Kubrick and Steven Spielberg. The former took a strong interest in him after learning that Pugh had been a talented amateur boxer – and had sparred with world light-heavyweight champion John Conteh. Kubrick was fascinated by boxing. Early in his career, as a photographer at *Life*, Kubrick took photos of the sport and made the short boxing documentary *The Day of the Fight* (1951), while his second feature *Killer's Kiss* (1955) is a crime thriller about a boxer. The American director would seek Pugh out to talk about boxing. The British props man witnessed his change in personality at first hand. Off set, Kubrick was gregarious and friendly. As soon as he started shooting, he changed. 'He could be your best friend in the morning and in the afternoon he would be so vitriolic, he destroyed people.' Once, he told Pugh to move an object six inches. Pugh did so. 'That's not six inches,' Kubrick complained. Pugh took out the tape measure. It showed exactly six inches. 'That was a bit of luck,' the director responded, as if the prop man had just got away with something. From then on, Kubrick insisted on Pugh having the tape measure wherever he went on set.

Kubrick was challenging to work for. The American director would be entrusted by his backers with the entire budget for the film, which he would distribute as he saw fit. Sometimes, Kubrick could be a penny pincher. At others, he would go to extreme lengths to achieve the effects he wanted. Pugh remembers one scene of Tom Cruise walking through a door on *Eyes Wide Shut* (1999), which took three full days to film even though it didn't feature any dialogue. This was a complete contrast to the films he made with Spielberg which would be shot at breakneck speed. 'You'd run from one set-up to the next because he [Spielberg] has got it all worked out how he wants to do it.'

By the time Pugh was hired for *A Passage to India* (1984), its venerated director, David Lean, was seventy-six. Lean had his 'cantankerous' moments but Pugh remembers him as 'a smashing guy . . . brilliant – he had everything worked out.' He expected the best from his technicians. Pugh tells a story about a carriage which is described as moving from a gravel to a sand road. The way it travelled across the ground changed slightly – and Lean expected Pugh to recognize that. 'It was close up so I am bumping the carriage,' he remembers. He asked the director if he should change the way he was doing it. 'Of course, my dear boy. You read the script!' came back the reply.

Sometimes, productions on which Pugh worked lasted for a small eternity. He had 'two birthdays' during the shooting of Warren Beatty's Russian revolution epic *Reds* (1981). On that production, he was working alongside legendary Italian cinematographer Vittorio Storaro. It was before the age of digital special effects. Storaro loved using smoke. That was why Pugh and his team were busy on his behalf using bee guns that would shoot off charcoal smoke and incense across the huge sets that Beatty had had constructed to re-create Russian in 1917. 'It wasn't too healthy . . .'

Another of his credits was *The Bounty* (1984), which Lean was originally intended to direct. In the end, the job was taken by Roger Donaldson. He became very friendly with Liam Neeson, who shared his passion for boxing, and with Daniel Day-Lewis (one of whose first films this was and likewise a boxing fan). His foresight with props also endeared him to the film's star, Mel Gibson, who played Fletcher Christian. In one scene, Christian was drinking spirits. Gibson wanted the scene to seem realistic. Pugh, who always carried whisky and brandy with him, was able to supply the Australian actor with what he needed. 'After he had drunk half the bottles, I said you can't have any more,' Pugh intervened when the alcohol began to get in the way of the performance.

Bernard Williams, producer of *The Bounty*, headhunted Pugh to be props master on Michael Mann's Hannibal Lecter thriller *Manhunter* (1986). Mann quickly warmed to his work ethic. 'In America whilst filming they have two "on-set dressers". In the UK the prop standbys do all the on-set prop dressing with no extra help.' Mann was also intrigued by the hand props and admired Pugh's eye for detail.

On Mann's Muhammad Ali biopic *Ali* (2001), Pugh's expertise gave the production an authenticity it might otherwise have lacked. He knew from his own boxing experience that in the early 1960s, the setting for part of the film, the thumb hung loose from the boxing glove. (Today, it is attached.) He also could remember when adrenaline used to treat cut eyes was kept by the trainers in phials behind their ears. He also knew that in the period before plastic bottles, the boxers would drink water out of a glass bottle but that the bottle would have tape wrapped around it so it wouldn't smash. Pugh explained that in those days the canvas was not non-slip like it is now. He therefore had made square wooden trays that could be used in shot and filled them with resin. The actors/boxers could get into their corners and stand in the trays filled with resin, grinding their boxing boots so the soles were covered in resin and would not slip. This was an example of the props man drawing on his own experiences to do his job better.

Ali's real-life trainer Angelo Dundee was startled to find someone on set who knew almost as much about the sport as he did. Mann was also impressed. 'He loved anybody who knew stuff that he didn't know. He wasn't one who would get annoyed.' Pugh was listed as technical advisor on *Ali* because of his knowledge of boxing and to differentiate him from the prop men already working in the US on the film.

As the industry changed, so did the tasks that Pugh was given. On *Lara Croft: Tomb Raider* (2001), starring Angelina Jolie, or *Mission Impossible* (1996), starring Tom Cruise, both films largely driven by special effects, a new job alongside his other work was to keep the 'blue screen' (used for projecting backdrops) clean.

The veteran props man's advice to newcomers in the industry is clear cut. Always do 'a little bit extra' and don't just walk away at the end of the day until you know exactly what you need for the following day. Study the script – read between the lines and anticipate what the production might need. Pugh himself had earned a privileged position. To get him to agree to work in their movies, filmmakers would consult him earlier and earlier in the process.

Photographs of Pugh on sets like *Braveheart* and *Air America* show him in the midst of the action, clearly trusted by star Mel Gibson. 'Mel's a great guy and really talented and has an intensity that means he does everything as on set with all his passion. He likes to get involved – and is pretty intense. In Thailand [for *Air America*], he got himself a motorbike. The producers went crazy. He wouldn't drive it carefully. He would think he was racing. He would bomb off down the road, stop at the local bar and then bomb off back. If he smoked, which he used to do, he would smoke full stop. He does everything to extremes.'

Pugh may have saved Gibson's life when the actor was playing William Wallace in *Braveheart*. 'We were about to do the scene of Wallace/Mel being hung, drawn and quartered. The famous first AD [assistant director] David Tomblin asked me to get changed into a costume so that I could be in the crowd, as close to Mel as possible whilst he was being hung, so that I could help him with any safety issues. Well, that was a good call as in the scene Mel wanted it to be very realistic and very nearly hung himself. I was able to race in and lift him to take the weight off his neck.'

Gibson wasn't the only hellraiser Pugh encountered. He worked with the notorious John Bindon, a flamboyant actor with close links both to the underworld and Princess Margaret, whose party piece when drunk was to hang half-pint beer glasses on his 'manhood'. 'He'd always do the trick in the pub, no matter where he was. He would get 'it' out and put it in the pint jug trying to reach the bottom and saying it's just trying to have a drink. He was a really strong guy. Three of us tried to get him on that film and throw him in the pool. I've always been quite fit but he just threw us off like we were nothing. It was me that ended up in the pool.'

Pugh also did a film (*The Prince and the Pauper*) behind the Iron Curtain in Budapest in the communist days with Oliver Reed. 'There was a big birthday party we got invited to. There was a great big long table with all the producers sitting at it. Halfway through, Ollie has just had a few drinks and he has got up and is running down the table, dropping his trousers. He was out every night causing havoc in a communist state. His stand-in, who was really his minder as well, had to do two weeks in prison for him.'

It's a measure of the relatively low regard in which props 'men' (there were very few women in the job) used to be held that their jobs didn't even have set names. Pugh would be styled as 'supervising standby' (head man on the floor on the set), 'prop master' or 'head of hand props'. But in his six decades in the business, Pugh ensured that props technicians were regarded as essential members of the filmmaking team with a key creative role to play. The man who started his working life on a building site as a sixteen-year-old had re-defined a job that, before he came along, had been taken entirely for granted.

9

Isaac Julien

When he contemplates his unlikely route into the British film business, artist and director Isaac Julien likes to quote a remark made by the black American novelist James Baldwin.

'He was being interviewed. It was a white male interviewer. He said to him [Baldwin], "It must have been very difficult and terrible [to be] born black, working class, homosexual, poor. That must have been really terrible." Baldwin turned around to him and said, "Actually, I think I hit the jackpot!"'[1] As a gay, black, British filmmaker, growing up in a working-class family in Hoxton, east London, Julien felt the same about his background as Baldwin once had. Being disadvantaged had its advantages.

Julien was the eldest of five children. His father was a welder in a Ford plant, his mother was a nurse. His parents worked nights and he often had to look after his siblings. As he noted in an autobiographical essay in *Riot*, a book accompanying his 2013 exhibition at the Museum of Modern Art in New York, his parents, who were from Saint Lucia, spoke French Creole to each other while speaking in English with their children.[2]

'Early on there were two central goals in my mind: I didn't want to live the life of my parents, nor did I want – ever – to work in a factory or a bank,' he wrote,[3] echoing a sentiment shared by several others in this book who found ways of escaping the lives and careers laid out in front of them and breaking

---

[1] Isaac Julien, interviewed by the author, Isaac Julien Studios, Hutley Wharf, Hackney, London, 24 July 2019.
[2] Isaac Julien, *RIOT* (New York: Museum of Modern Art), 2013.
[3] Ibid.

Isaac Julien. Photo: Clayton Chase/WireImage via Getty Images.

into the British film industry. He cites his O level art teachers as among the first who inspired him with the belief he could take a different pathway and he might be able to become involved in the arts himself. He had come across what he calls 'middle-class culture' and had met 'middle-class younger people doing to my mind fairly interesting things. All of that fomented the curiosity I had, which was really trying to think about the possibility for a cultural expression that would somehow articulate things I felt were not quite right in the culture. Also, I think it was one's own quest for self-representation.'[4]

Another 'lucky' accident was the fire which forced his family to move house. It seemed a disaster at the time but enabled Julien to move away from an area where he was mocked and harassed, referred to as 'that effeminate boy' or called 'secretary boy because I bothered to study'.[5] He went on to choose art and communications for his A levels. The latter course required him to make a film. He chose as his subject 'How Gays Are Stereotyped in the Media'. 'I don't

---

[4]Ibid.
[5]Ibid.

think I got a very high mark but I passed and I made this documentary,' he remembers. One teacher told him it was an interesting documentary but that maybe he should think about dealing with the experiences of black gays. 'I thought OK, I will have to think about that one.'[6]

Then, in 1980, Julien won a place at Saint Martin's School of Art in central London.

Julien's landmark feature *Young Soul Rebels* (1991) dramatized what it was like to be young, black and gay in working-class London in the Queen's Silver Jubilee year of 1977. A movie of tremendous energy and passion, it falls somewhere between a coming of age story, a celebration of soul music and pirate radio, a punk protest movie and a murder mystery. The film won an award in the Cannes Critics' week but was regarded with suspicion by British reviewers. 'Badly made ... trivialising ... incomprehensible,' was the waspish Alexander Walker's verdict in the London *Evening Standard*.[7]

Julien (born 21 February 1960) was a teenager in 1977. He wasn't as wild as the protagonists in his movie. He didn't drive cars or clamber up skyscrapers to erect aerials for illicit radio stations. 'But what I was involved in when I was seventeen was that I was exposed to filmmakers who I befriended who were part of a film collective called the Newsreel Collective,' Julien remembers.

These filmmakers, among them figures like Noreen McDowell and Joy Chamberlain, were mentors to the young Julien. Most worked in conventional jobs in the film and TV industry but were also part of the Collective, making political documentaries and dramas. Julien was an actor in one of their films, *True Romance*. There were some colourful figures linked to the Collective, including Astrid Proll, a German former political terrorist who had been part of the Baader-Meinhof gang in Germany and was now in hiding in London.

When he could afford it, Julien was going to clubs, among them Lacey Ladies (a soul club in Essex) and, more upmarket, the Embassy Club in Bond Street (whose patrons included Andy Warhol and Bianca Jagger). He was also starting to visit gay clubs. Julien was part of what he calls 'black and white soul

[6]Julien, interviewed by the author.
[7]*Young Soul Rebels* reviewed by Alexander Walker, London *Evening Standard*, 1991.

boy culture'. It was an exciting period. Punk rock was at its zenith and Julien felt he was in the middle of what he calls a big 'cultural explosion'. 'I was on the verge of coming out but, at that time, it tended to be bisexual. You had David Bowie and Marc Bolan and a lot of different representations that were being offered in pop music.'[8]

The young filmmaker was active in the youth wing of the 'Rock Against Racism' movement. This was also the beginning of the 'Black Action' film movement. Julien had grown up in an area in which the fascist National Front was very powerful and in which street violence and confrontations with the police were commonplace. Adding to the combustible atmosphere was the influx of Asian immigrants and the rise of the neo-Nazi movement. The old Jewish community was moving out. It was, he remembers, 'a highly charged environment'.

His studio is still based in east London, a sleek ground-floor space overlooking the canal, full of video screens and designer furniture, and just a few hundred yards from Gainsborough Studios where Michael Balcon and Alfred Hitchcock used to make films. Like other former film studios including Denham and Teddington, much of the Gainsborough site has been redeveloped with modern housing.

'I flirted with any organization that seemed interested in me,' is how Julien explained his involvement in so many oppositional groups. 'I was a very bored, alienated teenager.'[9]

The young artist and would-be filmmaker may have been a highly politicized 'soulboy' but he also liked his genre: blaxploitation and kung fu movies. During his time at Saint Martin's, he earned money to fund his studies by working as a 'dresser' for the West End production of *Evita*. It was a colourful experience and one that he later credited with teaching him about the behaviour and psychology of actors and the logistical challenges in mounting big artistic endeavours. By then, he was making 8 mm films. One was called *The Dresser*. Midway through his course, in 1981, there were riots all over Britain: in Brixton in London, Toxteth in Liverpool and elsewhere.

---

[8]Julien, interviewed by the author.
[9]Ibid.

One consequence of the riots was that 'all black artists were suddenly lumped together, we were all seen in the same frame of reference,' Julien later wrote.[10] To put it crudely, they were half expected to be making agit prop and for their work to rail against a white, racist system that was oppressing them. Julien didn't want to be classified in such a narrow way. However, while at Saint Martin's, he had made a documentary, *Who Killed Colin Roach?*, about the death of a 23-year-old black man shot outside an east London police station in 1982.

> The Colin Roach marches, organized by the Colin Roach family committee, had been taking place in Stoke Newington. It was a very politically charged moment. The issue had been going on a very long time, about young black men being killed in police stations ... this came a bit closer to home. It could have been my brother or myself. When I saw the family on the march, I thought, well that could have been my mother. That sprang me into action.[11]

The film was championed by radical listings magazine *City Limits*. It attracted the attention of Channel 4, and later helped Julien secure a place at the National Film and Television School in Beaconsfield (not that he would stay there for long).

After leaving Saint Martin's, Julien became a founding member of the Sanfoka Film and Video collective 1983. This was funded by the Greater London Council and was making work which, as historian Stephen Bourne noted in his study *Black in the British Frame: The Black Experience in British Film and Television*, 'challenged preconceptions about black identities'.[12]

Julien has written about how he and fellow filmmakers were 'running off to meetings with Channel 4, the ACTT [an industry union], and the Greater London Council for the Arts'. He thrived in the collective movement. He was an expert organizer who could negotiate his way through committees and was heavily involved in film education. He also enjoyed being part of an artistic

---

[10]Julien, *RIOT*.
[11]Julien, interviewed by the author.
[12]Stephen Bourne, *Black in the British Frame: The Black Experience in British Film and Television* (London: Continuum, 2001).

avant-garde. He was meeting and socializing with other important gay cultural figures, among them pop group Pet Shop Boys and filmmakers John Maybury and Derek Jarman. Like Maybury and Jarman, he was exploring different ways of shooting, using 8 mm and video as well as 16 mm celluloid. The formation of Channel 4 was a huge stimulus to him and his friends. Different voices were being heard and they were addressing different audiences. He was steeping himself in film theory and political theory, studying work by academics like Stuart Hall and Edward Said. In his 1984 film *Territories*, partly inspired by the work of Chris Marker, he explored race, class and sexuality in black British culture of the time. He took part in debates about black British film culture at events like the Third Eye Film Festival and the Edinburgh Film Festival. He met Spike Lee in Chicago in the mid-1980s when Lee was presenting his first full-length feature, *She's Gotta Have It* (1986).

Unusually for filmmakers in this period, Julien was steeped in academic film theory. He had read about semiotics, intertextuality and structuralism. Even so, he didn't want to be pigeon-holed as an experimental director any more than he wanted to be regarded as a campaigning one. He was also watching Hitchcock and Jean-Luc Godard films as well as studying structuralist filmmaking. He was intrigued by narrative cinema.

Julien's time at the National Film and Television School turned out to be extremely brief. In fact, he left the school after a single day. 'I decided it wasn't going to be for me. First of all, I hated where it was located: Beaconsfield. I thought it was completely boring, really not for me. I thought it was much more exciting to be commissioned by Channel 4 Television and to make my mistakes in public.'[13]

Instead of taking a directing course at the NFTS, Julien made films with the Sanfoka Collective and taught himself that way. 'It took a long time to think about how to articulate questions of black gay desire in film and to figure out what would be my strategy,' Julien remembers of the lengthy lead-up to *Looking for Langston* (1989), a forty-two-minute lyrical drama-documentary about the black gay American poet and leader of the 'Harlem Renaissance' Langston

---

[13]Julien, interviewed by the author.

Hughes (1902–67), which marked his international breakthrough.[14] The film, produced through the Sanfoka Collective, screened at the New York Film Festival, the Telluride Festival and the Toronto Festival.

'I was fascinated by the Harlem Renaissance and by Harlem and by black American culture,' he remembers.[15] The east Londoner was telling the story of an American icon. Hughes's family complained that he hadn't asked for permission to quote from Hughes's poems but the film was still given an enthusiastic reception in America.

Sanfoka received funding from the British Film Institute which was to back Julien's debut feature, *Young Soul Rebels*. The brilliant, polymathic English academic Colin MacCabe, Head of the Production Board at the BFI in the late 1980s and then its Head of Research and Education, was the executive producer on the film.

Julien has written of the inspiration he received from Stephen Frears's *My Beautiful Laundrette* (1985), scripted by Hanif Kureishi (see Chapter 18), which had dramatized life in Thatcherite Britain and had the chutzpah to show on screen a gay love affair between a white skinhead and a young Asian man. 'There began to be a feeling that independent film could change things ... Kureishi's film was proof that the rules could be subverted.'[16]

Young Soul Rebels seemed to herald the arrival of an important new black British filmmaker whose work could reach mainstream audiences. It was a ground-breaking film which, as Julien noted, aimed to champion 'black independent cinema which deals with questions of sexuality, gender and national identity'.[17] Through his work at Sanfoka, his documentaries and his campaigning, Julien had served an apprenticeship which had readied him to direct further features and to become a figurehead for black British film culture.

'It was a film that got away,' Julien says today. He talks of a meeting he had with Kureishi in a London restaurant not long after *Young Soul Rebels* and *London Kills Me* (1991), Kureishi's directorial debut, had come out. 'We were

---

[14]Ibid.
[15]Ibid.
[16]Julien, *RIOT*.
[17]http://www.screenonline.org.uk/film/id/497077/index.html.

both licking our wounds really in terms of [asking] what is wrong with the film establishment in terms of the journalistic response to the work.'[18] Both films had received very mixed receptions from the critics. 'We didn't believe our works were as terrible as they were being constructed. We knew that something else was going on,' Julien says. He suggests 'people were questioning the idea of authorship in black hands. There was a general antagonism and that antagonism never left.'[19]

It's a striking and dispiriting reflection that neither Kureishi nor Julien have directed second dramatic features. They looked to be at the front of a new wave of black and Asian British filmmakers but that wave soon lost its momentum. Both have had illustrious careers since the early 1990s but not as directors of mainstream narrative feature films.

Young Soul Rebels was distributed all over the world. Julien had the possibility of pursuing a career in Hollywood. 'When I went to LA, I didn't want to do a film called *The Babysitter*. I wasn't interested,' he says of the idea that he might have become a director for hire, even if this was simply as a means to an end. He was keener on what he calls a 'Derek Jarman model': an idea of making independent films which would 'tell a story and have a narrative inflection' but that at the same time would have their own 'signature'.[20]

By the mid-1990s, Julien had discovered the art world. 'In a way, it was a more attractive world to be involved in. I didn't have some producer telling me, "You can't do this", or commissioning editor exec trying to manipulate the story.' He had been developing various screenplays but had felt his creative autonomy was being questioned every step of the way and eroded as he did so. 'There was a lot of interference,' he says curtly.[21]

Julien has made further films, among them *The Darker Side of Black* (1993), about nihilism and violence in black culture, docudrama *Frantz Fanon: Black Skin, White Mask* (1997), *BaadAsssss Cinema* (2002), a documentary about blaxploitation, and *Derek* (2008), an archive-based documentary about his

---

[18]Julien, interviewed by the author.
[19]Ibid.
[20]Ibid.
[21]Ibid.

friend and fellow filmmaker, Derek Jarman. These, though, have been documentaries and art films.

'I just found it frustrating and I think I found England frustrating,' Julien recalls about the difficulty of finding backers for feature films. When he was offered the chance to work as a producer on a series called 'The Question of Equality', a 1995 history of the gay and lesbian movement in the United States, he took it. It gave him the opportunity to live in SoHo in New York. During this period, he discovered 'the relation between the art world and the moving image'.[22] He began to show his work in galleries rather than cinemas. He was one of the pioneers of multi-screen work.

Since then, Julien has flourished: he has been nominated for the Turner Prize and represented Britain at the Venice Biennale. He has been awarded a CBE. 'I did it because I felt a lot of things that were happening in the British film industry were really boring,' he says of his move away from British filmmaking. 'I just felt the film culture in Britain became really tedious and predictable. It was the same names. It became very claustrophobic. It didn't develop in the way it should have done.'[23]

Julien's misgivings about British cinema notwithstanding, he is still a pivotal and important figure in British film culture of the late 1980s and early 1990s: someone who found his way into an industry that initially seemed closed to him and who, in a short period of time, created a varied and intriguing body of work. He didn't come through film school (a day in Beaconsfield apart); he didn't have rich patrons or producers who opened doors for him. From his time as a teenager and then at art school, he worked in co-ops and collectives but still retained his artistic identity as he did so.

Put it to him that he has turned his back on cinema as a popular medium and embraced elitist and esoteric high art instead and he points out that when his immersive nine-screen film installation *Ten Thousand Waves* was shown in the atrium of the Museum of Modern Art in New York, it was seen by over 500,000 visitors 'who paid to see the work'. That's an aggregate that few British independent and arthouse films can match.

---

[22]Ibid.
[23]Ibid.

'I still see myself as involved in the film culture because I am still making films,' Julien says. His latest art installation project, *Lessons of the Hour* (2019), a poetic meditation on the life and times of writer, abolitionist and former slave Frederick Douglass, was filmed in Britain. This was shown as a ten-screen work but he is planning a single-screen version and sees no reason why it shouldn't be shown in cinemas or even turned into a Netflix series. He is heartened, too, by a younger British generation of filmmakers. 'The people involved in film seem more interesting,' he says. He also cites black British filmmaker Steve McQueen, director of *Hunger* and *12 Years a Slave*, who moves seamlessly between the film and art worlds, making films for cinemas, galleries and TV. 'In a way, that approach of a sort of bricolage is precisely the approach that lots of young people in the UK making work should have.'

In 2019, Julien was mentoring Stephen Isaac-Wilson, a young black filmmaker, as part of a course developed by BAFTA. He rails against the lack of support available for him. 'We are in a moment where you have anomalies,' he says of black Oscar winners like *Moonlight* (2016), whose star, Mahershala Ali, who picked up Academy Awards for Best Supporting Actor not just for that film but also for *Green Book* (2018). He ruminates:

> Until we get to a point where there can be films which are not special cases, then we are going to hear this question of the anomaly. The fact is that the majority of films made by white filmmakers are mediocre . . . in a way, it is generally accepted that they can exist. I am not suggesting we need to have mediocre films by people who are not white but I think it is a reflection of the film culture generally, the people who make the decisions. There is so much black talent.[24]

---

[24]Ibid.

10

Adrienne Fancey

Adrienne Fancey (1933–2013) earned her footnote in British film history as one of the first women to run a UK film distribution company. The fact she was born into the business doesn't lessen the achievement. Adrienne was the daughter of the egregious and outrageous E. J. Fancey (1902–80), the founder of New Realm, a production and distribution company. He distributed Hollywood B-movies, made some low-budget films of his own and was nicknamed Britain's 'King of Poverty Row' as a result.

'Around 1940/41 E.J. Fancey was prosecuted for stabbing his company accountant in the groin,' reads an entry on Fancey from one British film website. The accountant reportedly had had the temerity to suggest that Fancey ran his company a bit too 'close to the wind'. This anecdote is impossible to verify and may well be apocryphal but, as historian Adrian Smith has established, E. J. Fancey was in trouble with the law in this period, charged with fraud for receiving stolen cheques in 1940.[1]

The Times has a long and embroiled account of how Fancey, proprietor of 'Pall Mall Enterprises, 1933, Company, and New Realm Pictures, and a Director of Celluloid Despatch Services Ltd' fell in with Arthur Ruppen, a stockjobber's clerk from Sevenoaks, from whom he was alleged to have received the stolen cheques. 'He seemed quite a nice sort of fellow,' Fancey, then thirty-seven, told the court about Ruppen, who had already pleaded guilty to stealing the cheques from his former employers.[2]

---

[1] Adrian Smith, 'E.J. Fancey's Exotic Thrills: Selling Global Exploitation in 1960s Britain'. https://sussex.academia.edu/SmithAdrian.
[2] *The Times*, 16 February 1940.

Adrienne Fancey. Photo: Albert McCabe/Daily Express/Getty Images.

The case involved horse-racing tips, trips to the dog races and talk of setting up a bookmakers. It's as convoluted and confusing as the plot to one of New Realm's movies. Nonetheless, Fancey wriggled off the hook and his filmmaking career began in earnest. He had formed New Realm with his brother Sid in 1940. His first feature film as a producer, wartime comedy *The Balloon Goes Up*, was released by New Realm in 1942. The title refers to a colloquial phrase for a German wartime invasion of Britain. He had a Canadian, Reed Davis, to direct it and a reasonably well known lead in the form of Ronald Shiner.

Fancey operated in the era of 'quota quickies', when exhibitors would show low-grade British films in order to fulfil their legal quota requirements. Fancey, like others before him, spotted the gap in the market. Cinemas, terrified of losing their licences, weren't always discerning about what British films they showed – as long as they were British qualifying. If he could produce the films, he would have no difficulty in getting the circuits to book them on the bottom half of double bills.

Although he seemed to operate in the most disreputable corners of the British film industry, Fancey had an outer veneer of bourgeois respectability. As Talking Pictures TV pointed out, 'he owned a grand, castle-like mansion in Worthing'[3] which had a cottage on its grounds where he is supposed to have kept his mistress. He was well enough off to have race horses. Look through British newspaper archives and you'll find more references to his horses than to his films. He never wasted any opportunity to remind the racing journalists that he had bought one of his best horses, Eastern Imp, for a mere 45 guineas when he was six months old. 'I have won £12,000 in bets on this horse. We have him home every winter at Warnham, near Horsham, where I breed. Eastern Imp loves to be about in the mud and I think this is what keeps him so fresh for racing,' he proudly declared after Eastern Imp had won the Dover Handicap at Folkestone in June 1957.[4]

The British showman featured prominently in the BBC documentary *Truly Madly Cheaply* (2008), narrated by film historian Matthew Sweet. 'He was the most notorious producer of British B movies ever to break an employment law or fiddle the accounts and his name was Edwin J. Fancey, the Cecil B. DeMille of cheap British rubbish,' Sweet introduces Fancey in mock heroic fashion.[5]

New Realm had a sister company, SF Films (Small Films Company). Fancey's production credits included *Rock You Sinners* (1958), blatantly and very cheaply ripped off from *Rock Around the Clock* (1956) but still notable as one of the UK's first rock and roll movies, *The Goon Show* spin-off *Down Among the Z Men* (1952) and crime thriller *They Never Learn* (1956). As Sweet reveals, he took cheese-paring and money saving to extraordinary lengths, using and re-using the same sets, cheating on locations (for example, having East Grinstead in Sussex double for alpine Switzerland) and making cars drive on the wrong side of the road in an attempt to hoodwink British viewers that the

---

[3]https://www.facebook.com/TalkingPicturesTV/posts/spotlight-on-e-j-fanceye-j-fancey-held-so-many-positions-within-the-film-industr/848530595280931/.
[4]*Birmingham Daily Post*, 25 June 1957.
[5]*British B Movies – Truly Madly Cheaply*, BBC documentary, 2008.

action was taking place on the Continent. Paying technicians and actors a pittance was another way of keeping costs down. Using family members was another. His wife Beatrice was a producer and wrote screenplays under the name Beatrice Scott.

Always a chancer, Fancey provoked the wrath of Charlie Chaplin by releasing a compilation of his shorts without going to the expense or inconvenience of actually paying for any of them. Chaplin came to Britain to set matters right. 'When Charlie Chaplin came to England for the first time after many years in the early sixties, he got off the plane and reporters said to him, "why are you coming back Mr Chaplin?" Chaplin said "to sue that bastard EJ Fancey who has been making money by pirating my films,"' filmmaker Michael Winner, who worked with Fancey early in his career, recalled in his autobiography.[6] Fancey responded to Chaplin with typical chutzpah, threatening to sue the legendary comedian whose work he had been ripping off for libel.

'He [E. J. Fancey] was crazy about the film industry and he was a lot of fun,' Adrienne recalled of her father.[7] Not only did he give her a thorough grounding in every aspect of production and distribution. He also briefly made her into a movie star, casting her in some of his productions. Adrienne, who appeared on screen under the name 'Adrienne Scott', had the twin virtues of being genuinely glamorous and of being his daughter. He could get her cheap. She appeared alongside Jackie Collins, sister of movie star Joan Collins and later a hugely successful bonkbuster novelist, in *Rock You Sinners* (1957) and *They Never Learn* (1956), about a policewoman in north London taking on a gang of forgers. However cheapskate or eccentric his methods, Fancey had made enough money to give his daughter an expensive education at a Swiss finishing school – and she had poise in abundance. 'She was fairly tall, naturally blonde, absolutely full of life,' remembers one admirer who knew her well.[8]

Adrienne's acting career tapered off but she became a prominent distributor in the UK film industry of the 1970s and 1980s, taking over the running of her

---

[6]Michael Winner, *Winner Takes All: A Life of Sorts* (London: Robson Books, 2005), 68.
[7]*British B Movies.*
[8]Stuart Hall, interviewed by the author, 24 June 2019.

father's companies. Some sources suggest this was because E. J. Fancey (who died in 1980) had left home and run off with his secretary, setting up a new company, Border Distribution. Others state that E. J. Fancey had simply reached retirement age. New Realm, though, remained a family business. Adrienne's brother Malcolm was also involved at New Realm but Adrienne was the face of the company.

Adrienne's greatest coup was acquiring the UK rights to Just Jaeckin's softcore porn classic *Emmanuelle* (1974). The film had been made by French producer/financier Alain Siritzky, a one-time academic who used to lecture on political philosophy at the Sorbonne, in the wake of the *succès de scandale* of Bernardo Bertolucci's *Last Tango in Paris* (1972). Siritzky was originally planning to make a historical biopic about Marshal Petain and his experiences in the war years but eventually opted to produce *Emmanuelle* instead. The film, based on the racy life story of Emmanuelle Arsan, had very high production values compared with most previous sex films. Its crew members were more accustomed to working with François Truffaut than in making exploitation pictures. Its Dutch star Sylvia Kristel, who came to Britain to support the release, quickly turned into a household name. Critics in Paris sneered but when *Emmanuelle* was released in the summer, there were queues around the block. Businessmen took their secretaries. Then, when their wives came back from holiday and asked about this new phenomenon being written about in all the newspapers, these businessmen went to see it for a second time with their wives.

The New Realm boss had bought the UK rights to *Emmanuelle* for $5,000 reportedly on the basis of the script alone. Rival distributor Miracle, run by Michael Myers, had wanted to buy it too but had baulked at the price.[9]

There was a paradox about Adrienne Fancey. She was a well-spoken, home counties woman from a very middle-class background who made her living distributing softcore sex films. E. J. Fancey had lived in Worthing, Sussex, whilst she lived in Esher, Surrey. Her husband Gordon Bendon was a former Wasps and England rugby player who had been working as brand manager at Martini and later set up his own wine importing business. When they married in

---

[9]Martin Myers, interviewed by the author, 9 June 2019.

August 1958, they had a church wedding with all the trimmings. Jackie Collins was one of Adrienne's bridesmaids. At home, she was Adrienne 'Bendon'. At work, she was Adrienne Fancey. When she was acting, she was Adrienne Scott. As the changes in name attested, she was nothing if not adaptable and could play different roles. Nonetheless, sex movies were the bedrock of her business. As Adrian Smith noted, 'out of 160 films imported and distributed by New Realm between 1960 and 1979, 66% were rated X by the BBFC'.[10] These were films with titles like *Naked Slaves of Satan* and *Sex from a Stranger*.

Nonetheless, New Realm under Fancey also released some auteur-driven arthouse movies, such as Polish director Andrzej Zulawski's cult horror film *Possession* (1981), starring Isabelle Adjani.

'She [Adrienne] was very much a female operating in a boys' club,' says Dennis Davidson, founder of PR and marketing company DDA, of the British film industry in which she was working. Every part of that industry – production and exhibition as well as distribution – was dominated by men but New Realm's films tended to come from outside the UK. 'As a distributor in those days, pretty much everybody she negotiated with to get her films into cinemas would be a man. Wardour Street was all male . . . she was importing a bunch of European films and I suspect the Europeans were less misogynist than the British film industry at that time,' Davidson says.

Thanks to her personality and intelligence, she thrived. The bookers at the major cinemas, Bob Webster at ABC and George Pinches at Odeon, liked and respected her. 'She was able to use her feminine wiles in a nice way. If you're going to take somebody to lunch and you've got Bob Webster, George Pinches and Adrienne Fancey, you would choose Adrienne Fancey,' Davidson notes. 'She was running her own company. She wasn't just a figurehead. Anybody who thought she was a soft touch as an ex-actress and daughter of a man in the business, they certainly learned very quickly that was not the case. She was a very effective distributor and marketer.'[11]

Fancey booked *Emmanuelle* into the Prince Charles Cinema in Leicester Square. It stayed for over a year, becoming a runaway success in the process.

---

[10]Smith, 'E.J. Fancey's Exotic Thrills'.

[11]Dennis Davidson, interviewed by the author, May 2020.

'She came across as a very powerful businesswoman,' rival distributor Michael Myers's son, Martin Myers, remembers the only female executive in charge of an independent UK distribution company in the 1970s.

New Realm had somehow managed to persuade the British Board of Film Classification to give *Emmanuelle* a certificate (an X), ensuring it could be shown in a public cinema. 'In those days, these films were cut by hand when they had been to the censor. It was all done manually. You only needed two or three prints to make money because you showed them in the West End and a few provincial theatres,' Myers remembers. 'Today people would laugh at it because they were so silly those films. But because there was no internet and there wasn't much media and press, the only way to see a bit of "T&A" [tits and ass] was to go to the cinema,' he adds.[12] West End cinemas, among them The Moulin and the Eros, specialized in showing sex films.

Even if softcore sex films were briefly box-office staples for a period in the 1970s, they were never truly mainstream. Fancey was having to deal with some ruthless and cynical exhibitors. The Prince Charles was a first-run cinema, operated by Derek and Rodney Eckhart's Leeds-based Star Group. The Eckharts were keen gamblers and this was an era before credit cards were easily available. When they came down to London, Martin Myers remembers, the brothers would drop by the Prince Charles Cinema and take all the cash from the tills to use as their stake in the casinos. (They would replace the money later but their behaviour was still highly irregular.)

Fancey showed her business savvy not just by acquiring *Emmanuelle* but in her decision not to snap up the sequel, *Emmanuelle 2*, as well. This was eventually released by another company, Intercontinental Films, in 1982. By then, *Emmanuelle* was a phenomenon and the asking price for the new film was huge. Fancey realized, correctly, it would struggle to emulate the original and that she'd have only limited chances of turning a profit – and so she passed on it.

Around the time *Emmanuelle* was released, New Realm had another substantial hit with the German-made *Nurses on the Job* (1975), also X rated. Adrienne dealt tactfully with the fury of real-life nurses who tried to have it taken off screen. 'Thanks to films like this, everyone thinks nurses spend their

---

[12]Myers, interview.

time jumping in and out of bed with every Tom, Dick and Harry,' a union representative commented to the *Daily Mirror* which ran a story under the headline 'No Sex Please, We're Nurses'.[13] Adrienne parried the protests. 'It's meant as a little bit of fun and in no way to be taken seriously,' was the official company line.

The 1970s British distribution and exhibition sector was notorious for long lunches and a culture of very heavy drinking. Adrienne thrived in this environment. Her close friend Stuart Hall, head booker at cinema chains The Classic, Cannon, MGM and Virgin, tells colourful stories about her typical daily regime. 'The business became a kind of hobby to support her lifestyle,' Hall suggests.[14] According to Hall, a typical day would involve Adrienne arriving at the office at around 11.30 a.m. in time to go to lunch at 12.30 p.m. She would then head off home at 3.30 p.m. 'She had a team in the office who kept the wheels on the cart,' Hall remembers of her management style. 'If she didn't know how to do something, she knew somebody who did.'

He adds: 'In those days, she was a bit of a good-time girl. She liked a nice long lunch and a good bottle of wine.' Braganza in Soho Square was one restaurant where she might meet clients. Wheelers on Compton Street was another. She didn't especially like Quo Vadis on Dean Street but there were plenty of other restaurants dotted round Soho which enjoyed her custom. She ate and drank voraciously but kept her figure. 'She was one of those lucky people. I've only got to look at a sandwich and I put weight on.'[15]

Every summer, Fancey would head down to Cannes. 'You'd find her installed on the Rado Plage in front of the Martinez Hotel most lunchtimes,' according to Hall.[16] Other colleagues and friends point out her 'forceful' personality and her ingenious approach to marketing. Film financier and producer Guy Collins worked with her on the Jackie Collins adaptation *The World Is Full of Married Men* (1981), on which she was executive producer. The original star dropped out at the last minute, reportedly because she didn't want to do the nudity. The

---

[13] *Daily Mirror*, 9 January 1975.
[14] Hall, interview.
[15] Ibid.
[16] Ibid.

film had a red carpet market premiere in Cannes. Collins and Fancey persuaded Cartier to lend them some jewellery for the premiere.

'We duly pitched up at the Cartier shop [on the Cannes Croisette] on the morning of the premiere and were handed about half a million pounds' worth of jewellery for our leading lady which adorned her neck. We had to take with us an armed bodyguard,' Collins recalls. 'Then, at the end of the premiere, we had to get all the jewellery back to Cartier.'[17]

This was a typical day at the Cannes Festival for Fancey. She relished being at the festival; she would hold court at the Rado Beach restaurant and would party until late in the night before heading home to get ready for the next day's business meetings.

Back home in Esher, Adrienne had a very active social life. She was a member of the local golf club and hosted or attended her share of dinner parties. The success of *Emmanuelle* and some of her other exploitation pictures not only helped pay her children's school fees but enabled her to go on regular skiing holidays. 'They had a bloody good time.' She drove a Jaguar, 'E type, bright red,' Hall gives the specifics.[18]

Ask Hall if Fancey felt embarrassed about distributing exploitation films and he dismisses the thought. 'I don't think it crossed her mind. She would be more concerned about where she was having lunch the following day – and who with.' Gradually, the sex market shrivelled up. 'When Franco toppled in Spain, censorship was abolished. A lot of our patrons at the Moulin were either randy farmers or they were Spaniards,' Hall remembers the unlikely clientele which (he says) underpinned the success of exploitation pictures.[19]

The films tended never to be as explicit as the viewers had been led to expect by the advertising for them in the top-shelf magazines. The British titles, for example *Come Play with Me*, featured well-known British actors, such as John Le Mesurier and Irene Handl, who didn't realize they were appearing in a sex film. Hall says, 'They [the filmmakers] shot all the well-known people, their scenes, at a completely different time to when they were shooting the porno

[17] Guy Collins, interviewed by the author, 14 May 1920.
[18] Hall, interview.
[19] Ibid.

scenes.'[20] The sex films began to migrate out of cinemas and onto video – and to become more explicit in the process.

By the end of her career, Fancey was licensing films to cruise ships and airliners. She had moved away from the sex films. One of her more ambitious acquisitions was a kids' film about a family of seals. It was decently reviewed but did patchy business, performing far less impressively than titles like *Emmanuelle* had done a few years before.

When her husband died, Fancey remarried. Her new husband, Bev Peerman, was a former sales director at EMI. Her career went into gradual decline but her social life was as colourful and busy as ever. Her money ran out but he still had some cash and (as Hall puts it) was 'quite happy to let her spend it'.[21] Hall used to speak to her every day. 'She was very glamorous. You couldn't re-create her today,' he reflects. 'I don't think there was anybody like her in the British film industry at that time. She was completely unique,' Guy Collins agrees.[22]

Adrienne Fancey isn't the typical role model for a career in the British film business. She came into the industry first of all because her father was one of British cinema's most notorious hustlers and showmen. She didn't appear to have much passion for movies. She wasn't a feminist and she didn't make any fuss at all about the fact that she was one of the first women to run a British feature-film distribution company. Nonetheless, she knew the film business inside out. She refused to be patronized and she dealt with the chauvinism in a male-dominated industry by the simple device of ignoring it. As Dennis Davidson puts it, 'she was a pioneer without question'.[23]

---

[20] Ibid.
[21] Ibid.
[22] Collins, interview.
[23] Davidson, interview.

11

'Poppa' Day

The opening sequence of *Mattes & Miniatures*, a documentary about the Luton-born special effects maestro Walter Percy 'Poppa' Day (1878–1965), is revealing. It doesn't begin with a scene from the painted glass shots or magic trompe-l'oeil tricks he performed for filmmakers like Abel Gance and Powell and Pressburger. Instead, its first images are of a female nude and of a moustachioed man Day painted early in his career. In his own eyes, these paintings were just as important as any of the films he worked on.

Day was a hugely influential figure in the British film industry of the 1930s and 1940s but a largely unacknowledged one when he was still working – and someone almost entirely forgotten today. 'If we joined up the men and women to whom the British film owes most, we should find alongside Mr. Rank and Sir Alexander Korda, and next to our greatest stars and best directors, an inconspicuous little man in a paint bespattered overall, with a battered old hat on his bald pate and a rumpled tie around his open-necked shirt collar,' British magazine *Cavalcade* wrote of Day in the summer of 1949, by which time he was in his seventies.[1]

Day was nicknamed 'Poppa' because he worked closely with his sons, Thomas Day, a cameraman, Arthur Day, a draughtsman, and stepson, Peter Ellenshaw, who might best be described as the sorcerer's apprentice. Ellenshaw assisted Day on films like *The Thief of Bagdad* (1940) and *Black Narcissus* (1947), learned much of his wizardry and took it with him when he went to

---

[1]*Cavalcade*, 21 May 1949.

Walter Percy ('Poppa') Day. Photo: BFI – W. Percy Day Archive.

work for the Walt Disney Company on films like *Treasure Island* (1950) and *Mary Poppins* (1964). He was Disney's top special effects technician for some thirty years. Ellenshaw in turn passed on his wisdom to his son, Harrison Ellenshaw, a matte artist and visual effects supremo whose credits ranged from *Star Wars* (1977) to *Dick Tracy* (1990).

Follow Day's own career and that of his heirs and it is possible to draw a direct line which takes you from French silent cinema (Gance's *Napoleon* (1927)), through the glory days of British cinema in the Korda and Rank era right into the world of Luke Skywalker, originally produced at Elstree Studios. His influence was profound and long lasting. The irony was that he only entered the film industry under sufferance. He was a painter. Day had studied at Heatherley School of Fine Art and at the Royal Academy. As a teenager, he had also been apprenticed by his parents to his cousin, a photographer, an experience that would later help as he moved sideways into cinema. His father, Eli Day, was a craftsman who, according to his granddaughter Susan, produced handmade leather handbags and suitcases. The Days were a Methodist family with a very stern approach to life. They disapproved of drinking and carousing. Eli was a lay preacher.

Walter was considered to be a very precocious talent. He had fallen in love with Ada Chandler, a young, working-class woman he saw first by chance on the street. She was from a humble background. He was better off and better educated. He told her that he would marry her – on one condition. She needed to get herself educated to his level. 'Amazingly enough she did. She must have attended evening classes. She learned Italian and French,' Day's granddaughter Susan Day recalled.[2]

For several years, from 1908 to 1912, the couple lived together in Tunisia, where they married. She worked as a governess. He painted, specializing in portraits and oriental scenes. Eventually, when she became pregnant and Tunisia was going through a period of political unrest, they returned to London and Walter set himself up as a portrait painter in St John's Wood. He had many distinguished sitters including prominent businessmen and captains of industry. His work was exhibited regularly at the Royal Academy. He was a perfectionist who, his granddaughter Sonia Day later observed, would 'jump on his hat in a rage when a portrait wasn't "going right"'.[3]

Like many of the subjects in this book, Day came into the film business in a very roundabout way. During the First World War, he had attempted to enlist

[2]Susan Day, speaking in *Poppa Day: Mattes & Miniatures*, documentary by Dennis Lowe. http://www.zen171398.zen.co.uk/.

[3]http://www.soniaday.com/?page_id=45.

in the British army but had been turned down on medical grounds, having been tubercular as a child. Instead, he was put in a job in the drawing department of an aircraft factory. It was an environment closer to that of a film studio than that of the artist's studio in which he was used to working.

Day is written about with respect and awe in Michael Powell's autobiography. 'Poppa was the greatest trick photographer and double-exposure merchant that the movies have ever seen' and 'the greatest trick-man and film wizard I have ever known', Powell enthused.[4] Powell regarded Day as a necromancer, too, someone like Jules Verne who could transport the public into faraway realms. Day even dressed like a wizard. 'He used to wear lightweight floppy suits draped over a very thin body, so that you felt there was hardly anything there, and he had big round spectacles, which he wore over his nose, and a hat which he was continually dancing on in frustration.'[5]

The English director claimed Day had served his apprenticeship with silent film magician Georges Méliès in Paris in 1905. The truth was a little more prosaic. Day was a struggling British artist from Bedfordshire who had a young family to bring up. After the First World War, clients prepared to commission him to paint their portraits were in increasingly short supply. He needed work. According to the *Cavalcade* article about him written towards the end of his career, one of his sitters said to him: 'Mr Day, have you heard about the new process for screen photography? They're now holding up miniatures of paintings in front of the camera lens instead of building enormous sets.'[6] This sitter suggested he might be able to land a position with a film company.

Day had the perfect background for a job he ended up effectively inventing for himself. He had served a short apprenticeship in photography. He was a brilliant painter and draughtsman. His time in the aircraft factory had accustomed him to industrial production. He was brought in to work at Ideal Films at Elstree Studios in Borehamwood in 1919. At the time, special effects were not especially sophisticated. The most familiar technique was the so-called 'Hall' process which involved mattes being put in front of the lens to block out

---

[4]Michael Powell, *A Life in Movies: An Autobiography* (London: Methuen, 1986), 239.
[5]Ibid., 311.
[6]*Cavalcade.*

parts of the frame. (Mattes are a technique of combining two or more elements into the same picture.) Day would then paint over the darkened spaces and the work he did would be double exposed into the film. The attraction of the process was that Day did the work at his own leisure. He didn't have to hold up production, tinkering around on set. He could just as well paint the backdrops in his garden at home as at the studios.

The bosses at Ideal didn't take advantage of Day's expertise and ideas. He grew frustrated and moved to work in France, hoping for greater opportunities. His career began to flourish there. Day went on not only to provide effects for Abel Gance's masterpiece *Napoleon* but to play an important role, that of the English Admiral Hood, in the film. Day also refined the Hall process. Instead of using glass, he painted on cardboard. As Kevin Brownlow noted in his book on *Napoleon*, 'when the camera photographs the glass in perfect register with the set beyond, the effect is absolutely convincing'.[7]

The British visual effects artist also worked with other important directors, among them Jean Renoir and Julien Duvivier. He briefly returned home to the UK to join the crew on Alfred Hitchcock's silent boxing movie *The Ring*, for which he did visual effects on some of the Albert Hall fight scenes. His career in France stuttered with the advent of talkies. The 'stationary matte' techniques which worked so brilliantly on silent films weren't suitable for early sound cameras which, as his granddaughter explained, vibrated and caused the image to fall out of focus.

When Day returned to work for producer Alexander Korda in Britain in 1932, few in the local industry realized that he was English himself and had grown up in the home counties. Korda had hired him on the recommendation of cinematographer Georges Perinal, also working for Korda but who had collaborated many times with Day in France. Korda had procured new Bell & Howell talkie cameras which didn't suffer from the same 'jiggle' problems as the ones Day had been using in France. This meant that the magic could still work.

Although an Englishman, he was regarded as one of the wave of émigrés who galvanized British cinema in the 1930s. His granddaughter Susan Day

---

[7]Kevin Brownlow, *Napoleon* (New York: Knopf, 1983), 119.

recalls his complete lack of business pragmatism. When Korda offered him a pay rise, he turned it down. His one perk was a house in the grounds of Denham Studios. He was a patriarchal and aloof figure who, in the early years, didn't pay his sons, who were working for him.

'He was quite terrifying . . . really tyrannical,' Susan Day says of him. 'He was the arch Victorian who thought that children should be seen and not heard; he thought my sister and I were far too outspoken.' When she showed him one of her own drawings, he was dismissive in the extreme. He once put his foot through one of the portraits he was trying to paint of his granddaughters. 'He was always very grim and intimidating,' Susan says. He may have worked with his sons, but there was never any possibility he would teach his granddaughters the secrets of his craft. He wanted them to get married, preferably to the richest husbands possible. If he saw his female relatives wearing make-up, he would tell them to go back upstairs and wash it off so they didn't look like a 'Jezebel'.[8] As a teetotaller, Day would get into a fury when people consumed alcohol in his presence and his family learned to hide their drinks in the oven when he was on the prowl.

Susan writes of him in her family history:

The nickname 'Pop' or 'Poppa' Day conjures up the image of an elderly gent of kindly and avuncular disposition who bestows pats on the head and doles out sweets (or candy to our cousins across the pond) to the children clustering at his knee. I regret to shatter illusions but 'Pop' Day's persona did not live up to this idyllic vision. Inculcated with stern moral and social values, Walter Percy Day conformed to the archetype of the unbending Victorian patriarch. He cowed his entire family. No one would have dared address him in such a familiar manner, for fear of incurring one of his frequent temperamental outbursts. His children and stepchildren addressed him formally as 'Pa' and his grandchildren either as 'Grandad' or 'Grandpa'.[9]

---

[8] Susan Day, interviewed by the author, May 2020.
[9] Susan Day, *A Tale of Art, Infidelity and Betrayal: An Intimate Portrait of the First Family of Matte Painting* (unpublished, 2015), Chapter 1 'Dour Days and Creepy Crawleys'.

Day's work in British cinema of the 1930s and 1940s was astonishing. He did process shots and visual effects for such films as *The Thief of Bagdad* (1940), with its scenes of the caliph on horseback galloping across the sky; he provided futuristic effects for the H.G. Wells adaptation *Things to Come* (1936), battlefield scenes for Laurence Olivier's *Henry V* (1944), the famous whirlpool scene for Powell and Pressburger's *I Know Where I'm Going!* (1945) and the stairway to heaven that he helped production designer Alfred Junge build for the same filmmakers' *A Matter of Life and Death* (1946).

On *Black Narcissus* (1947), Day's brilliance enabled Powell and Pressburger to re-create the Himalayas in Pinewood Studios when the rest of the crew were convinced they would be obliged to travel thousands of miles eastward to shoot on location. 'What about the Himalayas? You can't build them,' the daunted camera operator Chris Challis asked his director. Michael Powell reassured him there wouldn't be a problem. 'Glass shots. Poppa Day and his two sons will paint them.'[10]

'The great Poppa Day looked quite venerable with long white hair and steel glasses, but he was truly a wizard with painted glass mattes for all kinds of trick photography,' cinematographer Jack Cardiff wrote of him, echoing Powell's description.[11] Cardiff won an Oscar for *Black Narcissus* but always maintained that the award should have been given to Day.

By the late 1940s, Day's importance to British film culture was finally being recognized. He was given an OBE in 1948 and one or two flattering profiles of him appeared in trade papers. Nonetheless, as Susan Day noted, film for him was really just a way of making a living. 'It is not exaggerating to say that his entire existence was bound up in his paintbrush. His family came a poor second. At the same time, painting would enrage and frustrate him. His epic rages had to be seen to be believed and were worthy of any screenplay. He would vent his rage on his old felt hat – which explains why it was so battered. When a painting did not conform to a preconceived idea, he would rip off his headgear, throw it to the ground and jump on it.'[12] His real passion had always

---

[10]Powell, *A Life in Movies.*

[11]Jack Cardiff, *Magic Hour: A Life in Movies* (London: Faber, 1997).

[12]Susan Day, *A Tale of Art, Infidelity and Betrayal.*

been his painting. He was an ornery and awkward personality who turned down requests for interviews, behaved with high-handed chauvinism towards female collaborators and would work himself up into enormous tantrums. There are tales of him putting his foot through paintings that didn't meet his exacting standards. 'He went out of his way to be as obnoxious as possible,' his granddaughter Susan later said of him.[13]

In his personal habits and demeanour, he was chaotic but when it came to his work, Day was an arch-perfectionist. 'Poppa Day's hat was not created for Poppa Day's head, but to be danced upon. Poppa Day's spectacles were made ready to be broken, Poppa Day's hair had never seen a brush and comb, Poppa Day's clothes, when he was in the studio, would have disgraced a tramp; yet he commanded respect and admiration from all who worked with him, because he knew,' Powell explained the way the artist's talent and technical knowledge atoned for any social deficiencies. The director regarded him as a fellow pioneer. 'He was ten or fifteen years older than me, but we both belonged to the miraculous period when everything had to be discovered, when the motion picture wasn't just a machine that turned at twenty-four frames a second, but a miracle box which could record movements at any speed that the operator wished to crank.'[14]

Day's is one of the more paradoxical careers chronicled in this book. He was involved in a key creative capacity in many of the greatest British films of his era. Those Korda- and Rank-produced masterpieces looked as awe inspiring as they did partly because of his extraordinary visual imagination and resourcefulness and yet few realized his contribution then and few remember his work today. He saw his film work as secondary to his painting and yet his feats in cinema easily eclipsed anything he achieved as an artist. His paintings, especially those he did late in his career, were undistinguished. For all his early promise and the times he exhibited at the Royal Academy, he was a run-of-the-mill artist at best. An outsider in the film industry, Day wasn't exactly an insider in the art world either. The Academicians would mock him because of his Bedfordshire accent and humble upbringing. He was a selfish and curmudgeonly

---

[13]Susan Day, interviewed by the author.
[14]Powell, *A Life in Movies*.

man and yet enabled others, from Abel Gance to Michael Powell and many others, to achieve the most startling effects on screen. Some of his collaborators were utterly dependent on him. 'I could not do this picture without your help and collaboration,' Alexander Korda wrote to him when he was preparing a never to be made ballet movie, *The Sleeping Beauty*, in the early 1950s.[15] Laurence Olivier was equally effusive after *Henry V* (1944).

In the days before CGI, you could trace a line through the history of VFX in cinema. Poppa Day had worked with some of the leading names of the silent era. He, in turn, passed his secrets on to a new generation of artists, among them Charles Staffell, whose credits ranged from Powell and Pressburger's *A Canterbury Tale* to *Batman* and the Bond films and rear projection on Stanley Kubrick's *Eyes Wide Shut*.

Day was one of the invisible army of British film technicians without whom many classic films would not have been made in the way they were. He was a relentless individualist who allowed others to realize their visions – and often helped mould those visions in the first place. His name may feature a long way down the credits but those who knew him best regarded him as a true visionary. His own granddaughter had little idea of the scope of his achievements. Susan Day talks of going to see Gance's *Napoleon* in Paris when the silent classic was re-released in a restored print by film historian Kevin Brownlow in the early 1980s and being startled to see her grandfather in a prominent role in the film.[16]

Poppa Day had worked with Hitchcock. He would also have met Hitchcock's wife, Alma, whose journey through the British film industry was as strange as his own.

---

[15]BFI microfiche on Walter Day.
[16]Susan Day, interviewed by the author.

12

Alma Reville
Mrs Hitchcock

Alma Reville (1899–1982) has not been treated kindly by posterity. Over the years of her very long marriage to Alfred Hitchcock, her own identity gradually vanished. Since her death, she has rarely been written about, discussed or portrayed as anything other than an appendage to Alfred Hitchcock – his wife, confidante, muse, chauffeur, chaperone and accomplice, the mother of his daughter (and only child) Pat, but rarely as a distinct artist or personality.

It is telling that the memoir about Alma co-written by Pat, *Alma Hitchcock: The Woman Behind the Man*, ends not with a summation of the triumphs of her sixty-year career in cinema but with a collection of her favourite recipes. Reville's versions of Vichyssoise soup, steak and kidney pudding, beef Beaujolais, fish mousse with pike and Yorkshire pudding ('Mr Hitchcock's Special Own') among others are all listed. 'My wife is an excellent cook and I could die eating,' Hitchcock confessed in one late interview.[1] His portly shape testified to the excellence of the food she prepared for him.

Whatever Reville's accomplishments in the kitchen, they pale next to what she achieved in her early career in the British film industry, before her name and reputation were swallowed up by that of her husband.

---

[1]Sidney Gottlieb (ed.), *Alfred Hitchcock: Interviews* (Jackson, MS: University of Mississippi Press, 2003), 60.

Alma Reville. Photo: Pierre Vauthey/Sygma/Sygma via Getty Images.

'Once they were married [in 1926], Alma's future as a producer and director in her own right – which was more than a possibility in the minds of producers like [Michael] Balcon and Basil Dean, and directors like Adrian Brunel and Henrik Galeen – was completely subordinated to her husband's career,' Donald Spoto writes in his biography of Hitchcock, *The Dark Side of Genius*. Spoto suggested the marriage was based on 'a kind of professional symbiosis rather than a grand passion'. If it was symbiosis, it was far more to his advantage than Alma's.[2]

There is a revealing and depressing scene in *The Girl* (2012), Julian Jarrold's drama about Hitchcock's obsession with his leading actress Tippi Hedren. Alma (played by Imelda Staunton) apologizes to the star that her husband (Toby Jones), then in his sixties and very overweight, has been harassing her. The implication is clear. She knew about his predatory behaviour – and she didn't do anything about it. 'You'd think she'd put her foot down, wouldn't you? I don't understand that relationship either. There you have it … one day she said to me, "I am so sorry you have to go through this".' Hedren remembered Alma's failure to intervene on her behalf.[3]

Hitchcock was famously devoted to Alma. When he received the American Film Institute Lifetime Achievement Award in March 1979, he gave a speech in which he referred to the 'four people' who had given him the 'most affection, appreciation and encouragement' in his career. 'The first of the four is a film editor; the second is a scriptwriter; the third is the mother of my daughter Pat; the fourth is as fine a cook as ever performed miracles in a domestic kitchen … and their name are – Alma Reville.' He talked of her 'lifetime contract' as 'Mrs Alfred Hitchcock'. This was Hitch's affectionate acknowledgement that her career had been intertwined with his for sixty years and that his towering achievements were built on her support and advice. Nonetheless, the very fact he needed to say it suggested how invisible she had become and how he increasingly began to take her for granted. Her film credits thin out over the years. By the mid-1950s, she is barely mentioned at all. It is easy to forget that at the start of their careers, she was the senior figure.

[2]Donald Spoto, *The Dark Side of Genius* (New York: Da Capo Press, 1999), 65.
[3]Tippi Hedren, interviewed by the author, *Independent*, 10 February 2012.

In her entry in the 1929 edition of the *Kinematograph Yearbook*, the bible for the UK film industry of the time, Reville is listed under her own name but the entry already adds, in parenthesis (Mrs A. J. Hitchcock), as if, even then, she couldn't be referred to without at least passing reference to the man she married three years before. However, the entry suggests that she had already built a very substantial career of her own. 'Expert cutter; began with London Film Co.; the first British lady assistant director; scenarist; did script of the Constant Nymph for Basil Dean.'[4]

Although Reville was born one day after her future husband (on 14 August 1899), she started in the film business four years before he did and she was a pioneer in her own right.

Alma grew up in humble circumstances. Her family lived in Nottingham. One grandfather, George Edward Reville, was an ironsmith while another, Thomas Bailey, was a nail-maker. Her father, Matthew, was a lace warehouseman and her mother, Jane Bailey Reville, was a hosiery worker. There was little in her background to suggest she would have any future in the British film business then springing up let alone soon become one of its leading figures.

The family had decamped to London where Alma's father had taken a job at the Twickenham Film Studios set up by cinema owner Ralph Jupp (co-founder of new production company London Film Company) just before the First World War. The company's home was in The Barons, St Margaret's, Richmond in a building that had once housed an ice-skating rink. According to her daughter, Pat, Alma cycled to visit her father at the studios and was fascinated by the rigmarole of filmmaking. She loved to watch the shooting outdoors. Her grandmother used to take her to the cinema despite other relatives warning that this was a dirty habit and she would only catch fleas. Alma was growing up 'alongside an industry that was practically her own age'.[5]

Jupp suffered ill health and the company foundered, causing him to sell the premises to a rival outfit, the Alliance Company, in 1918. By then, Alma had

---

[4]*Kinematograph Year Book 1929*, 'Who's Who in the Studio', 303.
[5]Patricia Hitchcock, *Alma Hitchcock: The Woman Behind the Man* (New York: Berkley Books, 2003), 22–31, co-authored with Laurent Bouzereau.

already been working at the studios for at least two years. After leaving school at fifteen, she had found work through her father in the editing room at the Twickenham Studios as a 'rewind girl' for London Film Company. 'In those days, films were cut and spliced completely by hand. No electricity was used. It was a very precise and tedious job, which probably and unfortunately, further damaged her [Alma's] eyes; she was farsighted and always had to wear glasses,' Pat Hitchcock wrote in her memoir of her mother.[6]

After she was promoted to oversee continuity as well as to edit, Alma's job was to make sure that scenes were shot in the right order and were consistent. 'The art of telling stories on celluloid was still in its infant years. They would shoot scenes wide, without doing close-ups on the actors. Therefore, no editing was needed, just the splicing of one scene to another ... at that point, the profession of "editor" really meant gluing the different parts together and was pretty much a technical job,' her daughter noted.[7]

The work may have been monotonous but the teenager threw herself into it. Reville had had a hankering to become an actress but was prepared to do anything. She volunteered for odd jobs. Her plan was to make herself indispensable. Diminutive, red haired, bespectacled, she would pop up as a floor secretary on one production and as a continuity girl on another.

Alma's enthusiasm impressed her employers. She was quickly assigned to major films, including the 1915 version of *The Prisoner of Zenda*. From today's vantage point, it can't help but seem bizarre that key editing decisions were made by a teenage girl who had only recently left school – and whose education had been interrupted for two years anyway by illness.

Editing is generally considered as among the most painstaking and delicate crafts in filmmaking. In the British film industry Alma entered as an editor/continuity girl, however, it was a matter of cutting pieces of film by hand and then joining them together. Early in the silent era, British filmmakers had learned how to use close-ups and parallel editing to heighten dramatic tension or to tell two separate stories at once. However, in 1915, when Alma entered the industry, they hadn't experimented with montage in the way it would be used

---

[6]Ibid.
[7]Ibid.

a few years later by the Soviet directors whose work Reville and Hitchcock saw at London Film Society screenings.

US company Famous Players-Lasky Corporation set up an offshoot in London in the spring of 1919. The company (eventually to be renamed as Paramount) was based at a new location on the site of a former power station in Islington. Reville came to work there in 1921 as 'floor secretary' to Donald Crisp, the prolific actor-producer-director who had worked with D. W. Griffith in the US but who came back to Britain to serve in army intelligence during the First World War.

Reville was learning from a mentor whose credits included such D. W. Griffith classics as *The Birth of a Nation* (1915), *Intolerance* (1916) and *Broken Blossoms* (1919). According to his *Times* obituary, the Scottish-born Crisp directed 'several of the memorable battle sequences in Birth Of A Nation.'[8] Alma edited *Beside the Bonnie Brier Bush* (1921) and *Appearances* (1921) for Crisp. The latter film is significant as one of Alfred Hitchcock's first credits. Hitchcock was responsible for the intertitle cards. Reville also worked directly for Griffith on *Hearts of the World* (1918), the propaganda film commissioned from Griffith by the British government as part of its efforts to drum up American support for the war effort.

There are few details about Reville's working relationship with Griffith or with Crisp. One of the frustrations concerning her early career is how reluctant she herself later was to discuss it. 'One thing I did notice about her was that she never talked about herself and she never talked about the past. She had been a pioneer in the silent era, but she never made a point of mentioning it,' a family friend who knew her many years later in Hollywood observed of her. 'Alma never talked about the past and she never pushed herself forward,' Jay Presson Allen, a screenwriter who worked with Hitchcock in Hollywood, agreed.[9]

Nonetheless, if you look into Alma Reville's career in the British film industry from the end of the First World War to the mid-1930s you realize that she was a substantial figure in her own right. One of her most notable qualities

---

[8] *The Times*, 28 May 1974.

[9] Cited in http://www.alfredhitchcockgeek.com/2011/08/remembering-alma-reville-born-august-14.html.

was her versatility. She is credited on different projects as a screenwriter, as head of continuity and as an editor. She had experience as an actress too, playing Megan Lloyd George in Maurice Elvey's *The Life Story of David Lloyd George* (1918) and taking bit parts in various other films too. 'Alma volunteered for odd jobs, trying to make herself useful to everyone. In the cutting room, she reached a technical proficiency so expert that she was entrusted with the cutting of the actual film negative, which also meant she was making more money,' her daughter recalled of her early years.[10]

In the early 1920s, Reville was with Hitchcock when both were sent by Michael Balcon to work at Neubabelsberg Studios in Germany. She too was able to mingle with and observe the working methods of the great German directors of the period, towering figures like F. W. Murnau and Ernst Lubitsch.

Reville's name became more and more familiar in the trade. She was one of the few screenwriters in the British film industry of the 1920s who were recognized by the film press. 'There were comparatively few people known by name as scenario writers in England at the time, and most of them were little more than hacks,' historian Rachael Low noted,[11] but cited Reville as one of the writers who were acknowledged and respected. Low also identified Reville as one of the first British film editors properly credited on screen. In 1925, *The Bioscope* referred to her as 'the only woman assistant director in the trade'.[12] She had managed, therefore, to excel in three separate fields.

If Hitchcock hadn't married her, it seems likely that she would have remained a major figure in British cinema.

Collaborators other than Hitchcock who worked with her, among them Elvey (for whom she edited several films), Adrian Brunel (for whom she co-wrote the successful 1928 feature *The Constant Nymph*), Miles Mander and Crisp, also spoke highly of her. Producers, notably Michael Balcon, trusted her. Reville helped the former exhibitor turned filmmaker Graham Cutts reinvent himself as a director. Certain sources suggest she did much of the work on his early films anyway. She was a key figure behind the success of Cutts's *Woman*

---

[10]Patricia Hitchcock, *Alma Hitchcock*.
[11]Rachael Low, *The History of the British Film, Vol. IV: 1918–1929* (London: Routledge, 1997), 240.
[12]*The Bioscope*, 22 October 1925.

to Woman (1923), on which Hitchcock had been appointed assistant director by producer Michael Balcon.

Trade journalist and screenwriter P. L. Mannock described her in very revealing terms in an article in industry magazine *Kinematograph Weekly* in 1925 as 'a striking example of those important assistant filmmakers upon whom the limelight of publicity seldom, if ever blazes . . . she had much to do with the finish of all Graham Cutts' big pictures'. He added that, 'Gainsborough is to be congratulated on the retention of her exclusive services, the value of which everyone who knows her will confirm'.[13]

In the same year, fans' magazine *Picturegoer* also highlighted her increasing prominence. 'Little Alma Reville is nothing like as unsophisticated as she looks, as some tough film guys have discovered to their cost,' the magazine wrote, describing her as always smiling, calm and efficient.[14]

As Hitchcock's biographers all point out, Reville and Hitchcock worked together on the same productions at Islington Studios in the early 1920s without establishing anything beyond the most cursory of relationships. 'Hitch and Alma worked at the same studio for two years, and to my mother's knowledge, in all that time, he never so much as glanced in her direction', Pat Hitchcock wrote.[15]

Until they collaborated on *Woman to Woman*, Alma was senior to the bashful young Hitchcock and he was seemingly too intimidated to talk to her. 'It was unthinkable for a British man to admit that a woman had a better position, and Hitch waited to speak to her until he had a better job than she did, until he was in a position of power,' Pat writes in her memoir of her mother of Hitchcock's decision to wait until after making his directorial debut with *The Pleasure Garden* (1926).[16] Alma was his assistant director before she was his wife.

After she married Hitchcock, Reville continued to work with other filmmakers but her independence was soon eroded. 'I had wanted to become, first a movie director and second, Alma's husband – not in order of emotional

---

[13]'Two British Production Units', *Kinematograph Weekly*, 8 October 1925, 49.

[14]'Alma in Wonderland', *Picturegoer*, December 1925.

[15]Patricia Hitchcock, *Alma Hitchcock*, 32.

[16]Ibid, 32–34.

preference to be sure but because I felt the bargaining power implicit in the first was necessary in obtaining the second,' Hitchcock explained with typical deadpan irony how his filmmaking and marital ambitions were completely intertwined.[17] He knew he needed Alma.

From Hitchcock's point of view, marrying Alma was an astute career move. Some have suggested that the so-called 'Hitchcock touch' evolved directly under her guidance. 'What we think of as "Hitchcockian" might well be the result of creative collaboration rather than isolated genius,' wrote critic Pamela Hutchinson when the British Film Institute restored *The First Born* (1928), a drama about a philandering politician directed by Miles Mander but co-scripted by Reville. 'There are combinations of shots, which elegantly condense the action and underpin what is really quite an intimate film. The structure of the film, the choices of shots and camera angles – things shown or suggested – can only have come from someone with a lot of screenwriting experience,' Hutchinson quotes the BFI's curator of silent film, Bryony Dixon, as saying of the film.[18]

Hitchcock was a grocer's son from Leytonstone, east London. Alma Reville was from a similarly unprepossessing background. In its early years, the British film industry may have been more fluid and open to outsiders than it later became. Nonetheless, neither Hitchcock nor Reville was ideally placed to prosper on their own.

Hitchcock was very obviously prodigiously talented but wasn't an especially astute judge of character. Nor did he always deal well with the politicking and hustling necessary to build a career. Older directors like Graham Cutts were jealous and suspicious of him. Distributors like C. M. Woolf distrusted what they perceived to be his pretentiousness.

Alma may have been the 'first British lady assistant director' as the *Kinematograph Yearbook* referred to her. That was a considerable achievement in its own right, but her husband, with four years less experience in the film business than she had, was still given an opportunity to direct a movie. She

[17]'London Film Festival Puts Spotlight on Forgotten Figures of UK Cinema', *Guardian*, 22 October 2011.
[18]Sidney Gottlieb (ed.), 'The Woman Who Knows Too Much', *Hitchcock on Hitchcock, Vol. 1: Selected Writings and Interviews* (Berkeley, CA: University of California Press, 1995), 51.

wasn't. Contemporaries called her Hitchcock's 'scrappy little watchdog'[19] and pointed out again and again that she was shrewder in business terms and more pragmatic than her husband. He could rely on her to advise him frankly both about potential collaborators and about the quality of his own work. She was his troubleshooter. If there were continuity errors or elements in a screenplay that didn't hang together, she would be first to spot them. 'My mother knew every single bit of the movie,' Pat Hitchcock later observed of how Reville immersed herself in Hitchcock's movies. Reville was 'able to pull out little things that weren't right and tell my father about them'.[20]

Away from the studios, Reville protected and encouraged her husband. Journalist Norah Baring wrote in a 1935 profile of the director in *Film Pictorial*:

> He [Hitchcock] is fortunate to have a wife who, far from resenting the intrusion of business into every hour of his life, encourages and sympathises with his enthusiasm. With true feminine intuition she can pick out the sheep from the goats in the crowd which inevitably surrounds him, thus saving his precious energy. It is all done so unobtrusively that one is never concerned of this selective scrutiny.[21]

During the 1930s, Reville had her successes apart from Hitchcock. She was one of the co-writers of *Sally in Our Alley* (1931), a film that helped launch the 'Lancashire lass' Gracie Fields as a star. She worked with other well-known directors from the period, among them Basil Dean and Norman Walker.

None of these films, though, had the critical or popular impact of her husband's films. In the second half of Hitchcock's career, when the couple moved to Hollywood, she worked only with him.

In a 1974 interview, Andy Warhol asked Hitchcock if he had ever considered using Alma in one of his films. After all, he always made cameo appearances himself. 'She wouldn't do it. She has been in movies longer than I have. She was a writer, she was an editor at 19,' Hitchcock replied.[22] On the face of it, this is

---

[19]Cited in Donald Spoto, *Spellbound by Beauty: Alfred Hitchcock and His Leading Ladies* (London: Arrow, 2009), 19.

[20]Patricia Hitchcock, *Alma Hitchcock*.

[21]Norah Baring, 'Hitchcock Profile: The Man Who Made *The 39 Steps*', *Film Pictorial*, 23 November 1935.

[22]Hitchcock, interviewed by Andy Warhol in 1974, included in Gottlieb, *Alfred Hitchcock: Interviews*.

surprising. Alma Reville had appeared in front of the camera several times at the start of her career and her initial ambition had been to become an actress. Their daughter had parts in some of his films. You might have expected Alma to make the occasional appearance too. Instead, she gave a virtuoso performance in the role of his faithful wife. 'I don't mind taking second place,' she said of the successes Hitchcock would never have achieved without her.

13

Val Guest

The prolific and versatile Val Guest (1911–2006) wrote and directed several of the very best genre films made in the UK in the 1950s and 1960s while also cheerfully churning out low-grade exploitation fare in between times. He was British cinema's answer to the girl in the Henry Longfellow poem:

When she was good,
She was very, very good,
But when she was bad, she was horrid.

The *New York Times* noted as much in its obituary, saying some of his work was 'remarkably good' and some of it was 'remarkably bad'.[1] Perhaps because his career was so uneven and so varied, encompassing everything from writing Will Hay and the Crazy Gang comedies in the 1930s to sci fi and hardboiled thrillers in the 1950s and early 1960s and then to softcore porn in the 1970s, Guest rarely received the credit that his achievements warranted. The longevity of his career and the sheer variety of the films he made testify to a relentless drive. Guest could not be stopped. He was determined to make films. Through sheer desire and force of personality, he managed to carry on doing so in different eras, for different bosses, working on different budgets.

As a young man, starting in the business, Guest had worked alongside Alfred Hitchcock and Michael Powell. If his filmography had consisted only of *The Quatermass Experiment* (1955), *Hell Is a City* (1960) and *The Day the Earth*

---

[1]Val Guest obituary, *New York Times*, 27 May 2006.

Val Guest. Photo: Pictorial Press Ltd/Alamy Stock.

Caught Fire (1961), all acknowledged as minor classics, he might have been regarded as the British equivalent of the great Hollywood B directors like Don Siegel, Jacques Tourneur or Sam Fuller. Dubious later works like *Au Pair Girls* (1972), a prurient comedy about Scandinavian nannies, *Confessions of a Window Cleaner* (1974), starring Robin Askwith as a randy young Romeo with a sponge and a ladder, and *The Boys in Blue* (1982), with British comedians

Cannon and Ball in a Will Hay remake, cast a different, murkier light on his reputation.

'Was I proud of them?' Guest reflected in an interview with me late in his life when asked about his late foray into exploitation. 'Not in the slightest. They were just something that happened in a long career. There are lots of other films I made that I wasn't proud of, and some of those are still making money too.'[2] The fact Guest made these films, though, testified to his resilience and his determination. These were the qualities that got him into the British film industry in the first place and kept him close to its centre for almost half a century.

Few of the subjects covered in this book found conventional pathways pathways into the industry. Guest's route was one of the strangest and most surprising but also one of the most straightforward. He was given his chance by a director whose work he savaged in a review he wrote for trade paper *The Hollywood Reporter*. The director read the review, contacted him and challenged him, if he thought the script was so lousy, to write a better one himself. He did so and very quickly proved himself as one of the most versatile and witty screenwriters in British production in the late 1930s. As a 'scenarist under contract at Gainsborough Pictures', Guest provided the words and ideas that gave comedians in the Gainsborough stable like Will Hay, George Formby and the Crazy Gang their biggest box-office hits. But Guest's conversion from trade journalist into leading British screenwriter wasn't quite as seamless as he sometimes liked to suggest.

Valmond Maurice Guest, as he was christened, was from a middle-class background. Born in Maida Vale, London, in 1911, he spent his early childhood in Calcutta where his father, John Simon Guest, was working as a jute broker. As far as the young Val knew, his mother, Julia Ann Gladys Emanuel, had died when he was only three years old. In fact, as he discovered when he returned to London, she was very much alive. His father had come home to England before the start of the First World War and little Val had been deposited as a boarder at Seaford, a prep school on the East Sussex coast.

The school's main claim to fame is that it was attended by Anthony Buckeridge (1912–2004), who was only a year older than Guest and whose

---

[2]'Confessions of a Serial Director', *Independent*, 4 September 1997.

time at the school overlapped with his. Buckeridge went on to write the hugely popular Jennings novels which were set in a school not unlike Seaford itself and chronicled the adventures of a mischievous schoolboy forever getting into scrapes. These novels, which Buckeridge started writing in the 1950s, shared much of the same knockabout humour found in the Will Hay and Crazy Gang comedies that Guest had helped script in the 1930s.

Guest gives only the most cursory description of his school days in his autobiography. He didn't enjoy school and talked in one interview about 'soldiering through it'. There are no stories about him getting into Jennings-like scrapes although he acknowledges he was a 'monstrously bad child actor'.[3] One revealing anecdote he shared with the British Entertainment History Project was that at school he used to sneak down late at night into the masters' common room and laboriously type out short stories on the school typewriter. This compulsive outpouring of creativity was typical of him. Whether as an unhappy schoolboy at a British boarding school or as a filmmaker working with sceptical financiers and producers, he would always find the way to complete a story or a script and to get a movie made.

In his autobiography, Guest mentions that he left school abruptly at the age of fifteen and went into the City, getting a lowly clerical job in the accounts department of the Asiatic Petroleum Company. It was a strange, sideways move for a youngster with creative yearnings but it gave him an independence that he wouldn't have had if he remained a schoolboy. By then, he had discovered his mother was indeed very much alive. They first met when he was twelve when she contacted him.

'She played the violin, wrote short stories for magazines, had a book of poetry published and, under the stage name of Anna Thayer, had starred as principal boy in many pantomimes produced by the eminent London impresario Julian Wylie. She had married again and was now wife of one Arthur Williams, a civil servant who worked in a government office,' the future director later recounted.[4] His mother had played the principal boy in

[3]Val Guest, interviewed for British Entertainment History Project, 17 August 1988, 23 August 1988, 30 August 1988, 6 September 1988. https://historyproject.org.uk/interview/val-guest.
[4]Val Guest, *So You Want to Be in Pictures: The Autobiography of Val Guest* (London: Reynolds & Hearn, 2001).

pantomimes, loved theatre and literature, and was as encouraging about her son's artistic aspirations as her father was discouraging.

The circumstances of his parents' separation aren't discussed but it was clearly a very bitter divorce. Guest's father had tried to scrub out the very fact of his wife's existence from his son's life. The mother had secretly contacted him and they used to have covert meetings in the school holidays at Lyons' Corner House or at the Regal Cinema in Marble Arch. Guest knew that his father would have been 'horrified' if he had known about these illicit trysts and so he kept them quiet.

Some of his mother's bohemianism and thirst for storytelling and performance rubbed off on the young Val. His father was an altogether sterner and more austere figure who had told him that it was 'the duty of all respectable people to keep their names out of the paper'.[5] This wasn't advice Val was ever likely to heed for long.

There is an Oliver Twist-like quality to accounts of his youth. He didn't stay working in the City for long. He was a restless, inventive character who, even in his school days at Seaford, had been writing those short stories. With his mother's help, he was able to buy his first typewriter. Showing the versatility and entrepreneurialism that would later sustain him throughout his fifty-year career in the British film industry, he started sending off unsolicited items to magazines, among them *Film News*, *The Sphere* and *The Illustrated London News*. He did caricatures for comics. A talented draughtsman, he was hired as a sign writer for shops. Gradually, as more and more of his work began to be published, he became established on Fleet Street. He ghost wrote Marlene Dietrich's autobiography for the *News of the World* and Mae West's for the *Sunday Dispatch*. His 'Behind the Scenes with Val Guest' articles, in which he provided inside gossip and insight about Hollywood, was syndicated in various British newspapers.

According to a studio biography published to promote one of his later films, at one stage during his attempt to establish himself, the young Guest was in the habit of writing 'eight regular weekly film columns as well as short stories for national daily newspapers'.[6] This may sound far-fetched, a piece of puffery

---

[5]Ibid.
[6]BFI microfiche cuttings on Guest.

dreamed up by studio publicists, but it chimes with his later behaviour as a screenwriter and filmmaker. He was very prolific, not always discriminating in his choice of projects and he worked extremely fast. He was funny and an inveterate gossip, one reason why the legendary New York based showbiz columnist Walter Winchell used him as a London correspondent. Readers of local papers from Sunderland to Falkirk were treated to his reviews and interviews. One titbit from *The Era* in 1933 mentions a make-up artist friend of Guest's, London Films' Jimmy Barker, asking why it was taking him as long as four weeks to complete the biography of Marian Marsh when he had managed to dash off Lubitsch's in only ten days.[7]

While churning out dozens of articles, Guest had a parallel career as an actor working on stage and appearing in such productions as *Unholy Orders*, the first play written by Arnold Ridley (later to achieve fame as one of the venerable stars of BBC TV comedy *Dad's Army*). Guest briefly landed a contract with Warner Bros. However, he had a low opinion of his own abilities in front of camera and soon quit. He liked to joke in later years that he already knew he was a lousy actor and decided to stop before 'anyone else found out'.

The young Guest flitted around the London journalism and entertainment world in such an erratic and energetic fashion that it was sometimes hard to keep tabs on him. He kept on popping up where you least expected. One of his other sidelines was writing songs, both music and lyrics, and he was successful at that, too. Collaborating with the American composer Manning Sherwin (who wrote 'A Nightingale Sang in Berkeley Square'), he continued to write songs and to be involved in hit musicals even after his film career took off. He wrote musical revues for the London Palladium.

One of the paradoxes about Guest is that he was active in so many fields that his achievements were continually overlooked. He was regarded as a bit of a flibbertigibbet. The French critics at *Cahiers du Cinéma* may have revered the work of his friend and colleague Alfred Hitchcock but they never paid much attention to Guest himself.

Guest's first big opportunity in the film business behind the cameras came through a girlfriend, the young Herne Hill-born actress Ida Lupino, who

---

[7] *The Era*, 13 December 1933.

introduced him to her uncle, comedian Lupino Lane or 'Nip' as he was nicknamed. He was working at British International Pictures (BIP), later to become Associated British Picture Corporation (ABPC). Lane needed a writer and recruited Guest. They worked together on the major musical *Maid of the Mountain* (1932), set in Ruritania but shot in Cheddar Gorge and in Shenley, and went on to collaborate on *Innocents of Chicago* (1932).

Lane had come back to Britain after a successful career in Hollywood and was beginning to write and direct films. Guest ghostwrote screenplays for him and didn't seem bothered about not getting credit. 'He was a nice little man,' Guest later recalled in memory of this early mentor. He regarded Lane's films as workmanlike at best but admired him hugely as a comic performer. Lane paid him, not the studio. 'If I got £50, I would have been very, very lucky,' he said of the going rate for a ghostwritten script.[8]

Guest wasn't just writing. Thanks to Lane, he was given bit parts in BIP films. 'It all seemed to be an awful lot of fun,' Guest said of his time working for BIP at Elstree under the studio boss John Maxwell's 'Scottish Mafia' as the executives at the company were called. 'There were no specific hours we had to work. Although at times it was hell, it was fun hell.'[9]

Colleagues at Elstree included Hitchcock, then making his thriller *Number 17* (1932) and who built a huge miniature railway for one of the scenes, and Frank Launder, a fellow screenwriter who was later to form a filmmaking partnership with Sidney Gilliat.

Robert Clark, later to become the boss of ABPC, was then a lowly accountant, the one who paid him his meagre cheques. Extras on some of the movies shooting at the studio would later go on to become big name stars in their own right, Stewart Granger and Michael Rennie among them. Michael Powell was working at the studios as a stills cameraman.

The one blight on what was generally a very happy workplace was the head of production, Walter Mycroft, a former writer (see Chapter 5 on John Maxwell). This was more than eighty years before the Harvey Weinstein scandal and the birth of the #MeToo movement. Nonetheless, Guest's remarks

---

[8]Guest, British Entertainment History Project.
[9]Ibid.

about Mycroft's behaviour to female staff members have a horribly familiar ring. 'Walter Mycroft was the most hated man there had ever been at Elstree by everybody. He was devious. His secretaries left one by one because they couldn't take all the fumbling that went on and he would fire them.' No film was made without the head of production's say-so.

Guest liked to tell a scurrilous story about what happened after the diminutive Mycroft had the lavatories at Elstree cleaned of graffiti. He put out an edict saying that if anyone drew or scribbled on the walls and was identified, they would be instantly fired. A week or two later, the slogan 'Mycroft is a shit' appeared on the wall of one of the lavatories. Before the diminutive Mycroft could have it erased, someone else drew in an arrow pointing to about 2 feet 6 inches off the floor where another slogan had been written, 'No, I am not'.[10]

The restless Guest didn't stay long at Elstree. He ended up being hired by Billy Wilkerson, owner and publisher of *The Hollywood Reporter*. 'Over our Grosvenor House lunch he told me his London correspondent was leaving them to become a screenwriter and possible director,' Guest remembered how he landed his next journalistic job.[11] The correspondent in question was John Paddy Carstairs, later to direct several hit comedies for Norman Wisdom.

While working for the *Reporter*, Guest was based in London but made occasional trips to Los Angeles. While there, he reviewed a Hollywood film called *Chandu the Magician* starring Edmund Lowe. He hated it. 'I had said if I couldn't write a better film than this with one hand tied behind my back I'd give up the business,' he later recalled of the general gist of the review. The film's director, Frenchman Marcel Varnel, had, by chance, just come to Elstree to shoot a film in Britain. Varnel contacted *Hollywood Reporter* publisher Wilkerson and said to him, 'If your reporter is so goddamned clever, let him write my next [film]'.[12]

Guest took this as a challenge. He hadn't been credited for his work on the Lupino Lane films and had no established reputation as a screenwriter. Wilkerson told him he had no choice – he had to write the screenplay or he

---

[10]Guest, *So You Want to Be in Pictures*.
[11]Ibid.
[12]Ibid.

would be fired anyway. Varnel, he soon discovered, didn't hold any grudges about the negative review. He liked the 'bite' in Guest's journalism and felt he might have potential to write movies as well. Guest described him as 'a small, cheery, chubby, slightly balding Frenchman with merry, twinkling eyes'.[13] Varnel was excitable but highly professional and took it as a matter of personal integrity and pride that his films would never go over budget or schedule.

The director's invitation to Guest launched the Englishman's career in earnest. He was set to work with a more experienced writer, Roger Burford, on a British war movie called *Freedom of the Seas* (1934) and made at Gainsborough Studios in north London. Burford taught him the rudiments of screenwriting. The film, also notable as David Lean's first film credit, albeit as a focus puller, turned out well. It was the beginning of what would turn into a long-standing partnership between the director and his young screenwriter. They worked on seventeen films together, including some very successful comedies featuring Will Hay, the Crazy Gang and others.

'When I joined Marcel, I went on every picture. I was general gag man. Perhaps [I would direct] an odd second unit shot here and there. I went through all of those pictures which was invaluable training,' Guest remembered of a period when he learned the skills that would later enable him to flourish as a director in his own right.[14] There may not have been film schools but this was the perfect apprenticeship. He was working under Birmingham-born studio boss Ted Black, an inspirational figure revered by Guest for his pragmatism and adaptability. Black could handle anything from the Varnel comedies to Carol Reed dramas, Hitchcock films and melodramas.

There were three other writers put under contract at Gainsborough alongside Guest: Launder, Gilliat and Marriott Edgar. They did sterling work without ever really being acknowledged for it. The Marcel Varnel comedies were fast paced and very funny but the critics were suspicious of them. *Oh, Mr Porter!* (1937), starring Will Hay as a bungling railway stationmaster, is nowadays acknowledged as a classic. On its release, it made a fortune at the box office but the reviews were patronizing and dismissive. Together with

---

[13]Ibid.
[14]Guest, British Entertainment History Project.

Edgar, Guest came up with the antic lunacy and surrealism of such films as *Gasbags* (1941), a wartime farce in which a British fish and chips van carrying the Crazy Gang floats into a German POW camp on the bottom of a barrage balloon, *Ask a Policeman* (1939), with Will Hay as bumbling police sergeant Samuel Dudfoot, and *Alf's Button Afloat* (1938), starring Flanagan and Allen and in which the Crazy Gang go to sea.

The comedians in the Crazy Gang were not easy to work with. 'They infinitely preferred their own lines to those in the script and when Val argued they ripped off his shirt, tore his trousers, and dumped him in a waste-paper basket,' one newspaper reported. True to form, Guest fought back. 'The same afternoon Val returned to the set wearing a brand new shirt and sweater and again began arguing. They fell on him with a howl and tore his clothing to bits – but Val just lafed and lafed and lafed [*sic*] – because they didn't know the clothes belonged to [Crazy Gang member] Teddy Knox.'[15]

'I much preferred writing for Will Hay,' Guest remembered of his stint at Gainsborough. 'He was a very firm character who didn't deviate from film to film. The Crazy Gang, though, were a handful. We had six people to deal with at any one time. We used to keep a chart in front of us while we were writing so we didn't leave one of them out for more than seven pages at a time.'[16]

Having cut his teeth writing Gainsborough comedies, Guest was eventually given his first chance to direct. The opportunity came in a typically haphazard fashion. The Ministry of Information recruited him during the Second World War to write and direct a short movie warning the public about spreading disease through sneezing. 'Constant sneezes spread diseases' was one line he wrote for it which, true to the subject matter, caught on with the public and became a well-known catchphrase. His first feature was *Miss London Ltd* (1943), a wartime music comedy starring popular music hall star Arthur Askey. 'In the euphoria of completing my first full-length picture . . . I careered on like a runaway train, writing and directing two more that year, one of them being the Jean Simmons debut *Give Us the Moon* [1944].'[17]

---

[15]*Evesham Standard & West Midland Observer*, 2 October 1937.
[16]Guest, *So You Want to Be in Pictures*.
[17]Ibid.

Actors relished working with Guest. He had been one himself and had an instinctive sense of their insecurity and what they needed to do their best work. He helped launch the careers of Jean Simmons and Michael Rennie among others and worked with Peter Sellers long before Sellers became a star. He gave pop star Cliff Richard one of his first big breaks in the cult Soho-based musical *Expresso Bongo* (1959), written by Wolf Mankowitz. For a while, Guest's second wife, the glamorous actress Yolande Donlan, was his muse. He later wrote:

> Actors are children, and no matter how big a star they are, they need their hands held, they have to be convinced they can do it. The director has to be father, mother, confessor, schoolteacher, lover, brother. I've worked with any number of so-called neurotic stars, but they are all manageable once you got their confidence. If someone is being difficult there is usually a reason and once you find out what it is, you can crack it.[18]

Guest may have cut his teeth in comedy but his best work as a director tended to be on genre films, cop thrillers like *Hell Is a City* (1960) or sci-fi horror like the *Quatermass* films and *The Day the Earth Caught Fire* (1961). *Hell Is a City* was a rarity: a British crime drama that was as gritty and hardboiled as the best in American film noir. It was set in Manchester, not London, and had a memorable lead performance from Stanley Baker as the tormented policeman hero. *The Day the Earth Caught Fire* wasn't just notable as a cleverly scripted and frighteningly plausible sci-fi drama whose themes seem more relevant than ever in an era of extreme anxiety about climate change. It also offered one of the best depictions on film of the world of Fleet Street journalism in its heyday, when journalists worked and drank to excess.

A sentiment which Guest expressed again and again in interviews and in his autobiography was his love of teamwork. He flourished when working in a studio environment with people he liked and trusted. Whether at BIP in the early 1930s or at Gainsborough Studios a few years later or at Hammer Films, where he began working in the 1950s, he always talked about the 'family atmosphere' in which he bloomed. Thanks to his grounding as a writer and

---

[18]Ibid.

actor and the opportunity he had to work on almost every part of the filmmaking process during his formative period at Gainsborough, he knew the business inside out.

Hollywood history is full of figures like Val Guest, directors who worked in multiple genres and who had no snobbery at all about the material they worked on. Such figures are much rarer in British film history. Compared to others profiled in this book, Guest's route into the business seemed relatively straightforward. He charged in at it from multiple different angles at once, as an actor, a writer and, finally, as a director. At any given time, he had so many projects on the boil that one or two were always likely to work, even when others stuttered. His peers liked him and always found him reliable. Like Marcel Varnel, the little Frenchman who gave him his biggest break, he brought pace and professionalism to all his projects. It was a measure of both his reliability and his uncanny knack to keep big stars happy that he was the one brought on to steady Charles K. Feldman's James Bond spoof *Casino Royale* (1967). Whether in the raunchy comedies he made in the 1970s or some of the more prestigious projects he directed for Hammer, his meticulous approach didn't change.

Like Varnel, Guest had his misfires. One of his later efforts, *When Dinosaurs Ruled the Earth* (1970), was described as being one of the 'worst movies ever made'.[19] That is a description not so far removed from the slating he gave films he didn't like when he was writing about them for *The Hollywood Reporter* in the 1930s. He knew better than to dwell on successes or failures. Regardless of whether his latest film had been received well or badly, he would always be straight on to the next one.

The *Independent* wrote in its obituary of Guest:

Discipline was the key to Val Guest's film work. He liked to create the original idea for a film or adapt a novel he had enjoyed. He would spend a solid four weeks writing the script. He directed, frequently produced and often supervised the editing. But the amazing thing about his whole career was the wide range of themes and styles: he switched from broad comedy to

---

[19] *Telegraph*, 16 May 2006.

situation comedy to crime and detective thrillers, from studio-bound productions to location dramas, from period musicals to science-fiction tales (of which the *Quatermass* films and *The Day the Earth Caught Fire* are among his best-known work), from pop musicals to bawdy escapades, from cinema to television series.[20]

He even directed episodes of TV's *The Persuaders*, starring Roger Moore and Tony Curtis.

When Guest was bad, he was bad but when he was good, he was very good indeed. He had a ferocious work ethic, a desire to create that couldn't be stymied by such small inconveniences as not having a typewriter when a schoolboy or secure backing for his films when an adult. Guest often anticipated public taste. His best films not only spawned many imitators but continue to be shown today.

---

[20]*Independent*, 15 May 2006.

14

Liz Wrenn[1]

Liz Wrenn's route into the British film industry was circuitous even by standards of other figures profiled in this book. The American founded and became managing director of Electric Pictures, one of the leading British independent distribution companies of the late 1980s and 1990s. It was a matter of chance and coincidence, though, that she was in Britain at all.

Wrenn was born in 1939 in Santa Barbara, California. She grew up in Alabama and then in Florida. Her mother was a housewife. Her father was in the car rental business (and held the franchise for Hertz in central Florida). She studied English literature at the University of North Carolina. There was nothing in her background that gave the slightest hint she would one day be releasing Pedro Almodóvar and Jim Jarmusch movies in British cinemas.

Wrenn married when she was young to a law student, John, also at the University of North Carolina. They had spent a few months in Paris early in their marriage, in 1964. Her husband had gone to France to study international law and her first child, Michael, was born in the country. The family then returned to the US. At one stage, John, a French-speaking, American-trained lawyer, was sounded out by Columbia University about taking up a job in the Belgian Congo to write a new constitution for the country. Liz was apprehensive but excited at the prospect and had even started buying malaria tablets. However, riots broke out and the leading members of the government were hanged in the town square. Columbia quietly shelved the constitution writing project.

---

[1]Unless otherwise cited, quotes in this chapter come from the author's interview with Liz Wrenn, London, October 2019.

Melvin Van Peebles' Sweet Sweetback's Baadasssss Song *(1971), programmed by Liz Wrenn at the Ritzy, Brixton. Photo: LMPC via Getty Images.*

John was on a paid two-year training course for lawyers in international banking. He was fascinated by international law, then in its infancy. The course gave him the opportunity to choose where he wanted to go. He chose New York. Relieved that they had escaped the carnage, the Wrenns set up home in Brooklyn. Her husband was employed by the Chase Manhattan Bank on Wall Street. They were there from 1968 until 1970.

Liz and her husband were gradually worn down by the aggression they encountered in their everyday lives. On nights when the husband worked late, he couldn't get home. No taxi would take him. On one occasion, Wrenn threw her sleeping kids into the back of a car and drove across town to Wall Street to collect him. En route, just as she reached Manhattan, a bomb went off above her and hails of glass fell on the car. With sirens blasting, she drove round and round in search of her husband.

In some ways, the life was stimulating. There were marches against the Vietnam War and passionate debates between feminists, writers and anti-war activists of the type captured a little later in D. A. Pennebaker's famous documentary *Town Bloody Hall* (1971). Nonetheless, Wrenn found the US of the period to be 'a very violent and materialistic society'. She and her husband hoped to find something different in Europe.

In 1970, the family returned to Paris. They spent six years there. Then her husband fell ill. He was eventually to die and she was left on her own, a single mother with two young children. 'In '76, I washed up in the nearest English-speaking country which was this one,' Wrenn, sitting in a cafe on the Euston Road, gestures around at the London streets. The future distribution boss arrived in the UK with her sons, then aged twelve and ten. She had nowhere to stay and no job. She was also in the country illegally. She had French residency papers and a US passport. Her prospects could not have been grimmer. 'We did not have any money. We had suitcases,' Wrenn remembers the circumstances in which she arrived in the UK. She eventually found a flat to rent in north-west London, near Gospel Oak School.

For the first two years she lived in Britain, Wrenn would leave the country every six months and come straight back again. Doing so enabled her to get her passport stamped again and allowed her leave to remain. She soon developed a routine. She would go back to France with her sons in the cheapest way possible, spend the weekend with friends and then return to Britain.

On one of those trips, on the ferry on her way to the UK, she met, completely by chance, Tasmanian artist Rodney Pople, who was then studying at the Slade School of Fine Art. He became a friend and eventually provided her with an entrée into the film industry.

Wrenn had found piecemeal work as a sub-editor at *Time Out* magazine, working for the then editor John Fordham. She was also teaching English as a foreign language and writing news reports from Britain for English-language French publications.

Nonetheless, she realized that if she didn't find a more secure way of making a living, she would have to return to the US, where she would be allowed legally to work. In the meantime, during one summer, Wrenn left the children staying with a friend and went back to France where she found work with another friend at Sigma, one of the big photographic agencies. It was then that Pople called. He told her that his landlord was part of a group of people planning to open a cinema in the West End. One of their investors had dropped out and they were looking for a replacement.

Wrenn was intrigued. She had long held the dream of running a bookshop in a cinema like the one found in the Entrepôt in Paris, run by Frédéric Mitterrand, nephew of former French president François Mitterrand. Maybe this was her chance. The investors came to her little flat in north London, climbed the five flights to the top and told her what they were planning. They were going to take over the lease for the Tottenham Street venue of what had been The Other Cinema (run by Nick Hart-Williams, Paul Marris, Peter Sainsbury and Tony Kirkhope). The plan was to re-open the venue as the Scala Cinema. The Other Cinema (1976–77) became the Scala in June 1978.

The investors were looking for someone to invest £3,000. Thanks to having recently sold some property in the US, Wrenn could just about scrape that much money together. It was all she had. She told the investors, led by Nick Hart-Williams, they could have the cash – on the condition they gave her a job. In effect, she was buying her way into the British film industry. The investors asked her what job she wanted. She replied off the top of her head that she could do press and marketing.

Wrenn's fellow investors, now her employers, assured her they would apply to the Home Office to ensure she was granted permanent residency. She talks of endless trips to an immigration advice centre in Holborn. In the end, though, she won legal status to stay in Britain not through her work at the cinema but through a loophole for self-employed people. Friends and colleagues lobbied on her behalf, making promises that they would employ her at some future date.

In the meantime, the investors in the Scala, including Wrenn, went to visit businessman and entrepreneur Richard Branson, founder of Virgin, on his barge in Maida Vale. Branson agreed to provide some backing. 'I was following on, realizing that I knew absolutely nothing about anything and that I would have to hold on for dear life,' Wrenn recalls her initial steps into the industry.

Once the Scala was up and running, Wrenn began teaching herself the rudiments of press and marketing as she went along. She quickly decided that if she was doing the job, she'd like to have a say in what she was promoting. That led her to programming. At this stage, she didn't have specialist knowledge of film but she had been a regular cinema-goer during her years in Paris. Everyone in France seemed to go to the movies. It was part of the way of life. There seemed to be cinemas on every street. There had been a cinema club at her university. During her time in New York, she and her husband had carried on seeing movies.

Stephen Woolley, soon to become one of the UK's most prolific producers, was working front of house alongside Paul Taylor, later to have an important job in the British Film Institute's distribution division. Wrenn was startled by the breadth of their film knowledge. In a bid to catch up, she would go to screenings at the cinema whenever she could. Other London repertory cinemas at the time, among them the Electric, the National Film Theatre and the Everyman, would allow her into screenings free of charge. Wrenn was conscious that she had 'bought' her way into her job and that she needed to learn fast. That didn't just mean building up press contacts, acquiring the skills to write the best press releases and learning when and where to advertise. She also wanted to steep herself in cinema, to read as much as possible and to learn the business.

Wrenn was friendly with Tony Rayns, *Time Out*'s then film editor, and Scott Meek, then working for the BFI archive but later to become managing director of production company Zenith. 'Back then, in '78, I was an outsider, a good ten to fifteen years older than the other people starting out,' Wrenn, born in December 1939, remembers. She had two children to look after, very little money and she was always pressed for time. Nonetheless, Rayns and Meek encouraged her. Other journalists like Derek Malcolm at the *Guardian*, Alexander Walker at the *Evening Standard* and Philip French at the *Observer* supported her too and championed the new venue. They liked the idea of a cinema supporting independent films which otherwise would have struggled for distribution in the UK.

Not that the venue was making any money. Soon, it was teetering close to bankruptcy. As other colleagues left, Woolley and his business partner Nik Powell (Branson's partner at Virgin, overseeing the mogul's investment into the cinema) were taking on more and more responsibility. Nick Hart-Williams was pushed out. Wrenn started doing front-of-house work, including the 'all-nighters' for which the Scala became famous. However, she wasn't 'a night person' and had two pre-teen children to look after. She didn't have the same freedom as some of her other colleagues.

The Scala Cinema Club moved to its more famous home in King's Cross in 1981. Wrenn soon found herself the only one of the original team in place but then her job was made redundant. Woolley and Powell (soon to set up their own distribution company, Palace Pictures) were developing the Scala brand with new backing from Chris Blackwell, the Jamaica-based mogul behind Island Records. They already had a press and marketing executive. The fact that she was one of the owners, having invested that £3,000, was forgotten. Her papers weren't in order and, at this stage, she didn't yet have a proper work permit – so it wasn't clear that she could work legally anyway.

Out on her ear, Wrenn managed to get an administrative job for an arts organization in Hammersmith. She also approached a new cinema, the Ritzy in Brixton, that had just opened in the building of an old cinema after a young south London cinephile called Pat Foster had persuaded Lambeth Council this was the best use of the site. He had set up the cinema as a co-operative. Wrenn volunteered to write a brochure about the new venture on the understanding that she would be given a job if the brochure boosted attendances. That was how she became programmer, booker and marketing manager at the Ritzy.

Thanks to her experiences at Scala, Wrenn had a sense of what worked with audiences and what didn't. She was from the Deep South of the US having spent time in Florida, Alabama and North Carolina, and warmed to what she calls 'the black cultural mix' of Brixton. One coup early in her career at the Ritzy was persuading the producers of Melvin Van Peebles' cult blaxploitation thriller *Sweet Sweetback's Baadasssss Song* (1970) to send in a print to show at the Ritzy. This was the film that effectively ushered in the Blaxploitation genre of the early 1970s. Dogged by controversy and heavily censored when it was first shown in the US, *Sweet Sweetback* had not then had a proper release in UK cinemas. Wrenn was in charge of daytime programming at the Ritzy. Clare Binns, eventually to become Joint Managing Director of Picturehouse Cinemas, did the evening programming. The cinema survived the Brixton riots in 1981. 'No one harmed the Ritzy because the Ritzy was really part of the community. We knew that if we worked front of house and there was an incident, the last thing you would do would be to call the police. That would not be possible. It just wouldn't work for our communities.'

However, profit margins were minuscule. The co-op behind the Ritzy wasn't sure it could afford Wrenn's salary. The solution it came up with was to share her with the Everyman in Hampstead. She began to programme for both cinemas – and the Everyman paid some of her wages. The Everyman, located in an affluent part of Hampstead, had been open since the 1930s. It had once been a thriving venue but Wrenn discovered a cinema stuck in the past. When she arrived, the Everyman had never played an 18-certificate film. The programming was staid and conservative. The venue had conspicuously failed to pick up on the new waves in European cinema. It didn't take much to revitalize the Everyman. Wrenn began to show the best independent movies.

Wrenn's programming empire soon expanded. She had an assistant, Penny Ashbrook, who helped her as she took on programming duties for the Electric Cinema in west London and the Barbican (which opened in 1982) as well. Her living conditions improved as well. She had lost her rental flat but, in 1984, was able to get a Camden council flat for homeless families. She was doing her office work half in the Everyman and half in the new flat.

From a standing start, Wrenn quickly established herself as a force in British independent exhibition. However, programming arthouse cinemas in London was very different from setting up your own distribution company. By her own admission, she was very shy and had no background in business. Every year, Wrenn's treat to herself was to take a holiday at the Venice Film Festival. She had managed to sort herself out a press badge and cheap accommodation on the Lido. For ten days every autumn, she would watch films without any pressure to programme them or write about them. By chance, at a lunch during the festival, she met Derek Hill, then about to start as the film buyer for Channel 4 Television. She remembers asking him, 'How does it work? How do you sell to television?' Hill explained the ins and outs. In this period, no distributor would acquire a film unless it could be sold on to television to defray the cost. That is still the case now. Distributors need as many windows of opportunity as possible. However, during the mid-1980s, TV sales were absolutely crucial to independent distributors – the bulwark of their businesses.

As an experiment, after speaking to Hill, Wrenn acquired UK theatrical rights to a small Japanese film (paying nothing for them), showed it at the Academy Cinema in central London and then managed to sell the film to TV. Once the marketing and print costs were factored in, she broke even. At this stage, though, she had no particular plans to leave programming and set up as a distributor instead.

In Venice, the great French New Wave auteur Agnès Varda (1928–2019) had won the Golden Lion, the festival's biggest prize, for *Vagabond* (1985). The film had already been bought by Channel 4 but had no one to release it in British cinemas. Carole Myer was then head of sales at Film Four International and was looking for someone to take Varda's film into British cinemas. She knew that Wrenn had distributed one film. She therefore called her, inviting her to make an offer for *Vagabond*. It was an excellent film with an obvious appeal but no other British distributors wanted to pay to acquire it because they knew the TV rights (on which they had the best chance of making a profit) were already gone. Wrenn suggested £1,000. 'Big spender!' Myer replied with obvious sarcasm but let her have the film anyway.

At first, the other distributors were angry that Wrenn had nabbed such a good title from under their noses. They hadn't realized that Wrenn was waiting in the wings. Artificial Eye's Andi Engel had thought if he delayed coming in for the film for long enough, Myer would let him have Vagabond for free, just to ensure it was seen on British screens. (Unlike most other distributors, Artificial Eye had its own cinemas.) Whatever his disappointment at losing out to Wrenn, Engel agreed to show the film at the Renoir, Bloomsbury, one of the sites which Artificial Eye then ran.

Wrenn was up and running as a distributor. She bought a limited company 'off the shelf' at Companies House and changed its name to Electric (after her favourite cinema in Portobello which she was also programming). Unlike some of her rivals, she had realized there was a huge Spanish population in west London, one reason she took rights to so many Spanish and Cuban films – and later did such strong business with the work of Pedro Almodóvar. The Electric Cinema is still in existence (and there is now a White City venue as well as the Portobello site) but although she borrowed the venue's name, Wrenn didn't own the exhibition business. As Electric Pictures grew bigger, she realized she no longer had time for programming.

Vagabond was a solid theatrical hit. Wrenn's posters for it were in black and white (she couldn't afford colour). However, by the time of the film's release, she had recruited Elizabeth Draper to handle marketing for the film and Emma Davie to do the press. Channel 4 provided the prints, free of charge. She brought over Varda to support the film, which opened at the Gate, Notting Hill, as well as in Bloomsbury.

Shortly before Cannes in May 1986, Contemporary Films, one of the UK's oldest independent distribution companies, set up by industry veteran Charles Cooper in 1951, had come to Wrenn with a proposition. Cooper and his wife Kitty, with whom he ran the company, were keen to step back but didn't want to leave the business. They said to her that they would underwrite her acquisitions – and then they could split the profits.

In Cannes, Wrenn acquired another film, Lizzie Borden's *Working Girls* (1986), a feminist drama about upper-class prostitutes. This was also acquired by Harvey Weinstein's Miramax for the US. Wrenn remembers Weinstein (later disgraced after years of sexually harassing staff and actresses) as 'an enormous bully'. He was 'charming, vastly intelligent but a terrible bully to anyone who worked for him and to anyone else'. Weinstein's expertise at marketing helped get *Working Girls* noticed. Electric Pictures used a poster Miramax had designed. With *Vagabond* and *Working Girls* behind it, Electric Pictures became 'a real distribution company'.

Electric went on to release Gus Van Sant's *My Own Private Idaho* (1991), starring Keanu Reeves and River Phoenix, Jane Campion's *Sweetie* (1989), Sally Potter's *Orlando* (1992) and many of the best Asian films of the early 1990s. The company brought Iranian cinema to the UK, successfully releasing Jafar Panahi's *The White Balloon* (1995) and Amir Naderi's *The Runner* (1985). Electric released Larry Clark's *Kids* (1995) and several titles by Pedro Almodóvar. Wrenn and her team supported British talent too, picking up Shane Meadows's early film *Small Time* (1996) and maverick arthouse director Andrew Kotting's eccentric road movie *Gallivant* (1996).

'These are very particular movies, movies that wouldn't otherwise get on to the screen. We will probably lose money on both but we'll try to make it up somewhere else because we think that distributing these films is the right thing to do,' she said at the time. 'Distribution can't be just about money.'[2]

The Electric boss also supported the best in US independent cinema in the period and was given 'special thanks' on the credits of Nicole Holofcener's wry romantic comedy *Walking and Talking* (1996), which she distributed.

She took particular pride in releasing debut features from directors whose talent she believed in. Some major names had their first films released in British cinemas thanks to her intervention, among them French director Claire Denis with *Chocolat* (1988), Belgian Jaco van Dormael with *Toto the Hero* (1991), British filmmaker Michael Winterbottom with *Butterfly Kiss* (1995), Swede Lukas Moodysson with *Show Me Love* (1998) and Canadian Mary Harron with *I Shot Andy Warhol* (1996). She also handled early work from revered festival favourites like Lars von Trier and Catherine Breillat.

At the same time she championed new directors, Wrenn, after all those years programming rep cinema, was always on the lookout for interesting back catalogues. She picked up older titles like Federico Fellini's *La Dolce Vita* (1960), several classics from Luis Buñuel and early John Cassavetes and Louis

---

[2]Quoted in I. Q. Hunter, Laraine Porter and Justin Smith (eds), *The Routledge Companion to British Cinema History* (Abingdon: Routledge, 2017).

Malle movies. These did strong business on video and DVD. Some were re-released theatrically too.

Several of the Electric films had censorship 'problems'. Wrenn, though, had a friendly and firm working relationship with James Ferman, director of the British Board of Film Classification, dating from Electric Pictures' early days, because of Lizzie Borden's *Working Girls*.

'Since I liked new and unusual films, there were often British censorship issues to confront. Censorship was strict with sexual images in those days, and Mr Ferman was (quite rightly) extremely sensitive to violence against women. Violence in general, except for cockfights, was not such a concern,' Wrenn notes drily.

The film which gave Electric the most trouble with the censors was also a first film – John McNaughton's *Henry: Portrait of a Serial Killer* (1986). 'I'd happened to be seated next to James Ferman at a lunch and mentioned to him that I had just taken *Henry* for UK distribution. Somewhat to my surprise, he had already seen the film, and he was very very opposed to it. I said I admired it because Henry, unlike other fictional serial killers, was not falsely redeemed by the love of a good woman. I also said that I thought the grotesque "death by television set" scene was comic horror, and that personally I laughed out loud, but Mr Ferman definitely did not see the humour.'

Neither did Wrenn's colleagues Elizabeth Draper and Emma Davie, so Electric hired Mark Borkowski to do the PR. Somewhere in the process she agreed to do a 6 a.m. telephone interview from the LA American Film Market without asking much about it. 'I expected some sort of soft publicity chat. The programme was *Today* and the interviewer was John Humphrys,' she remembers her encounter with the BBC's fiercest interviewer who accused her of corrupting the nation.

When Palace Pictures, the company formed by Woolley and Powell (who had ousted her from the Scala), collapsed in the early 1990s, a gap opened up in the market. That enabled her to acquire quirky French black comedy *Delicatessen* (1991), which became one of Electric's biggest hits.

Electric Pictures was a training ground for executives who went on to have very notable careers in the UK film industry, among them Alex Hamilton, eOne's former Managing Director in the UK, Andy Leyshon, in 2020 Chief Executive of the Film Distributors' Association, and Laura De Casto, formerly Managing Director of Tartan Films.

Wrenn was running a prominent UK film distribution company and was becoming involved in bigger and bigger projects. She had secured financial support from Jorg Judin, a Zurich-based exhibitor and distributor. With the backing, Electric moved from north London into smarter offices in Fitzrovia. 'It was the early 1990s. Everything we distributed seemed to do very well.'

It was quite a transformation from the period when Wrenn was a homeless single mother, arriving in London with two young sons and a couple of suitcases. By her own admission, she had no particular management expertise. Her skill was in spotting new talent and in finding unsung films that resonated with audiences. In the mid-1990s, as Electric grew, she worked closely with PolyGram Filmed Entertainment, a giant company then trying to establish itself as a European studio on the scale of a Hollywood major. There was talk that Electric might become part of the then rapidly expanding PolyGram empire.

In their period of the 1990s, the economics of UK indie distribution were shifting. US companies were moving into the market for independent films, often buying for all territories, and prices were escalating. Electric was (by comparison with its rivals) undercapitalized, one reason for looking to join with PolyGram. Wrenn remembers being blindsided by what happened with Baz Luhrmann's debut feature *Strictly Ballroom* (1992). During the Cannes Film Festival, she had put in a bid which she thought had been accepted. She knew the Australian producers. Channel 4 was committed to taking the UK TV rights. When the broadcaster fretted that the money they were putting up was more than the movie probably cost to make, she told them that wasn't relevant. The film (which she adored) was bound to be a hit. However, she paused and didn't sign the contract immediately. The next morning, Rank Film Distributors offered a figure that blew Wrenn and her company out of the water. 'I had to have a minder with me all weekend. I was broken hearted.'

Wrenn had started her company releasing titles for which she had had to pay almost nothing. Now the risks were huge. This led to a more conservative and mainstream buying strategy. Another change as competition intensified, ironically one which intensified risk taking, was that instead of being able to license films after seeing them, the emphasis was now on pre-buying, at script stage. Her job became more about reading than about watching.

Eventually, in 1998, Wrenn sold Electric to major Canadian company Alliance-Atlantic, which was looking for a foothold in the UK and had hoped (forlornly as it turned out) to win one of the lucrative lottery production franchises offered by the UK government in 1997. The deal didn't make her rich although it ensured that all her staff held on to their jobs, but it proved an anti-climactic end to her glittering distribution career. She was kept on by Alliance-Atlantic as managing director but didn't enjoy the corporate way the company did business. There were still high points, though.

As mentioned, another of Wrenn's tendencies had always been to pick up films by new directors. She 'smuggled' a tiny budget, London-set British black-and-white film called *Following* (1998), which had screened at the International Film Festival Rotterdam, into Alliance-Atlantic. Its promise was obvious, even if its commercial prospects seemed extremely slender and the Canadian bosses definitely didn't want it. This was the debut feature of a writer-director who had just finished his English literature degree at University College London. His name was Christopher Nolan. By 2020, thanks to *Dark Knight, Interstellar, Dunkirk* et al., his films had grossed an estimated $4.7 billion at the global box office. Wrenn had played her part in kick-starting his career.

In the end, in spite of such successes, when Alliance-Atlantic wanted to bring in PolyGram executive David Kosse as managing director, Wrenn's contract was paid off early in 2001.

The company that the American single mother had founded in north London in 1986 grew and changed under its new owners. It was rebranded as Momentum Pictures and released multi-Oscar and BAFTA winner *The King's Speech* (2011). Alliance was acquired by Entertainment One in 2013 and eOne (the notable UK distributor of *The Twilight Saga, The Death of Stalin, Stan & Ollie*, Oscar winner *Green Book, 1917* and various Ken Loach films) was acquired in turn by giant toy company Hasbro in 2019 for a reported $4 billion (£3.3 billion). The little acorn turned into an enormous oak. Wrenn came into the industry with no experience but left an indelible imprint. Both her sons work in the film business (Michael is a producer while Brennan is a film buyer for Australian broadcaster SBS). Thanks to Wrenn, British cinema audiences discovered filmmakers (from Larry Clark to Sally Potter, from Jafar Panahi to Gus Van Sant) who are now revered. She became a key player in a period when independent distribution in the UK was at its most adventurous.

15

Karel Reisz

Karel Reisz (1926–2002) was behind some of the best British films of the 1960s: gritty, realist, quintessentially British affairs like *Saturday Night and Sunday Morning* (1960), which he directed, and Lindsay Anderson's *This Sporting Life* (1963), which he produced; he also made playful whimsical dramas like *Morgan – A Suitable Case for Treatment* (1966). He seemed to have an intimate, first-hand understanding both of northern working-class life and of swinging London. He was an accomplished journalist, reviewer and film curator and programmer. Together with Lindsay Anderson, whom he had met on a Green Line bus to Aston Clinton,[1] where the British Film Institute (BFI) archive was then based, he worked on *Sequence*. This was the polemical film magazine set up by Anderson and several fellow Oxford undergraduates, among them Gavin Lambert, Peter Ericsson and Penelope Houston. On the face of it, his route into the British film industry was the same as theirs.

In fact, Reisz's pathway into British filmmaking was a very strange one which owed as much to Hitler and family tragedy in Eastern Europe as to the BFI. He had been born in 1926 in Ostria, a small industrial town in Czechoslovakia which, in later life, he liked to compare to Sheffield. His father was a lawyer. Karel led a relatively idyllic and uneventful childhood as a middle-class Jewish kid. There is a plaque outside the old family home which has a photograph as its centre showing Reisz as a young boy with his family. They look contented and prosperous, a happy bourgeois family. That was before the Nazi invasion of Czechoslovakia in 1938. By then, Reisz's older

---

[1]Brian McFarlane, 'Karel Reisz profiled', *The Encyclopedia of British Film* (London: Methuen, 1997), 475.

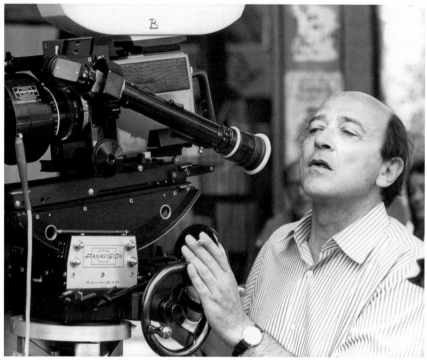

Karel Reisz. Photo: Michael Ochs Archives/Stringer via Getty Images.

brother had already been spirited out of the country, sent by his parents to Leighton Park School, a Quaker boarding school, in Reading, England. Reisz eventually followed him, arriving in Britain in June 1939 on the Kindertransport as a refugee.

The British filmmaker was one of the 669 children in Czechoslovakia rescued by Sir Nicholas Winton (1909–2015), the self-effacing London-born humanitarian later dubbed (much to his annoyance) the 'British Schindler', after Oskar Schindler, the Polish businessman who saved thousands of Jewish lives during the Second World War.

In 1939, Winton, then in his late twenties, had been working as a stockbroker in London. He arrived in Prague in 1938. His friend Martin Blake was a teacher at Westminster School. Winton was due some time off and had originally planned to help Blake take a group of children from the well-known public school on a skiing holiday. Instead, Blake summoned him to come to Czechoslovakia.

'Nicky's change of plan led him to Prague on New Year's Eve, to a meeting with Doreen Warriner, the volunteer head of the Prague office of the British Committee for Refugees from Czechoslovakia (BCRC) who Martin was assisting,' Winton's daughter, Barbara Winton, told the story.[2] The committee was trying to help refugees who had been forced to leave the Sudetenland after British Prime Minister Neville Chamberlain's infamous 1938 agreement with Adolf Hitler, which ceded the region to Nazi Germany.

'Their work was mainly with those on Hitler's "wanted list" – basically anyone who had criticized him, particularly Social Democrat politicians, communists and other intellectuals, who would be arrested if they fell into German hands,' Barbara Winton explains.[3] Her stockbroker father threw himself into the work. He was appalled by the suffering he saw around him. Families were living in desperate conditions in displaced persons camps. Winton was struck in particular by the plight of the refugee children.

Reisz was better off than many of these other children. His family hadn't been forced to leave home. However, his parents could see the dangers ahead and were determined to protect him. His lawyer father had no illusions about what might happen to Jews in Czechoslovakia. Chamberlain's 'peace in our time' speech didn't inspire confidence that the UK or anybody else would intervene to save them.

The future filmmaker was therefore sent away on the fifth of the Kindertransport, the eight trains that Winton organized to take children from Prague to the UK. He was twelve at the time, one of the older children. (The young refugees ranged in age from three to sixteen but some seventeen-year-olds were also smuggled aboard.) He had been taken to the dentist before he departed and had some gold implanted in his teeth so that he wouldn't arrive in Britain with no wealth. This was a detail which emerged during the research for *The Power of Good* (2002), a documentary about Winton made by Slovak director Matej Mináč to which Reisz contributed.

On arriving in England, Reisz joined his brother at the school, where he stayed for just over four years. Aged seventeen in 1943, Reisz enrolled in the

---

[2] http://www.barbarawinton.co.uk/Nicholas%20Winton.htm.
[3] Ibid.

Czech branch of the RAF. He qualified as a pilot just before the war ended but didn't see active combat.

The young immigrant spent the war not knowing what had happened to his parents. As soon as peace was declared, Reisz travelled to Poland to search for them but discovered they had both died in the Nazi death camps. He had no relatives left in Eastern Europe and came back to England, where, with the help of his foster parents, he secured a place to study for a chemistry degree at Cambridge University. He had a scholarship. His guardian had been a chemist, one reason he was drawn to science. After the trauma of war and of coming to Britain as a refugee, he settled down to a typical British university existence, playing rugby, socializing, becoming involved in left-wing politics. Most importantly for his future career, he also joined the university film society. He spent the holidays in East Grinstead in Sussex, in the heart of the home counties. Gradually, his central European accent (which had been very distinctive when he first arrived in Britain) faded. He sounded as English as the other students.

'I came down in 1948. Like everybody else, I couldn't get a job in the film industry,' he later remembered.[4] Instead, for several years, he worked as a supply teacher at various secondary schools, teaching physics, chemistry and maths. He slowly began to secure freelance writing work as a reviewer for the *Monthly Film Bulletin*. He taught courses in community centres on film appreciation. In old regional newspapers of the period, you find listings referring to him as 'Dr Karel Reisz'. By chance, through a friend, Kumari Ralph, who worked at the British Film Academy, he was commissioned to write a book on film editing. He later described this 'as a gift from heaven'.[5] He was paid to watch films on a Moviola, analyse them and write about how they had been edited. This was his equivalent of film school. The book turned out to be hugely influential, partly because it was so lucid and well written and partly because there were few other studies on the same subject. It was around this time, in the early 1950s, that Reisz met Lindsay Anderson on that bus route and started contributing to *Sequence*.

---

[4] Reisz interview, British Entertainment History Project, 17 April 1991. https://historyproject.org.uk/interview/karel-reisz.
[5] Ibid.

Reisz was now able to secure jobs in the public film sector, first as assistant curator at the National Film Archive and then as the very first programmer at the National Film Theatre on London's South Bank. He continued to write for *Sequence*, which was self-consciously polemical. Anderson would write fierce diatribes against class-based British cinema ('all those pictures about country houses with comic servants or stiff upper lipped officers and Cockney conscripts,' as Reisz described them to Brian McFarlane[6]) while trumpeting the glories of great Hollywood directors like John Ford and Preston Sturges and of leading French and Russian filmmakers. The magazine's approach was auteurist. The British directors *Sequence* championed were individualists who had a social conscience and a distinctive visual style, directors like Humphrey Jennings and Alexander Mackendrick.

Reisz and Anderson were British equivalents to the New Wave directors in France (filmmakers like François Truffaut and Jean-Luc Godard) who started as critics, writing for *Cahiers du Cinema*, and then moved sideways into film production. That was precisely what they did too. Together with Tony Richardson, they applied to the BFI's 'Experimental Production Fund' for backing for a documentary. They received £300 and made *Momma Don't Allow* (1955), a half-hour documentary about a north London jazz club.

At the NFT, at around the same time, Reisz put on a programme of films called 'Free Cinema'. The idea was to provide an alternative to the sometimes stuffy, snobbish, studio set British cinema of the period. The name stuck. Reisz, Richardson and Anderson emphasized the importance 'of the everyday', and went against the grain of British documentary making at the time which they felt to be polemical and rigid. They much preferred the visionary, freewheeling filmmaking of Humphrey Jennings (1907–50), who had made such distinctive and personal films as *Listen to Britain* (1942) and *Fires Were Started* (1943) that had what he called 'a poetic response to reality'.[7]

In time-honoured fashion, Anderson and Reisz were carving out a space for themselves in the industry by attacking the status quo. They were demanding the right to be able to make films on their own terms. The former was irascible

---

[6]McFarlane, 'Karel Reisz', 476.
[7]Reisz, British Entertainment History Project.

and polemical. The latter was famous for his mildness and equanimity. 'There is no temperament, there are no tantrums while Reisz is at work,' the *Daily Express* reported after one of its journalists observed him on set. 'He is a gentle man. The West End doesn't tempt him. He has never been inside a nightclub,' the profile continues.[8]

There was, though, nothing precious about Reisz, who took a job as films officer at the Ford Motor Company, making commercials about cars, in order to underwrite his own work. The young director negotiated the right to make one sponsored film a year which wasn't advertising driven. This was how his friend Anderson, with his support, was able to make *Every Day Except Christmas* (1957), about Covent Garden fruit and veg market, and how he found the funding for *We Are the Lambeth Boys* (1959), set around a youth club in south London and the lives of the teenagers who frequent it. The Ford Motor Company thus played an important role in a transformative period in British filmmaking. Ford sponsored the films as part of a 'Look at Britain' series which made a considerable splash. Critics and audiences always noticed the company name at the end of the credits. The films were shown in cinemas. The benefit to Reisz and Anderson was obvious but Ford did well out of the documentaries too. The films made their corporate sponsor appear open minded and supportive of the burgeoning new youth culture.

It wasn't just cars. Reisz also directed films about washing products. 'I do not feel ashamed about going from a film like *Saturday Night* to making shorts about detergents in the back gardens of Cricklewood,' he insisted. 'Detergents to me mean as much as 100 pounds a day – enough to allow me to be able to choose carefully the feature films I make.'[9]

Reisz talked about 'pricking the balloon' of ABC and Rank, who were the dominant duopoly at the time, and getting away from the 'Pinewood' aesthetic and the complacency of so much 1950s mainstream British filmmaking. 'We were film lunatics. Our gods were [Marcel] Carné and John Ford and [William] Wyler and so on,' Reisz remembered the fanaticism he and Anderson showed towards cinema.[10] They were turning out feature film scripts and saw the

---

[8]*Daily Express*, 6 January 1961.
[9]Karel Reisz, BFI microfiche cuttings.
[10]Reisz, British Entertainment History Project.

documentaries as 'stepping stones' which would eventually allow them to make dramatic feature films. Their timing was impeccable. Novelists like Alan Sillitoe and John Braine and playwrights like John Osborne, Arnold Wesker and Harold Pinter were also railing against the cultural establishment of the time.

Reisz and Anderson had nothing to do with Jack Clayton's *Room at the Top* (1959), famous as one of Britain's first commercially successful X-rated films and for its frank account of a northern working-class man trying to climb the social and career ladder. However, the film's success, and that of Tony Richardson's screen adaptation of Osborne's *Look Back in Anger* (1959), shifted attitudes. Richardson invited Reisz to pitch projects. He wanted to make a film of Sillitoe's *Saturday Night and Sunday Morning*. The rights were owned elsewhere but Richardson and his producer partner Harry Saltzman bought it on Reisz's behalf.

One irony about the success of *Saturday Night and Sunday Morning* (1960) lay in the casting. Reisz wasn't interested in stars but this was a movie with a fantastic, larger-than-life performance from Albert Finney as the rebellious, hard-drinking anti-hero Arthur Seaton, a factory worker who seemed like a cross between Marlon Brando and Falstaff. This was, according to Reisz, 'a very, very simple film' and 'a little working class fable', and yet, thanks to Finney, it 'caught fire'.[11]

Reisz had never even worked with actors before but still elicited searing performances from all his cast. 'There are things you can do the first time when you don't know the problems,' he said of a confidence built on ignorance that allowed him to tell seasoned cast members what to do. It helped, too, that he was such a calm and likeable presence. The film had a freshness and offbeat quality that is rarely found in movies from more experienced directors, who find conventional but predictable solutions to problems they might encounter on set. He was known for his belief in 'maximum realism and continuity'.[12] On *Night Must Fall* (1964), a psychological thriller also starring Finney and about a killer, there were stories in the press about take after take of a scene involving a roast chicken. A new chicken was freshly cooked for each take and 19 were

---

[11]Ibid.
[12]*Thanet Times*, 3 September 1963.

served up in the course of a morning at Borehamwood British Studios. (The cast members were nauseous by lunchtime.)

The Rank Organisation was 'absolutely horrified' by *This Sporting Life* (1963), which Reisz produced and Lindsay Anderson directed from the David Storey novel. Reisz talked of an early screening attended by Rank's famously brusque and ruthless managing director John Davis. He hated the film but his then wife, actress Dinah Sheridan, liked it so much that he had to 'spike' his guns and release it against his better instincts.[13]

Without Winton's intervention and his parents' decision to put him on the Kindertransport, Reisz would have had nothing to do with the British film industry – and possibly would not have survived the war. Not only was his route into the industry surprising. He inspired several other careers. One of the most notable is that of Stephen Frears, director of *My Beautiful Laundrette* (1985), *Dangerous Liaisons* (1988) and *The Grifters* (1990). Frears has often acknowledged that he wouldn't even have considered working in cinema if Reisz hadn't invited him to work as his assistant on *Morgan – A Suitable Case for Treatment*. At the time, Frears had been working at the Royal Court Theatre. 'He took me into his family and changed my life.' On the BBC radio show *Great Lives* (2012), Frears speculated that Reisz's difficult background had turned him into a wise, kindly and very brilliant man'. Author John Lahr, who lived in the same house for several years, described him as 'an artistic father'.[14] Reisz mentored Frears, who, as his career gathered momentum, would show the older man his films and ask for advice.

There was a touch of Hollywood about Reisz's life. Reisz's wife was Betsy Blair, who had formerly been married to Gene Kelly. He was revered by younger artists and filmmakers.

Reisz's filmography is relatively slight. Over thirty years, between 1960 and 1990, he made ten films. They were all very different from one another and include angry young man British social realism, a Vietnam movie (*Who'll Stop the Rain* in 1978), a country-music drama (Patsy Cline biopic *Sweet Dreams* in

---

[13]Ibid.

[14]Both cited in *Great Lives*, BBC Radio 4, 11 September 2012. https://www.bbc.co.uk/programmes/b01mk4mw.

1985, which earned an Oscar nomination for Jessica Lange), a dance film (*Isadora* in 1968), a Dostoevsky adaptation (*The Gambler* in 1974) and a John Fowles adaptation (*The French Lieutenant's Woman* in 1981). For the latter, Meryl Streep won her first BAFTA and received the first of her many Oscar nominations for Actress in a Leading Role, although she had already won a Supporting Actress Oscar for *Kramer vs. Kramer* (1979). Actors trusted him and responded to his passion. He wasn't the kind of director to browbeat them or treat them like cattle. He was interested in their craft and put them at ease. Male and female stars from Finney, James Caan and Nick Nolte to Meryl Streep, Vanessa Redgrave and Debra Winger did some of their most striking work in his films. 'He knew what he wanted but it was also very much about letting them find their own truth in the characters,' his son Matthew Reisz says of his approach to directing actors.[15]

Reisz was never doctrinaire. He was as comfortable working on stage as on screen, in making documentaries as in directing dramatic features. When he made *The Lambeth Boys*, he spent months before shooting began getting to know his subjects and their world. In advance of *Saturday Night and Sunday Morning*, he lived for a few weeks in a mining village in Nottingham.

Reisz devoted much of his later career to theatre. His flexibility was underlined when he directed two productions of the same Harold Pinter play, *A Kind of Alaska*, one in London and one in the US. Each production was completely different. He was an unobtrusive figure, always keeping out of the limelight. 'Theatre and film director Karel Reisz is hardly a household name in this country, or anywhere else,' the *Sunday Independent* (Dublin) noted of him in an admiring article.[16] His low profile gave him artistic freedom. Nobody tried to pigeonhole him. He could move between stage and screen and deal with very different subjects without drawing attention to himself.

The one subject Reisz steered away from in his films, though, was his own childhood, background and the bizarre and tragic circumstances in which he arrived in Britain in the first place. 'A Czech Jew by birth who lived in London for more than fifty years except when away on location, he never made a film

---

[15]Matthew Reisz, interviewed by the author, October 2019.
[16]*Sunday Independent*, 10 March 1996.

that dealt in any obvious way with the events of his own life,' Matthew Reisz wrote of him in *The Times Educational Supplement* on the tenth anniversary of Reisz's death.[17]

One of the stranger and more poignant aspects of the story of the Kindertransport was the reluctance of anyone to talk about it. Winton himself would mention his role on his CV when he was applying for new jobs. This had been a significant moment in his life and he wasn't ashamed of it. However, he wasn't inclined to boast about it either. There were others involved in the rescue mission, many of whom took greater risks than he did, and he was uncomfortable about soaking up the praise.

The children themselves had often either been too traumatized or too saddened by the wrench of leaving their homeland to want to discuss it. Some had been so young that they couldn't really remember the circumstances in which they arrived in England. Like many of the others who had been on the transports, Reisz didn't discuss the experience. 'He found it very difficult to talk about,' Matthew Reisz remembers.[18] In interviews, if he was asked about the Kindertransport, he didn't avoid the question, but dealt with the episode in a dry and factual way.

In 1988, when a scrapbook which detailed Winton's involvement in the rescues fell into the hands of BBC show *That's Life*, Winton became acclaimed as a hero. This exposure had come about after Winton's wife Grete had found papers about the rescue in the family attic and gave them to Dr Elizabeth 'Betty' Maxwell, wife of the disgraced newspaper magnate and former *Daily Mirror* owner, Robert Maxwell. Betty was a renowned Holocaust researcher. She showed the information to her husband, then at the peak of his wealth and influence. Stories about the 'very reluctant hero', as the British press invariably characterized Winton, began to appear in Maxwell's newspapers and elsewhere. The BBC picked up the trail.

'I remember hearing Karel Reisz's story. He saw the programme or saw something about it and it was an opportunity for him to talk to his family about his story which he hadn't really talked about before,' Barbara Winton

---

[17]https://www.timeshighereducation.com/features/a-voyage-round-my-father/421859.article.
[18]Matthew Reisz interview.

recalls.[19] Her father went on to meet Reisz at reunions of the Kindertransport children. Matthew Reisz remembers that his father hated Rantzen's programme, which he found saccharine and manipulative, 'the worst kind of schmaltziness'. Nonetheless, he later met Winton at one of the private events organized for families of the Kindertransport children. Matthew Reisz and his siblings attended too. 'That was a very moving event. It is obviously true that quite a lot of the "kinder" went on to do remarkable things in this country but it was equally clear from that event that some had been very traumatized and remained very traumatized. There were [some] very twitchy, anxious people.'[20]

The publicizing of the Winton story helped Reisz to address his past. He was an Anglophile, 'slightly starry eyed about how the British system works,' as his son puts it, but he now took the time to remember his central European roots. 'A lot of his friends were surprised by how pro-British he was. But I think he always felt like an outsider. He always said all his films were about outsiders,' Matthew Reisz states.[21]

Such films as *Saturday Night and Sunday Morning* and *The Lambeth Boys* dealt with British working-class life in a fresh and irreverent way. 'He was passionately concerned to explore his adopted country,' Matthew Reisz suggests.[22] However, it is too simplistic to pigeonhole him as a quintessentially British director. He saw himself as being as much an outsider as the protagonists in his movies, especially characters like Arthur Seaton in *Saturday Night and Sunday Morning*, with his mantras 'I'm me and nobody else; and whatever people think I am or say I am, that's what I'm not, because they don't know a bloody thing about me' and 'All I'm out for is a good time – all the rest is propaganda'.

Reisz was equally single minded. However, having endured such tragic upheaval early in his life, he looked for routine and stability. He lived in the same house in Hampstead for many years. He supported Tottenham Hotspur's erratic and often struggling football team with a dogged patience. He went to cricket matches at Lord's. Matthew Reisz talks of his father's passion for

---

[19]Barbara Winton, interviewed by the author, October 2019.
[20]Matthew Reisz interview.
[21]Ibid.
[22]Ibid.

gardening. Reisz had worked in Hollywood and had directed some ground-breaking films but he was never bitter about the reversals along the way or how his filmmaking career tailed off. 'He wasn't terribly interested in, you know, events in his honour or anything like that,' his son said of him.[23]

Interviewed four years before his death by the *Daily Telegraph*, Reisz talked about 'a small English film' he was planning but also made it very clear that he wouldn't mind if it never happened. As you 'get older', he told his interviewer, filmmaking gets harder. 'Somehow you feel you're operating in a foreign country,' he commented with a very knowing irony.[24]

---

[23]Ibid.
[24]*Daily Telegraph*, 16 May 1998.

16

Constance Smith

Movie star stories are often presented as gilt-edged fables. In Hollywood, Lana Turner was supposedly discovered sipping soda at Schwab's drugstore. There are many other similar Cinderella-like accounts, heavily embellished by studio marketing departments, of ingénues plucked from obscurity and turned into global celebrities overnight. Of course, the reality tends to be grimmer and far more prosaic. Stars aren't born. They have to hustle and work hard, and rely on lucky breaks and the support of casting directors. The British industry has been notably less successful at creating them than its Hollywood counterpart. After all, in its heyday, the US studio system was built around stars. MGM liked to crow that it 'had more stars than there are in Heaven', a boast that no British company could match. However, the British have tried to create their own stars and have sometimes succeeded.

One of the stranger and sadder careers in British film history is that of the Irish actress Constance Smith (1929–2003), who really was plucked from obscurity in the way that film fan magazines like to pretend that all film stars are – but which, in truth, hardly ever happens. This book is full of the stories of outsiders who showed incredible resourcefulness to break into the film industry. Smith fell into it almost by accident and briefly seemed set to be very successful but ended up being spat out. Hers is a cautionary tale, included here as a counterpoint to the accounts of striving writers, producers and distributors who ultimately managed to control their careers or set up their own companies. Smith had steeliness and ambition; she pursued her career in three different countries – the UK, the US and Italy – and three different film cultures but she was always working at the behest of others.

Constance Smith. Photo: Hulton Archive/Getty Images.

The Limerick-born soldier's daughter was the first of eleven children. Smith grew up in near poverty. As a teenager in Dublin (where her family had moved), the convent school girl worked in the local fish and chip shop. Her father had died when she was fifteen.

Everyone used to comment on Smith's striking looks and to say that she was the spitting image of Hedy Lamarr. In February 1945, Irish film magazine *The Screen*, which had offices in Dublin, held a talent competition. 'Do YOU resemble a film star?' was the headline on the top of page fifteen. 'If so, here is your chance to win fame, a cash prize and to meet a real Film Star in person.'[1] Entrants were not supposed to use make-up. They had to send in a photograph

[1] *The Screen*, February 1945.

with the name of the star they looked like on the back. It seemed a typical marketing wheeze – a way for the editors to get lots of pictures of aspiring young hopefuls they could publish in the next edition of the magazine and thereby boost circulation. The notion that the competition might lead to a career in London or Hollywood would have seemed simply absurd.

The neighbours rallied round to buy the teenager a dress. According to one account, her formidable mother, strict but ambitious on Constance's behalf, entered the competition for her and paid the admission fee. Another source suggests she was discovered by a 'famous English photographer', for whom she modelled clothes and who put her forward for the lookalike competition. Whatever the case, she won it: she was 'first prizewinner in the Ladies' section'. She really did look strikingly like Hedy Lamarr. When the magazine published the photograph of the teenage fish and chip shop assistant and the Hollywood star side by side, it was almost impossible to distinguish between them. Husband and wife team star Anna Neagle and producer Herbert Wilcox came to Dublin to present her with her award at a 'Screen Ball' in Clerys Ballroom. Thanks to her triumph, she was also given a screen test with the Rank Organisation in London and drafted into the Rank Charm School in Highbury.[2]

This was the age of austerity, a period when Britain, hugely in debt after the First World War, craved escapism. Under the formidable Molly Terraine, the Rank Charm School taught its students deportment and elocution. They fenced and walked around with books on their head to improve their posture. They had dentists. They had make-up artists. Sometimes, some of them (Anthony Steel, Diana Dors and Christopher Lee among them) would be given parts in Rank movies, generally second features. They were also there to open village fetes and lend a little colour to a country desperate for it. The public may not have yet known who they were but when they turned up at fairs and openings of shops and department stores, they were still treated like minor royalty. They were symbols of a world of affluence and glamour that seemed a very long way away in an era when even bread was still rationed.

---

[2]Details are included in the documentary *Constance Smith – Hollywood Tragedy*, directed by Brian Reddin, 2018.

As Irish filmmaker Brian Reddin pointed out in his 2018 Irish TV documentary *Constance Smith – Hollywood Tragedy*, Smith was immediately deracinated. Her family, who were very poor, expected her to send money home. She, though, had moved into another world and the plight of her siblings, cousins, aunts and uncles back home in Ireland wasn't uppermost in her mind. She ignored them. She may not yet have been the name above the lights but she was given small but noticeable roles in such films as Gainsborough melodrama *Jassy* (1947), the Boulting brothers' *Brighton Rock* (1948) and *To the Public Danger* (1948), which was shot at Rank's B studios, also in Highbury. Directed by Terence Fisher (later famous for his Hammer horror movies), scripted by novelist and playwright Patrick Hamilton (*Rope, Gaslight*), this was a drama intended to warn the British public of the dangers of drink-driving; it was one of the Rank Organisation's earliest second feature releases.

But Smith never came close to fitting in with the other Rank starlets or with the Rank senior hierarchy. She was far too fiery and opinionated. There are pictures of her parading with other starlets, like Joan Dowling, dressed in feathers and furbelows as if she is a character on leave from a Jane Austen novel, or in strange bathing suits, 'a brief brassiere, slim fitting shorts, demure bolero and full gathered skirt',[3] and she is regularly described as 'demure' or 'gorgeous-eyed'. She is said to have objected when her Rank employers tried to make her change her Irish accent. Her contract was soon terminated. However, just when it looked as if her movie career was about to end ignominiously only shortly after it had started, Hollywood came calling. Fox put her under contract. Darryl Zanuck signed her up after seeing her playing a maid in *The Mudlark* (1950), a period drama starring Irene Dunne as Queen Victoria and Alec Guinness as Benjamin Disraeli. Nunnally Johnson, the producer of the film, called her 'a beauty in the classic tradition of Helen of Troy – an actress who draws upon a bottomless well of emotion'.[4]

Smith became engaged to John Boulting, with whom she had worked on *Brighton Rock*. Again, she seemed on the up. However, Boulting left her for another woman. She met young British actor Bryan Forbes shortly afterwards.

---

[3] *Hartlepool Northern Daily Mail*, 8 May 1948, 5.
[4] Ibid.

He was on the rebound too. They quickly married. The wedding was captured in a cinema newsreel. She had a fur coat. He was young and dashing. They looked a very glamorous couple. In Hollywood, her progress could be measured by the fact that she was chosen to present an Oscar (for Best Editing) at the 1952 Academy Awards. She was a rising young star. Her biggest break yet came when she was cast opposite Tyrone Power in the remake of *Berkeley Square, I'll Never Forget You* (1951). However, just as had happened in the UK, she lost the role and was replaced by Ann Blyth.

'She was immediately reduced to the status of a road sweeper, all privileges were withdrawn overnight, and the army of sycophants and glad-handers avoided us like the plague,' Forbes, who was in LA with her, remembered in his autobiography.[5] Forbes had to return to Britain to play a part on stage in a touring production. She went back with him but was told by Fox that if she didn't return to Hollywood immediately, her contract would be terminated. She left the decision to Forbes. He encouraged her to return. She did so. Again, her prospects appeared to be improving. She was working again. However, the films she made weren't distinguished.

Her marriage was faltering. She had become pregnant but the studio (it is rumoured) forced her to have an abortion. Her strict Catholic background made this traumatic for her. It also put further pressure on her marriage, which was soon to end. (Forbes was later to marry another actress, Nanette Newman.)

Smith was adrift in Hollywood, a very long way from home, still in her twenties and having to deal with callous studio bosses at the same time her marriage was crumbling. In 1953, she left Fox, came back briefly to Britain where she made one of her best films, *Impulse* (1954), but then headed off to Italy to try to rebuild her career yet again. Again, it looked as if she had the chance to achieve the success that she had been diligently pursuing for a decade or more. She remained defiant. 'She's Italy's Irish Rebel' was the headline in a 1955 story on her in *Picture Post*. 'I'm myself. I'm Irish. I'm wild. I'm an actress,' she told the press. Smith was labelled 'the girl who hates to pose'.[6] In interviews at least, she suggested she was finally happy and professionally

---

[5]Bryan Forbes, *Notes for a Life* (London: Collins, 1974), 206–7.
[6]*Picture Post*, 15 October 1955.

fulfilled. However, if she was happy, her contentment was very short-lived. Smith married for a second time, to Italian journalist and photographer Arnaldo di Crollalanze, whose father had been a prominent fascist, a minister in Mussolini's government. Her husband's family rejected her and refused to recognize the marriage. In the spring of 1958, she made a first suicide attempt. As Reddin's documentary makes clear, the suicide attempt was regarded with complete horror by her Catholic relatives, just as the abortion had been a few years before.[7]

Smith headed back to Britain where somehow, in the late 1950s, she met Paul Rotha, the 'doyen of British documentary', who was over twenty years older than she was and was already married. The relationship between Rotha and Smith was like a messier, more destructive and incongruous version of the one between Richard Burton and Elizabeth Taylor, one marred by violence and mental illness.

Rotha had plans to take Smith back to Ireland and to direct a film with her, an adaptation of Frank O'Connor's story *Jumbo's Wife*, about a man who beats up and abuses his wife and is then out-foxed by her. Yet again, it looked as if Smith was doggedly looking to relaunch her career, this time back home in Ireland and with a director, at last, who put her interests first. The film never materialized.

In late 1961, Smith, then thirty-two, attacked Rotha, fifty-four, in a drunken rage with a knife at Rotha's London flat. She slashed her own wrists and then called the police. Rotha was rushed to St Bartholomew's Hospital.[8]

'Constance Smith is remanded again,' was the headline at the bottom of the front page of one newspaper a few days after the attack. The story came below a picture of Pat Phoenix, one of the stars of TV's *Coronation Street*, signing pin-up photographs of herself for soldiers from the King's Own Yorkshire Light Infantry. Smith's lawyer didn't apply for bail. The journalists couldn't forget Smith was a movie star. She 'appeared in the dock in dark, tight slacks and a brown coat,' they reported, still fascinated by what she wore.[9]

---

[7] *Constance Smith – Hollywood Tragedy.*
[8] *The Times*, 22 December 1961.
[9] *Herald Express*, 29 December 1961.

At the time, Rotha was making a documentary about Hitler. He had taken Smith with him to Germany during his research for the film and she had visited Dachau. In court, a psychiatrist suggested the visit had had 'an absolutely terrifying effect on her'. She became afraid to leave her flat and 'saw every German as a storm trooper . . . she felt she was living a comfortable life in what she called "the graveyard of innocent victims"'.

At the trial, her defence counsel, Michael Sherrard, played on the court's sympathy. 'The situation is this, that it really is a story of a poor and beautiful girl who was squeezed into a situation of sophistication and fame when emotionally quite unable to cope with it,' he explained. Smith, he said, had made 'two previous attempts on her own life in moments of great distress'. The magistrate, Sir Ralph Perring, told the court that 'he hoped that while in prison she would be in the hospital'.[10] In January 1962, Smith was sentenced to three months in Holloway jail for wounding Rotha. Her mother was in the court weeping as she was led away to the cells.

Rotha, who had refused to testify against her, kissed her in front of the cameras before she went into prison and was waiting for her outside the prison gates when she was released. There was something bizarre about the highly distinguished, pipe-smoking former head of documentary at the BBC being drawn into a lurid tabloid scandal. He freely told the press that he adored Smith and would stick by her whatever happened. 'I shall be waiting for her when she comes out of jail . . . I still love her very much . . . I shall visit her in Holloway as much as I can.' The stabbing, he suggested, 'changes nothing between us'.[11] At the time, his then wife, Margaret, was dangerously ill in Stoke Mandeville Hospital. Rotha was visiting her frequently and trying to make sure she didn't hear that Smith had attacked him.

When Smith was released, he was even more effusive. 'I love her now and I will love her till I die. Despite everything that has happened I know, as Connie knows, that we need each other. We are devoted to each other. While she has been in custody she has written me three, sometimes four letters. They were all

---

[10]*Aberdeen Evening Express*, 11 January 1962.
[11]*The Times*, 12 January 1962.

beautiful love letters,' he stated.[12] The couple also informed the press that they would marry as soon as Smith's marriage to di Crollalanze was dissolved.

Once Smith was out of prison, she became one of the directors of Rotha's production company. On 23 August 1962, they announced plans to *The Stage* to make a Second World War drama about the Dutch resistance and to adapt Edna O'Brien's *The Lonely Girl* for the screen. Neither project came to fruition.

A few years later, by which time they were living in Manchester, where Rotha was a research fellow at the university, Smith stabbed him for a second time and was placed on probation for three years at Manchester Crown Court. 'Mr. Justice Fisher, after hearing of their "tempestuous association" punctuated with rows and violence, made a condition that Miss Smith, aged 39, did not reside with Mr Rotha during the probation period,' the newspaper reported. 'There can be little doubt there has been a love–hate relationship,' the psychiatrist summed up the case. Both Rotha and Smith, he added, had unstable backgrounds and Mr Rotha's heavy drinking 'had aggravated the situation'. The culmination, the judge was told, came in February when 'during a row after a drinking party, Miss Smith plunged a steak knife in Rotha's back and he had to be given two blood transfusions'.[13]

Again, Rotha stood by her. She was making suicide attempts. He still harboured hopes of making her a star again. They were both alcoholics and were both devoted to one another in their own idiosyncratic way. They continued to live together after the probation period ended, and eventually married. There weren't any more film roles though. In the late 1970s, Smith and Rotha featured in the press when they were evicted from the cottage they shared in a village in Oxfordshire. They were living in poverty and squalor. Rotha died in 1984. Smith, who was to live for a further two decades, drifted towards obscurity. The Reddin documentary has a poignant story about how she became a cleaner in a psychiatric hospital and the patients there recognized her from a film that was showing on television. There are accounts of her living rough. At the end of her life, she was based in a council flat in Islington. She

[12]BFI microfiche cuttings on Constance Smith.
[13]*The Times*, 4 October 1968.

died in the summer of 2003, aged seventy-four, and was cremated in Islington Crematorium. It was an anonymous and solitary death.

Smith's story has more pathos than glory in it but it is still a remarkable tale of someone who came from nothing, tried three times in three different cultures to establish herself as a star and eventually ended with nothing. She had beauty and talent and far more resilience than her detractors at the Rank Organisation or the US studios ever acknowledged but a career that took her from Limerick to Hollywood foundered all too quickly.

17

Anthony Minghella

When Anthony Minghella (1954–2008) was growing up on the Isle of Wight, he used to stand on the beach with his friends and gaze in yearning at the horizon. The island was less than ninety miles from London and only four miles from the mainland but, to Minghella, England seemed impossibly far away.

Minghella was born in Ryde, the biggest town on the Isle of Wight, in 1954. His parents, Edward and Gloria Minghella, both of Italian immigrant stock, ran a cafe which sold its own name brand ice cream. The family lived above the cafe. There was a cinema, The Commodore, next door. As a child, Minghella had access to it. The cinema's projectionist was a lodger with the Minghellas and used to give young Anthony film posters, with which he decorated his room.

Anthony loved movies from an early age and was sometimes traumatized by them. He used to talk in interviews about being left at home on his own when his parents were busy working. He had turned on the TV once and seen, completely by chance, a broadcast of Josef von Sternberg's *The Blue Angel* (1930), starring Marlene Dietrich and Emil Jannings. A story about a school teacher (Jannings) who becomes obsessed with a cabaret performer (Dietrich), the film was a tragicomic study in masochism and sexual humiliation – not at all what you expected an eight-year-old to be watching. The fact that he had seen it on his own made it all the more tantalizing and terrifying.

The film both shocked and fascinated him. When his parents returned, they found him in a pitiful state. 'What I remember was that it was the first time a piece of fiction had had such a devastating emotional effect on me,' he later recalled. 'It was the first time I realised there was an adult world – that adults

Anthony Minghella. Photo: Mike Marsland/WireImage via Getty Images.

could damage each other or destroy each other emotionally.' *The Blue Angel* taught him that love could be 'a rupturing and damaging emotion' as well as a 'healing' one. He also had youthful intimations of the film's erotic power, a sense that it was dealing with forbidden but tantalizing subject matter.[1]

When he wasn't at school, Minghella would be working in the family cafe or selling ice cream in the cinema. However, he had a bohemian side. He loved art and music and liked to hang around the art department at school, smoking cigarettes and listening to jazz. He had become interested in poetry through listening to the music of Leonard Cohen and then buying a book of his verse.

He had a piano and bass guitar. He was good enough as a teenager to play in a band that landed a record contract but the band 'fell apart' before managing to complete the album it had been signed up to record. He was later to become a successful playwright and one of the most celebrated British film directors of his era but, at this stage of his life, he claimed, it didn't even occur to him to think about writing or filmmaking as careers.

---

[1] In Geoffrey Macnab, *Screen Epiphanies: Film-makers on the Films that Inspired Them* (London: BFI, 2009).

Minghella may have lived next to a cinema but he didn't have a clue how films were made. He might have enjoyed reading but he didn't have much sense of the process that went into writing or publishing books. As he put it of his family and friends, 'we were just receivers of culture. We were lucky if we ever saw any. I don't mean this was some kind of privation. It was simply a way that you experienced culture merely as product.'

The most obvious outlet for Minghella's artistic ambition was music. He knew people who were songwriters and was sometimes hired to play the piano in bars and restaurants.

Minghella called himself an 'inadequate pupil' but had always been bright, doing well at both Sandown Grammar School on the island and at independent school St John's, Portsmouth. Dreams of musical stardom fast receding, he eventually enrolled at Hull University to study drama. His parents were confused by his choice. They wanted him to stay at home on the island and work in the family business. Celebrated English poet Philip Larkin was the university librarian. Minghella liked his work. 'I realised that the guy who made these books also walked around and did his shopping. He must have therefore sat down at some point and written these poems. It started to occur to me to make a deconstruction of the finished article,' Minghella remembered the process through which he realized that art, including cinema, was made: it wasn't just dropped down a chimney by a stork. It had to be created, produced and then distributed. He started to write and put on plays.

His parents may have been immigrants who sold ice cream but he was sent to good schools and was given opportunities. 'I think that the entitlement that you require to have to think you can tell somebody a story, that was something that didn't even occur to me. I didn't think I would ever be in the position to have the authority to tell a story. I was in a culture and social territory that wasn't empowered in any shape and form,' the director later claimed. 'It never occurred to me until I went to university that ordinary people could have access to the complex club that is the world of cinema.'[2] However, he had forged himself multiple points of entry to the arts. He was a musician (his

---

[2]Ibid.

Guardian obituary talked about his early dreams of being a pop star[3]), a writer and an academic.

Minghella was especially intrigued by cinema because he felt it was the medium in which his literary and musical ambitions and skills could best be combined. He was pragmatic enough to realize that openings for young writer-directors in 1970s British cinema were in very short supply. 'If you were in your early twenties in 1975 to 1978 and were looking for a professional apprenticeship as a writer, the cinema wasn't an option,' he told interviewer Timothy Bricknell. 'You couldn't say, I'm going to go and work as a movie-maker. You got a job writing for studio theatre. That's where you got your opportunities.'[4]

As it turned out, the Hull University Drama Department provided an excellent space in which to experiment. Sure enough, the department had a Bolex camera and a Steenbeck that students could use to shoot and edit film material, even if only to be used as short excerpts in their stage productions. During his time as a student at Hull, Minghella produced his first play, a stage adaptation of Gabriel Josipovici's story 'Mobius the Stripper'. He also made his first film, *A Little Like Drowning*, which was filmed on the Isle of Wight over fifteen days in 1977, and which he later turned into a play. He had borrowed the money to make it and it took him years to pay it back. This wasn't an auspicious beginning but the fact he had made it shows both his versatility and his resilience.

Minghella's pathway towards the film business came partly via children's television. He honed his screenwriting skills on the long-running BBC TV drama *Grange Hill*, devised by Phil Redmond and set in a secondary school. Minghella was the show's script editor. Under Minghella, the series became known for the skilful and sensitive way it broached hard-hitting social and political issues. This may have been a series about teenage school kids but it was topical as well as entertaining. During the 1980s, Minghella also wrote episodes of soap opera *EastEnders* and detective series *Morse*. There was no cultural snobbery about him. He may by then have been an academic, steeped in the works of Samuel Beckett and an expert in medieval theatre, but his

---

[3]https://www.theguardian.com/uk/2008/mar/18/filmnews.theatrenews.
[4]Ibid.

collaborators on *Grange Hill* found him inspirational (see Chapter 23 on Amma Asante).

He always remembered his roots. 'I have never resented my childhood. It was a blessed childhood in the sense that I had a wonderful family. I don't resent the lack of cultural information I had as a child. It made me enquiring and curious. I've always imagined that you find your culture rather than receiving it on a plate,' he later explained to director Alan Parker just why he was so fascinated by everything from opera to soap opera, from modernist fiction to kids' TV.[5] Having grown up without easy access to books, films and art, he had no preconceptions or prejudices. He was enquiring and enthusiastic about all forms of culture, high or low, popular or esoteric. In the 1980s, Minghella was busily writing theatre plays and radio plays as well as TV scripts and screenplays.

Look at the films he went on to make and you see that he had a chameleon-like quality. His first hit, which suggested he might have potential as a movie director, was the small-scale, very intimate *Truly, Madly, Deeply* (1989), a poignant comedy-romance about a woman (Juliet Stevenson) trying to get over the death of her boyfriend (Alan Rickman). The film was made quickly for the BBC but was shown at the London Film Festival and released in cinemas. The film won BAFTAs and Minghella was heralded as 'Most Promising Newcomer' at the Evening Standard Film Awards.

The film also caught the eye of the US producer and distributor Harvey Weinstein. He wrote in *The Times* after Minghella's untimely death following what had seemed to be a routine tonsil surgery operation:

> My acquisitions executives in England passed on the film; two weeks later an assistant at Miramax named Anne Greenhaul called me herself and said: 'You must see this movie.' So I screened it. I laughed and I wept. And celebrated. By the morning I tracked down the director, Anthony Minghella, and called him. 'I must have your movie.' 'You're too late,' he said. 'It's gone.' He had already made a deal with another company. 'I will never be late for you again,' I said.[6]

---

[5] *Minghella on Minghella*, Timothy Bricknell (London: Faber, 2005). Anthony Minghella, an appreciation, by Sir Alan Parker, March, 2008. http://alanparker.com/essay/anthony-minghella-an-appreciation/.
[6] *The Times*, 10 April 2008.

Weinstein was to become a reviled figure, a convicted sexual predator whose reputation fell apart when multiple witnesses testified to his abusive behaviour. However, in the 1990s, he was a dynamic figure in the US independent film world with a genius for marketing. One of the more benign acts of his career was to champion Minghella. The British director may have made his name with a chamber piece but, once he began working with Weinstein's company, Miramax, he made some very ambitious films. There was his multiple Oscar winner *The English Patient* (1996), his Patricia Highsmith adaptation *The Talented Mr. Ripley* (1999) and US Civil War drama *Cold Mountain* (2003). These were all big, star-driven international productions. Minghella showed a Lean-like flair for set-pieces involving armies of extras but all these films were character-driven at core and had the same emotional intimacy that had characterized *Truly, Madly, Deeply*.

At the same time he was directing films, Minghella was producing them. Alongside his friend and fellow filmmaker Sydney Pollack, he was a partner in Mirage Enterprises. He was also directing operas and even, on one occasion, a party political broadcast. He was at once a very British figure, alert to the subtleties and ironies of the class system, and an international one. The glib explanation is that he drew the best both from his experiences as a boy on the Isle of Wight and academic in Hull and from his Italian background. He was both disciplined and flamboyant. He thrived in the solitary environment of the writer and in the middle of the biggest and most chaotic film sets.

By 2003, Minghella, the boy who didn't even know that such a thing as a career in the film industry was possible, had moved into the heart of the British cinema establishment. He served five years as Chairman of the British Film Institute (2003–7), proselytizing tirelessly on behalf of British film culture and protecting the BFI from the machinations of the UK Film Council, the public industry body for film.

Like other subjects in this book, Minghella came into filmmaking in a very roundabout way. The first step was getting off the island. Then came drama and academia. Every step of the way, he was refining skills which would eventually enable him to direct films on the scale of *The English Patient* (1996) and *Cold Mountain* (2003). He wrote and wrote. There was radio and TV drama; there was children's TV. As the obituaries noted after his untimely death in 2008, he had gone from script-editing *Grange Hill* (the long-running children's TV drama produced by the BBC) to writing and directing Oscar-winning epic films on a scale that might have made even David Lean blink – and it all started with a boy on an island staring across the sea at the mainland and wondering if he could ever get there.

18

Hanif Kureishi[1]

Novelist and playwright Hanif Kureishi had a transformative effect on the British film industry of the 1980s without having had any particular desire or intention to work in that industry. His screenplay for *My Beautiful Laundrette* (1985), which he wrote while visiting relatives in Karachi, gave the sector a much needed boost at a time when cinema admissions were at one of their lowest points. This was a comedy-drama about a love affair between a young Pakistani man and a white English skinhead. It was subversive, wryly satirical about the greed and selfishness unleashed in Thatcherite society, and very funny. It also confirmed Daniel Day-Lewis, who played the skinhead, as a major British movie star.

Kureishi soon wrote a follow-up, *Sammy and Rosie Get Laid* (1987), set against the backcloth of Thatcher-era riots in London. The eminent British historian Norman Stone railed against the film in an article in *the Sunday Times*, bemoaning its 'overall feeling of disgust and decay' and its 'sleazy, sick hedonism', and lumping it together with other anti-Thatcher movies of the era that he deplored almost as much. 'For pointless sensationalism, sloppy attitudinising, and general disgustingness it deserves some sort of prize.'[2]

While being attacked by right wing journalists like Stone, Kureishi also provoked the wrath of certain Muslim groups, who protested against what they perceived as the lax sexual politics of his films. 'If you get that kind of

---

[1]Unless otherwise cited, quotes in this chapter come from the author's interview with Hanif Kureishi, London July 2019.
[2]*Sunday Times*, 10 January 1988.

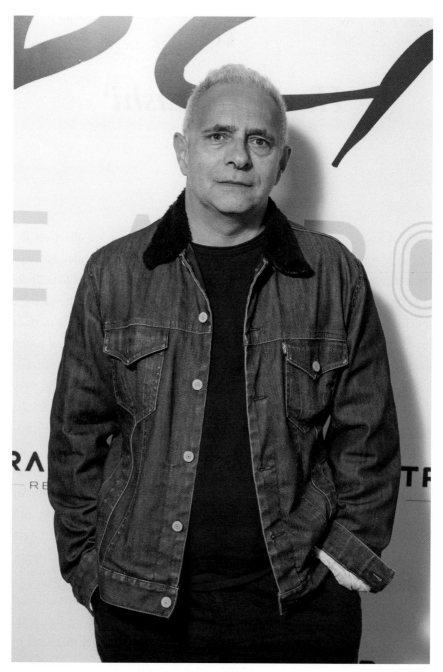

Hanif Kureishi. Photo: Jeff Spicer/Getty Images.

result, you're probably doing something that's right. It doesn't bother me. It makes me laugh. I am pleased that people are engaging with one's work. It means that it has hit home in some way,' Kureishi says of the angry reactions to his first two features. In later years, he would occasionally meet Norman Stone through his publisher, Matthew Evans at Faber, and enjoyed their encounters. 'He used to come to Faber parties and dinners. He was always drunk but he was a clever man and good fun in that old-fashioned, drunken hooligan way. He just liked to make trouble and annoy people – and we didn't mind being annoyed.'

On the day Kureishi is interviewed for the book, Boris Johnson had just been confirmed as the new British prime minister. To Kureishi, this was a sign of how reactionary attitudes like those displayed by Stone have become increasingly mainstream. 'In those days [the 1980s], somebody who was as absurdly right wing as Norman Stone was laughable. Now they're prime minister!'

Kureishi (born in 1954) acknowledges that he wouldn't have started writing for cinema if it hadn't been for Channel 4, the UK public broadcaster which first went on air in 1982. He was a young writer who had grown up in relatively humble circumstances in suburban Bromley. 'I am a mixed race kid from south London,' he declares, as if it is a badge of honour. 'I didn't go to Oxbridge. I didn't go to public school. I got three O levels.'

His Pakistani father, Rafiushan (Shanoo) Kureishi, was from a distinguished family which had been displaced by partition. He was working as a clerk at the Pakistan Embassy. As they built a new life in England, the Kureishis went on occasional family trips to the cinema, maybe to *Zulu* (1964) or *Lawrence of Arabia* (1962) ('"Florence of Arabia" as we called it'). They watched westerns on TV together, generally siding with the Native Americans rather than the cowboys. 'My dad always identified with the Indians. Even if they were red Indians, they were still Indians.'

Growing up in Bromley, Kureishi felt he received a terrible education. 'In south London, in the 1950s and 1960s, the education was shit. No wonder you turned into Tim Roth or Gary Oldman,' he name checks the actors who played young skinheads and thugs in Alan Clarke dramas. 'I am glad to be out. It [Bromley] was very, very anti-intellectual. They hated you if you said you listened to Beethoven yesterday. They'd go crazy. They hated it, thought you were a snob and getting above yourself. Also, they hated Pakis. So there wasn't much there for me.'

Nonetheless, the young Kureishi was part of the burgeoning punk-driven youth rebellion. He tells colourful stories about taking LSD as a young teenager with future rock star Billy Idol. 'We went camping to Bournemouth. We dropped acid. We set our tents up and tripped out all night. We woke up in the morning and the cops were looking in the tent. We realized we had camped in a park . . . we thought we were in the wilds and it was going to be like Dennis Hopper but we were in a park and the cops sent us home. They rang up our mums and said, "We've found your son tripping off his head in a park in Bournemouth".'

He was connected to local bands like Siouxsie and the Banshees (he had been at primary school with the bass player and founder of the band Steve Severin) and he had friends who ran away to work for Vivienne Westwood or Malcolm McLaren. He was part of the 'Bromley contingent'.

Although his father's relatives had had strong involvement in Bollywood, cinema was not a major actor in Kureishi's upbringing. 'What influenced me, I guess, was British television: *Play for Today*, the Ken Loach stuff, Alan Clarke, Stephen Frears and the work he did with Alan Bennett, early Stephen Poliakoff and so on.'

Kureishi didn't start watching movies in earnest until he came to London in the mid-1970s, when he was doing a philosophy degree at King's College and was working as an usher at the Royal Court. He'd watch Godard and Bergman films at the Academy in Oxford Street or at the ICA. 'But there was no way you would see Bergman films in Bromley.' One film the 'Bromley contingent' did admire was Bob Fosse's *Cabaret* (1972), starring Liza Minnelli as Sally Bowles, the flamboyant nightclub artist in Weimar Berlin. To Kureishi and his friends, this was a movie with a punk sensibility, an anti-fascist attitude and an enjoyable whiff of decadence. They also liked *The Night Porter* (1974) and *The Damned* (1969) for similar reasons. 'Although it [Croydon] was shitty, it was quite lively. There were bands. We got dressed up, came up to London.'

Eventually, Kureishi and his friends decamped to the capital to live. He eked out a precarious existence writing pornographic stories for *Game* magazine. It was a heady period. 'We were all on the dole. It was the time of The Clash and The Jam when London was really wild and dirty and cold. We were living in freezing cold places, [it was the time of] the Sex Pistols, The Damned and Derek Jarman.' Music, film and fashion intermingled.

The precocious Kureishi had started writing novels when he was still a teenager and had begun writing plays for the Royal Court Theatre at a very young age. There, he encountered venerated (and very 'posh') figures from British film and theatre like Lindsay Anderson, Tony Richardson, Bill Gaskill and Anthony Page. He went on to work at the Riverside Studios in Hammersmith and to have a play produced by the Royal Shakespeare Company (*Outskirts* in 1981) when he was still in his twenties. Prolific and successful though he was, it didn't even occur to him to try out the film business.

Script editor and publisher Walter Donohue, whom he had met at Riverside in the late 1970s, recommended him to Channel 4, thereby setting in motion the events that would soon lead to his Oscar nomination. 'I think in those days, I got most of the ethnic work. In those days, when Channel 4 started, they had to have an ethnic minority [representation]. In fact, they had an ethnic minority department, run by Farrukh Dhondy. I refused to go in there. I wouldn't go in the room at all. I said I am not going to be in the minority room. Besides, Kureishi points out, he was only 'half a minority'. His mother was white English. If he was going to go near the room, he would put only one foot in it.

Whatever his reservations about the 'minority' department, Kureishi accepted the commission to write what would become *My Beautiful Laundrette*. At the time, he thought he was writing it for TV. He associated British cinema with Goldcrest and David Lean movies, not with the project he was embarking on. 'I never thought of writing a David Lean film because that world wasn't accessible to me.' He felt a much greater affinity with Alan Clarke's TV movies like *Scum* (1977) and *Made in Britain* (1982), featuring punks, skinheads and delinquents ('rough white boys beating people up') who reminded him of the people he grew up alongside in Bromley.

One of the attractions of the film business was the money. Kureishi was paid £20,000 for scripting *My Beautiful Laundrette*, a fortune compared to what he received for his plays. Once he had completed a draft, he discovered the home address of director Stephen Frears from David Gothard, who ran Riverside

Studios, and posted the *Beautiful Laundrette* script through Frears's letterbox. 'I loved his work, mostly the Alan Bennett stuff,' he explains his course of action.

Frears was immediately enthused. He had been making occasional pop videos for a thrusting new production company called Working Title, run by Sarah Radclyffe and young New Zealander Tim Bevan. 'Being Stephen and a bit perverse, he said let's go with these kids [at Working Title]. They've never made a movie but I am sure they would be good at it.' That was how the production company which went on to make *Notting Hill* and *Bridget Jones* and to earn billions at the box office received its first big break. At the time, Kureishi remembers them as 'scruffy kids in a scruffy office and with no money whatsoever'.

The writer's own situation wasn't much better. 'I was on the dole. I had literally no money,' Kureishi remembers of the period before his amazing windfall from Channel 4.

> I had never thought I would be a screenwriter. I just wrote this film because they asked me and I needed the money and I had these stories from my past that I hadn't really got hold of yet. I had this 'uncle', a friend of the family who was running laundrettes. My dad thought I was never going to make a living as a writer and so he sent me off with my uncle. He thought I could run laundrettes.

Kureishi wrote the screenplay for *My Beautiful Laundrette* in Karachi partly as a way of dealing with his boredom and insomnia while staying there. The story came to him easily. As for the specific technique of screenwriting, that was something he had taught himself by watching videos while studying classic old screenplays (some of which Faber had started to publish in book form). The concept was simple enough – a gay Pakistani and a skinhead running a laundrette together. He was used to writing dialogue. He just needed to find the structure. 'It is not more difficult than writing a play.'

Frears kept his young writer on set throughout shooting. 'Stephen wanted me to be around because he didn't know anything about Pakistanis. I didn't know a huge amount about Pakistanis myself but I knew more about it than he did.' Kureishi helped with the casting, bringing actors he'd worked with previously like Saeed Jaffrey and Rita Wolf. They would meet at Frears's house and the director would ask them: 'Do you know anyone else? Do you have any mates who are actors?' This was Frears's way of dealing with the lack of established British-Asian actors.

'There weren't many young [British-Asian] actors around because there weren't many jobs for them. It was all a bit chaotic. Also, it was made as a television film. It wasn't made for the cinema. It was shot on Super 16 mm. It wasn't shot on 35 mm like a proper movie. It was just going to be shown on Sunday night at 10 o'clock.' This was a 'scruffy little' film about a gay love affair between a skinhead and a Pakistani. 'Proper' British movies didn't deal with this type of subject matter. Kureishi learned on the job. If a scene didn't work, Frears would get him to 'go round the back' and rewrite it.

When *My Beautiful Laundrette* was selected for the Edinburgh Film Festival, Kureishi and his collaborators travelled up to Scotland for the premiere. In Edinburgh, he ended up sharing a single room with Tim Bevan and the film's star, Daniel Day-Lewis. Kureishi insisted on having the one bed and left the other two to sleep on the floor.

> I said, fuck it, I am going into the bed – I am the oldest. Dan and Tim looked a bit bewildered and I got into the fucking bed and went to sleep. We stayed there for about three days. We had a really good fucking time. It was a real laugh. But we all slept in one room. Can you believe it? Tim and Dan were lying on the floor next to me, in their sleeping bags.

The Edinburgh screening was to transform the lives of all three of them. Its reception was so enthusiastic that Channel 4 realized it might be worth blowing up the film to 35 mm and putting it out in cinemas. Day-Lewis, who also starred in Merchant–Ivory's E. M. Forster adaptation *A Room with a View* (1985), released a few months later, was emerging as a major star. *My Beautiful Laundrette* was full of zest and humour but also captured perfectly the spirit of the times. 'I remember a friend of mine, [playwright] Nicky Wright, who worked at the Royal Court, saying he went to see the film and it seemed to him that it was exactly what Britain seemed to be like today.' Kureishi realized that the film was (as he puts it) 'just ahead of the zeitgeist'.

Oscar-winning producer Donna Gigliotti (who had worked with Martin Scorsese on *Raging Bull* (1980)) helped secure US distribution. The film was released theatrically in the UK after Edinburgh by Romaine Hart's Mainline Pictures – and Kureishi remembers that Hart was able to re-decorate her kitchen three times on the back of its success. Suddenly, Kureishi was the toast of New York as well as London. Soon, he had an Oscar nomination to his name. 'Everything completely changed for me,' the writer remembers.

Hollywood soon came calling. Kureishi went to Los Angeles to test the water. 'They said to me, "Come and live here. Sit in one of those cabins and type away. We can get you a job doing this, that and the other."' Spending time in California reminded him that his real desire was to write about Britain. He didn't want to be just another ex-pat British writer 'tapping away' on a typewriter in a cabin, on call for the studios.

> I thought I am really interested in Britain and in London. I am really interested in race so why would I want to see in Los Angeles and write about all that stuff. I'd rather sit in Shepherd's Bush and write about it. That's my subject. You move to Los Angeles as a British writer and you lose your subject. You don't have roots in your area any more. The idea of me sitting in Los Angeles, writing about the experiences of Pakistani immigrants in London would have been almost impossible. I was still researching, thinking and learning about that.

Kureishi had 'grown up with street fascism' in the Bromley of the 1960s and had witnessed at first hand the intimidatory behaviour of organizations like the National Front and British National Party in the 1970s. He was drawn to the left politically and wanted to be in the thick of the action, writing about sex, class and racism, dealing with 'contemporary stuff'.

Back to Britain Kureishi came. Margaret Thatcher was still British prime minister. 'She was great for the arts,' Kureishi remembers of the right-wing Iron Lady. Thatcher was detested by many of those working in film, TV, fashion and music but their animus against her inspired some of their very best work. They also shared her entrepreneurialism. 'You could say Channel 4 was a Thatcherite idea. It was a little business ... it was the beginning of the idea of production companies. There had never been production companies before. Now, there are hundreds of production companies in Soho, each one a little business.' He continues: 'Thatcher was fantastic for dissent. She really created this wall of fury which came out of British youth culture . . . she was great, very stimulating. Our hatred was very useful at that time.'

Bursting with anti-Thatcher energy of his own, Kureishi wrote his second screenplay, *Sammy and Rosie Get Laid* (1987), also directed by Stephen Frears and which Kureishi described as a 'declaration of war on the British establishment'. The film combined the portrayal of the very complex lives of middle-class couple Sammy and Rosie (Ayub Khan-Din and Frances Barber) with an apocalyptic vision of a riot-torn London. 'It was more like an agit-prop film, if you know what I mean: one of those instant films like you see in the theatre. There could be a play about the miners or about Thatcher or about school teachers or about strikes or whatever whereas *My Beautiful Laundrette* really came out of my childhood,' the writer says of the scattergun satire in his second screenplay.

After *Sammy and Rosie* came *London Kills Me* (1991), a picaresque London street fable set among the homeless and drug addicts. By then Frears was in the US, directing films like *Dangerous Liaisons* (1988) and *The Grifters* (1990). Producer Tim Bevan therefore suggested that Kureishi should direct the new film himself. 'I don't think I am very confident as a film director and I don't think I am a natural film director but I had a go.' The film was panned by critics and struggled at the box office (although it did acquire a cult status in later years).

Kureishi was peeved by the failure. 'I remember Stephen Frears saying that wanting to make films in Britain made him feel like a freak, as if it were an unnatural activity,' he wrote in the *Guardian* about the difficulty of getting any cinemas to play his directorial debut.[3] At the same time, though, he was half-accustomed to empty houses. 'I had worked in the theatre and so I was used to not having an audience. *My Beautiful Laundrette* was an exception. 'Mostly, you did a play at the Royal Court, at the Theatre Upstairs, or the Donmar Warehouse. You didn't get big audiences and you didn't make money. It was life as normal for me. Doing *London Kills Me* was no different from doing a play at the Soho Poly.'

Even so, he decided the film business was a dead end. Instead, he would try to sum up his experiences growing up in 1960s and 1970s Britain as a

---

[3]*Guardian*, 16 October 1991.

mixed-race kid in a novel: 'to say it all in one book,' as he puts it. This was *The Buddha of Suburbia* (published in 1990). 'It was partly the story of my childhood. It was to do with punk, it was to do with race, it was to do with sexuality . . . I would rather do that than become just another re-write man in Los Angeles.'

It was telling that Kureishi didn't feel that cinema could do justice to the themes of *The Buddha of Suburbia*. There were offers to make it into a movie from David Byrne (the lead singer of US new-wave band Talking Heads and also an occasional film director) and Hong Kong-born but US-based director Wayne Wang. 'But I really wanted to do it as a telly [drama] because it would be four hours. Four hours is longer than two hours – and so you could tell more of the story.' By then, he had been talking to director Roger Michell, whom he had first encountered at the Royal Court. Michell seemed a good fit for the material. He understood the ironic British humour and local references in a way an American outsider wouldn't have done.

Kureishi had entered the British film business at a time of extraordinary fluidity and new opportunity. As he recalls it, 'there wasn't an establishment'. Companies like Working Title were just starting out. The days of big Goldcrest and David Lean movies were over. Low-budget features like *My Beautiful Laundrette* and *Letter to Brezhnev* were being made by irreverent young filmmakers. The BBC and Channel 4 were backing young talent.

Thirty years on, the writer continues to work occasionally in cinema. He is a cinephile with a passion for film noir, 'corrupt, lonely gunmen, insurance scams and all that shadowy filth'. His 2017 novel *The Nothing*, whose main character is an elderly, wheelchair-bound filmmaker terrified of being cuckolded, is written in the spirit of noir. Other filmmakers look to adapt his work. The French director Patrice Chéreau had a notable success with his film version of Kureishi's 1999 novel *Intimacy* (2001), an intense drama about marital break-up and infidelity which won the Golden Bear at the Berlin Festival while sparking controversy because of its explicit sex scenes.

Kureishi had mixed feelings about Chéreau's film. 'French directors are much more arty than someone like Stephen Frears,' he suggests. 'Frears is a much more down-to-earth, cor blimey kind of filmmaker. They [French directors] are much more arty, much more self-conscious. They're auteurs.

Stephen hates the idea of being an auteur. He'll slap you if you call him an auteur. He is just a filmmaker who wants a job.'

He admired Chéreau's taste and intelligence but baulked at the lack of humour in *Intimacy*. 'I said to him that if I had written it [the screenplay], I would have put at least one joke in.' Kureishi's work is notable for the frank way it addresses sexuality but, as he puts it, he uses the sex as a 'social device'. In *My Beautiful Laundrette*, the affair between the Pakistani and the white skinhead allowed him to make observations about race, immigration and the disenfranchisement of white working-class boys. These boys might have grown into thugs but Kureishi had known them since they were five. 'I used the sex to make numerous points about social change in Britain. I don't think Patrice was interested in that. He was just making a film about a couple who fuck.'

The writer was far happier with the 1997 film version of his story *My Son the Fanatic*, which he scripted and which was directed by Udayan Prasad. A prophetic drama set in the north of England and made several years before 9/11, this was the story of a very worldly, hard-drinking Pakistani-born taxi driver in love with a prostitute, and his zealot of a son who becomes a religious fundamentalist. The son is disgusted with the decadence of Western living. The film deals with similar themes to those explored in his 1995 novel *The Black Album* (1995), about the radicalization of young British Muslims after the fatwa issued against writer Salman Rushdie.

'I had got very interested in taxi drivers. That's what mostly Muslim men in the north of London do as jobs. We drive all the taxis. If you take a minicab in London, it is probably one of our boys. Taxi drivers are mobile … they go everywhere and know everybody,' Kureishi explains the themes of *My Son the Fanatic*.

Kureishi remembers that George Faber, the BBC executive who commissioned the project, came to Halifax during shooting and was utterly flabbergasted by the hostility with which some of the Muslim locals treated him. 'I remember a fundamentalist running at him and attacking him, saying you BBC Jews come up to our town – you can fuck off! George was absolutely shocked. Nobody had spoken to him like that in his life.' Although he grew up in south London, Kureishi spent several months as a student at Lancaster University, taking a philosophy degree. (He was thrown out for not doing any work.) He understood the mentality of the northerners and their suspicion of London-based media folk.

Kureishi has had a prodigious career as a novelist and playwright but still sounds wary about a British film business in which, at one point, he looked likely to become a pivotal figure. 'I haven't written a film for ages. I don't really work in the cinema any more. It is partly because it is such a dodgy business,' he suggests. He likes to write 'on spec'. He has completed his screenplays for projects like *The Mother* (2003), *Venus* (2006) and *Le Week-End* (2013) and then taken them to Roger Michell. 'And Roger gets them made.' He says he is 'too old' to spend months working on a film project which may never get made. 'I am more likely to write essays or stories or a novel or whatever than to spend all that time on a movie which may or may not be made. I can't waste all the creativity on something that may end up sitting in a drawer.'

The veteran writer adds that he can't think when he last saw a good British film.

> I don't think the British film industry is very good on the contemporary and I don't think it is good at bringing new people on. One of the biggest, most interesting things that has happened in Britain since the war has been black music, urban music, hip hop and you never see that in the British cinema. That whole area of British life, which is what Ken Loach would have been doing if he was twenty-five, has not really been done. I haven't seen a great Brexit film. I don't feel the British cinema is engaging with the contemporary in any interesting way at all.

19

Julian Fellowes[1]

Julian Fellowes's path towards the top of the British film and TV industry could hardly have been more circuitous. Fellowes was a moderately successful, middle-aged actor and occasional writer when he won an Oscar for his screenplay for Robert Altman's *Gosford Park* (2001). That unlikely success was to transform his career and eventually to establish him as one of the key figures in the flourishing of British film and TV drama over the following two decades. The TV drama he later created, *Downton Abbey*, which ran for six series between 2010 and 2015 and later spawned a 2019 film, turned into a full-blown cultural phenomenon – the most popular costume drama of its time in the UK and a runaway hit in the US as well. His story is one of talent, perseverance and a series of lucky accidents.

Unlike many of the other figures covered in this book, Fellowes comes from a privileged, upper-middle-class background. His father, Peregrine Fellowes (1912–99), was a diplomat and businessman who worked for the Foreign Office and for Shell. Peregrine had no connection with the British film industry whatsoever other than a friendship with a neighbour, David Kingsley, who happened to be managing director of British Lion, one of the leading production companies of the time. However, he did like the cinema. 'My parents were very film-minded which actually, for the kind of people they were, was rather unusual for the 1950s and 1960s. Most of their friends probably didn't see a film more than once or twice from January to December but they used to go and take us to films pretty regularly.'

---

[1] The material in this chapter comes from the author's interview with Julian Fellowes, London, July 2019.

Julian Fellowes. Photo: David Livingston/Getty Images.

In Fellowes's early childhood, the family home was in South Kensington and his parents would whisk the children off to the Forum on the Fulham Road or to a cinema in Putney almost every weekend. These were the 1950s and few films were shown on TV. If you missed a film during its initial run, you would probably never see it again. 'We used to go quite a lot to Putney which was the last stop before they [film releases] left London. We would race over the bridge and see things just before they were finished.'

When Fellowes was nine, the family moved into a country house in Sussex and the cinema visits became markedly less frequent. Nonetheless, Fellowes had already acquired the film-going habit. He had a maiden aunt who also loved the movies. When she was asked to look after him and his siblings, she would often pass the time with a cinema visit. He talks with nostalgia of the films he saw in this period, among them *Seven Brides for Seven Brothers* (1954) and *The King and I* (1956). The aunt didn't much like children's films and so would take the Fellowes children to musicals instead. His parents were more adventurous and he recalls seeing many double bills, often with British B movie crime dramas starring Bonar Colleano accompanying the main attraction.

As an English literature student at Cambridge University in the late 1960s, Fellowes was an ardent cinema-goer, seeing films 'eight, nine, ten times a week'. A moment of epiphany came from a very unlikely source. One evening, he saw Michael Winner's *I'll Never Forget What's'isname* (1967), starring Oliver Reed as a despairing young ad agency executive and Orson Welles as his overbearing boss. 'For some reason, I was completely obsessed by this film. I've watched it since and I don't really understand why.' He went to see it again and again and again. By the eleventh viewing, he had made the life-changing decision that he didn't have to find 'a job of some grown-up nature and then have my interest on film on the side'. Instead, he could try to work in the film and television business himself. He was eighteen at the time and not very aware of anyone's role in film beyond that of the actors.

Another indirect influence on this decision was Kingsley, the family neighbour who ran British Lion and sometimes had Peter Sellers to stay for the weekend. Without really understanding what Kingsley did, Fellowes realized that there were ways of making a living in the film business. The English literature student who also performed in the Cambridge Footlights decided that he would become a professional actor, go to Hollywood and become 'a great success'. The only problem was working out how.

Being posh, Fellowes recalled, wasn't an advantage for someone who aspired to work in British cinema at the time he left university in the early 1970s. The anti-'posh' animus didn't necessarily come with a malicious side to it but simply reflected the attitude that, if you did come from the upper rungs of society, 'you were bound to be useless. You weren't going to be talented. You had been too protected. You weren't made of the right stuff.' The film world (Fellowes felt then and still feels now) was the preserve of 'the left-leaning intellectual urban elite. Those were the people who are largely in control of it.'

Fellowes portrays a film and TV establishment in which access was strictly policed and the new entrants were expected to be

the daughters and sons of school teachers and professionals. They [the establishment] have very fixed political and philosophical views that are acceptable within the world of what come to be called the 'luvvies'. It is pretty didactic. There is no one so illiberal as a liberal. And if you don't agree with them, you're wrong. There is no way round it.

If you didn't fit into the 'intellectual, urban, upper-middle-class mould', Fellowes discovered, you struggled to break into the industry. It didn't make any difference whether you were from an impoverished working-class background or you were trying to gatecrash the film world from the world of advertising (as David Puttnam did) or if you had been to one of the top public schools. You simply wouldn't fit in. 'That was what Puttnam was pressing against but it was also what I was pressing against.'

Fellowes sees the Tony Blair years as the 'apotheosis' of this liberal, metropolitan elite – a time when the 'values of what came to be known at one time as the champagne socialists were reflected wherever you looked. It didn't matter whether it was the head of the Royal Shakespeare [Company] or the head of the National Gallery, they were all Blairites.'

In his early seventies, when he gave an interview for this book, Fellowes looked as if he might have walked out of a P. G. Wodehouse Blandings novel. He sits in the House of Lords, on the Conservative benches. Dressed immaculately in a grey suit, sipping tea and nibbling shortbread in a Sloane Square brasserie, he was every inch the English gentleman. Nonetheless, as he points out, he would never have had a career in the film and TV industry without the 'help of America'. 'America, they don't really care about any of that stuff. They care about whether you are any good and if you can do something better than other people can do it. You're just as harshly judged but you're judged by your work. What was your last picture, what have you got lined up, who wants to work with you – all of that. That may be snobbish and rather limited in its way too but at least it has the benefit of being connected to the standard of your work as opposed to your philosophical position.'

After leaving Cambridge, Fellowes was accepted by the Webber Douglas Drama School. 'I didn't tell my parents until that point because I thought why have the row if I don't get in anywhere.' He started drama school in January 1971, finished in June 1973 and then launched himself on the profession in earnest. Although he wrote three romantic novels under the pseudonym Rebecca Greville which were published by Robert Hale, earning him some much needed 'pocket money', he hadn't contemplated scriptwriting or directing. His focus then was entirely on the acting career.

Starting out in provincial rep, Fellowes had a perfectly respectable career as a character actor. In the mid-1970s, he was cast alongside Hayley Mills in West End play *A Touch of Spring* at the Comedy Theatre. The run lasted a year. He went to work at Harrogate Rep, landed parts on TV, among them a role in BBC-produced drama *Kean* (1978) alongside Anthony Hopkins and Robert Stephens, and then went back on stage. He had more long runs in the West End, among them a role in the 1979 London production of Alan Ayckbourn's *Joking Apart* with Christopher Cazenove and Alison Steadman, and, a little later, a run at the National Theatre in a production of Dusty Hughes's *The Futurists* alongside Daniel Day-Lewis and Jack Shepherd. All these credits added a little more 'lustre' to his name.

'By that time, I had become not in any sense a star or even a minor name but I had become a working actor; I had joined the community of actors who get cast.' In this period, Fellowes still wasn't thinking of producing, writing or directing. His focus was always on the next role. 'You do have the sense that you want to keep on moving forward,' he says. 'Rather like an animal that has a basic need to get as much food as possible, and all they do when they have food is eat it, as a young actor, you just want to get work. And you want the work to be as good as it can possibly be.'

The 'odd' film began to come his way. For example, he had a role as a library assistant in Richard Loncraine's *The Haunting of Julia* (1978), a horror picture starring Mia Farrow. Its producers were still trying to cash in on her success in *Rosemary's Baby* (1968) a decade before. 'If you're cast in a picture, you hope it will get made. You hope it won't collapse, you hope it won't fade away.'

When Fellowes was starting out as an actor in the 1970s and early 1980s, there were two ways for British actors to reach Hollywood. 'You either went when you were young and very pretty and you become a kind of faux American like Pierce Brosnan or Jane Seymour or something. Or you wait to be brought by the industry.' Fellowes didn't do either. Instead, he arrived in Los Angeles as a jobbing character actor in 1981, looking for work. He found it but not the plum roles he had hoped for and so he headed back across the Atlantic to Britain where he continued to rack up the film, TV and stage credits. He was consumed with the desire, as he put it, 'to get on'. The American experience helped him – and it was to be an American director who finally gave him the big opportunity he craved.

For fifteen years after beginning in earnest in the business in 1973/74, Fellowes had thought about 'nothing but getting my next job'. By the late 1980s, though, he began to think that he might need a 'plan B'. The work was still plentiful but Fellowes felt he had reached a plateau. He was a respected and well-liked character actor, now in middle age – and that was it. His original plan had been to become the new Peter Ustinov or Robert Morley but that clearly wasn't going to happen.

One potential new avenue was to become a producer. Fellowes had 'done a lot' and felt that he understood how the business worked. He therefore joined with director Andrew Morgan (who had directed him in two kids' TV series, *Swallows and Amazons* (1984) and *The Knights of God* (1987)) to form a company, Lionhead Productions Limited, 'for the production and exploitation of literary, television and cinematographic works within the United Kingdom', as the company's accounts described it. (The name Lionhead came from his family crest.)

Their first project was *Little Sir Nicholas*, an adaptation of a Victorian novel by C. A. Jones. This was commissioned by the BBC in 1990. The original writer didn't 'work out' and Fellowes reworked the scripts, uncredited. 'Not to put too fine a point on it, we had run out of money and we needed somebody to do it for nothing.' Earlier in his career, he had been associate producer on a Piers Paul Read adaptation *A Married Man* (1983), a TV drama series starring Anthony Hopkins on which he had worked as a script editor. He realized he had an innate understanding of story structure. 'When you are an actor, you do inevitably learn quite a lot about the shape of narrative and what is said in dialogue. An actor can usually spot the speech you can't say.' Just as with *Downton Abbey* twenty years later, Fellowes's main interest was in what he called 'character narrative'. 'It is getting people interested in this woman, this man, this boy or whatever. You then follow them through a series of adventures.' The trick is to hook the viewers to the protagonists and then to take them on a journey with those protagonists.

Little Sir Nicholas was a resounding success. Fellowes was then given a commission to write a new version of Frances Hodgson Burnett's 1886 children's novel *Little Lord Fauntleroy*, for the BBC's children's drama department. It was at this point that Fellowes collided with the liberal elite establishment. The new project was caught in the crossfire of an ongoing battle between the BBC drama department and the children's drama department, which was still then autonomous. The executives at one department told Fellowes that the series would be a failure because no one was interested any more in 'class-based historical drama'. In the event, the series was still made on the say-so of the other department – and attracted the largest audience the BBC had ever then had for a children's drama. Thanks to its success, Fellowes, who was still acting, discovered he was now being taken seriously as a writer.

Fellowes's next mooted project was an adaptation of *The Prince and the Pauper*, again for the BBC. However, Lorraine Heggessey, who became Head of Children's BBC in 1997, wasn't supportive. 'I like Lorraine very much and think she was a very good leader of that department but she didn't really want my stuff. She didn't want Kleenex and Christianity. She was looking for something rougher and more streetwise. Not very surprisingly, she did not turn to me.'

As that avenue closed, Fellowes looked for other opportunities. US producer Ileen Maisel, based in London and who worked for New Line Cinema, recruited him as a script advisor. In this period, he was writing and co-writing various film screenplays, none of which were made. One or two were later revived. *Separate Lies* (2005), adapted from a Nigel Balchin novel, was put into production much later with Fellowes as director as well as writer. By then, though, he had an Oscar to his name. The script for *From Time to Time* (2009), which he also directed, was likewise completed at this time.

At the turn of the century, Fellowes was a recognized actor who had played character parts in everything from a James Bond film (*Tomorrow Never Dies*, 1997) to an arty French drama starring Catherine Deneuve (*Place Vendôme*, 1998). He had the beginnings of a career as a TV writer but no movie script credits behind him.

One of the scripts Fellowes had written was an adaptation of Anthony Trollope's 1871 novel *The Eustace Diamonds*. This was never made but it had been commissioned by American actor/director Bob Balaban. At that time, Balaban was busy trying to set up an English-country-house murder mystery for the maverick, Kansas-City-born, jazz-loving director Robert Altman, famous for his freewheeling and subversive approach to genre. 'What Altman liked to do was take an accepted form and turn it on its head. He would take a western like *McCabe and Mrs Miller* that wasn't really a western and a thriller like *The Gingerbread Man* which wasn't really a thriller,' Fellowes notes.

Altman couldn't find a writer for what would be his only UK movie. Tom Stoppard turned it down. So did Christopher Hampton. Thanks to Balaban, Fellowes was brought on board to write the mystery, which turned into *Gosford Park* (2001). 'He's this writer that you'll never have heard of and who has never had a film made but this is his sort of territory and he does know about it,' Balaban explained who Fellowes was to Altman. In this case, for once, Fellowes's gilded background counted in his favour.

Altman told him early on during a conference call that this wasn't a whodunnit . . . it was a who cares whodunnit. Altman's real interest was in class, character, the tensions between upstairs and downstairs and the way British society was changing in the early 1930s, the period in which the drama was set. At first, Altman commissioned him to write a series of character vignettes. When they turned out well, he commissioned a first draft of a full screenplay.

For many reasons, the film was a struggle to make. Altman, then seventy-one, had had a heart transplant and was impossible to insure. Only when Stephen Frears, a British director of a similar stature, agreed to be on standby in case Altman had health problems were the producers able to get the go-ahead. Financing was an uphill struggle. 'I never for a moment thought it would happen. I think I had a lot of luck. Altman and I were never a natural pair. He was a creature of the sixties, you know, dope and freedom and let it all hang out. Nevertheless, in certain areas, we were very similar. He also believed in character narrative. All his films are character narratives. The plot is often quite subsidiary. In some of them [Altman's films]', it is hardly resolved,' Fellowes remembers.

Altman also shared Fellowes's obsession with detail. Fellowes made it clear that *Gosford Park* would only work in his opinion if it was a very accurate depiction of the way of life it showed. Altman agreed completely. The problem came when Altman wanted to do something that was historically inaccurate and Fellowes, who stayed on set throughout the movie, would immediately put a stop to it. The intricacies of British class and etiquette baffled and exasperated the director. 'It was quite a stressful twelve weeks. There was I, a completely anonymous and unknown figure in film land, a supporting actor, instructing this world famous director in what he could and couldn't do. As you can imagine, it set up a certain amount of tension.'

Fellowes insisted the actors stick to the script and not improvise (as they often did on Altman's other films). This was a very complex screenplay with many interlocking plot lines and the screenwriter felt it would crumble if the ensemble cast didn't approach it with the right discipline and fidelity. Whatever his frustrations about the restrictions Fellowes placed on him, Altman proved a loyal and inspiring collaborator. He dismissed the studio's attempts to bring on a more established writer to give the script a polish or to re-do it entirely. 'I can tell you most directors would cave in to the studio but Bob did not and he said, "Either we make this guy's script or we don't make the film".'

Without Altman's support, it is conceivable that Fellowes's writing career would never have taken off – and there would have been no *Downton Abbey*. The writer suggests that there is obvious overlap between *Gosford Park* and *Downton Abbey* in their portrayal of masters and servants but that the former was far harsher and colder than the latter. *Downton* had 'a sense of warmth' that made audiences come back, week after week. *Gosford Park* was also set towards the end of an era. The Second World War was just a few years away and the old style of country-house living wouldn't survive it.

Fellowes grew up after the war and his family didn't have armies of live-in servants. However, he became very interested in the world of his parents and grandparents when he was still a little boy. He was close to a great-aunt who was born in 1880 and had various elderly cousins. He was able to talk to them about their lives before the First World War. The great-aunt would tell him stories about how she had been presented at court to Queen Victoria in 1898. He also knew about life between the wars because 'that was very much my stepmother's life. She had been presented to George V and Queen Mary.'

His luck, as he saw it, was that he asked the right questions when he was still alive. Once, he asked a relative why a drawer in the kitchen was full of tea spoons of different shapes. 'Because they are not all tea spoons,' came back the response. She started to explain that one was a melon spoon, one was a tea spoon and another was an egg spoon. As he listened, Fellowes began to appreciate the intricacy of this life. 'I had only just missed it. I was born as it was fading away. Where I was very lucky with the offer of the film that became *Gosford Park* was that I was asked to do something that I was already interested in and already had something of a gift for and a certain amount of empathy with those people.'

During filming, Fellowes was offered advice on the period from a professor of 'social something or other' from Essex University. He turned it down but instead brought onto set people who had worked as kitchen maids, house maids, butlers and underfoot men and who had been employed in the great country houses. 'They were giving us advice on how it really was which, of course, was a thousand times more interesting than some old professor imagining they knew when they didn't.' The idea was to provide the audience with an exact sense of how life really was lived. The question wasn't whether audiences approved of this vanished world but whether the world had been created with as much authenticity as possible.

Gosford Park was supported by the Blairite UK Film Council that Fellowes so disapproved of. 'They were hopeless,' he remembers. 'And they later claimed it as one of their triumphs. The only reason they gave any money at all was that Robert Jones [head of the UK Film Council's Premiere Fund] gave some money. And he was heavily criticized by members of his own Council for giving money to such a right-wing and ridiculous film. It was only afterwards, when it won an Oscar and was nominated for several, that it [the Film Council] started to claim it.' The only script note that Fellowes remembers seeing from the Film Council said simply: 'too much like *Upstairs, Downstairs*. Altman is a nightmare.' 'Really what they [the Film Council] did was to make a large amount of unwatchable and unreleasable films coming out of lottery money, which was just idiotic.'

Fellowes's remarks hint at just what an outsider he felt in a film industry he believed was entirely dominated by the 'liberal left elite'. He kept on encountering funders and commissioners who made it clear they felt 'the past doesn't work, only the present works' in drama. 'And in the past, everybody was either persecuted and unhappy or triumphalist and lording it over people who were morally their superiors. Generally, the whole thing was completely horrible, from soup to nuts,' he characterizes the view of the commissioners.

As Fellowes's dramas try to show, English history was far more nuanced and complex than such a world view allowed. 'If you can go far enough back, you can do a drama, particularly an adaptation, where all the upper classes don't have to be horrible. You can do Jane Austen's *Emma* and Mr Knightley's very nice. But the more modern they are, the less they will accept that. You can do *Lady Chatterley's Lover* because the Chatterleys are hopeless, everyone is wretched and the only morally superior person is basically the gamekeeper,' is how the actor turned writer sums up the attitudes he encountered from patrons and commissioners. 'It is a real prejudice. Of course, it is also very childish to think there is any class or colour or group or nationality or religion where everyone is either bad or good. This is a very fundamental fallacy. Evil and good, like good looks, are pretty evenly distributed between the social groups as anyone with a brain can tell you. But this is not the thinking among the urban left-leaning elite who still hold mighty sway in British show business.' In American show business, he continues, there 'isn't the terror about a drama about the upper middle class that you will find here'.

After *Gosford Park*, Fellowes had an Academy Award to his name. 'I was a totally unknown element and suddenly this unknown element had walked out from the back of the wardrobe and taken an Oscar. What it does for you in that sense is it makes you a player, you are a quantity.' On the night of the seventy-fourth Academy Awards, he found himself making small talk backstage to other guests during a commercial break at the ceremony. 'And I suddenly realized I had been talking to Robert Redford and Barbra Streisand. There was something wonderfully *Alice through the Looking Glass* about it.' He thought back to when he was sitting on his own in a little room, typing away at the screenplay to *Little Sir Nicholas*. Now, here he was, with 'Robert Redford holding his Oscar [for Lifetime Achievement] and I was holding mine. That was really rather marvellous.'

Soon after *Gosford Park*, Fellowes consolidated his reputation by writing the script for the new stage production of the musical *Mary Poppins* then being hatched by Disney and West End impresario Cameron Mackintosh. This touched on similar territory to *Gosford Park*. As with Altman, he put his opportunity partly down to luck. Disney owned the songs. Mackintosh owned the stage rights. They hadn't been able to come to an agreement for years but at the precise moment they did so, he was available, an Oscar to his name and ready to be hired. The show was a big hit and Fellowes had managed to prove that he was more than a one-trick pony. 'When you've got two [hits] under your belt, you're not an overnight sensation.'

Fellowes calls his film *Separate Lies* his 'favourite' among his realized projects, even if it did only modest business. He was in demand as a writer. Among his credits were *Young Victoria* (2009), starring Emily Blunt and produced by Martin Scorsese, and *The Tourist* (2010), directed by Florian Henckel von Donnersmarck and starring Angelina Jolie and Johnny Depp. The latter wasn't a film he was especially proud of but he 'made the most money out of it'.

In his work, Fellowes will rarely include violence and he expresses incomprehension about the levels of it found in contemporary movies. 'This insistence on violence,' he says, frowning. 'Our lives are lived without violence for most people. I am not saying there is absolutely never a violent incident that you witness but it's pretty rare. I have probably seen a real fight twice in my life – and yet I am expected to watch six a night and I don't really understand the logic of that.'

During the years he was making *Downton Abbey*, Fellowes came to the conclusion that TV was the medium for him. He didn't like special effects-driven Hollywood blockbusters and nor did he enjoy depressing indie dramas in which 'everything is bad, now it is worse, now it is terrible ... the end' as he sums up their usual trajectory. However, he relishes long-form TV dramas in which he can lose himself like *Mad Men, The Good Wife, The West Wing, Grey's*

Anatomy and others. 'I love getting drawn into a world and I suppose it makes sense that I should try to draw people into my world.'

Ask what advice he would give to others looking to find a pathway into the industry and whether they can learn from his example and he pauses. 'There is no logic to it,' he says of his career. 'For almost anyone who has known success, there will be a split response within you. Part of you will be saying, "Is this for me? Are you sure? Have you made a mistake?", and the other half is saying, "What took you so long!"'

Fellowes still bristles at the liberal elite deciding from on high who gets ahead and who doesn't ('a kind of cockroach at the heart of our industry') but sees some cause for optimism. 'My feeling is that with the young, this is loosening and the more the young go through the system and come to the top, I think that will get better. The simple volume of people they need means they have to let in more people of all types.'

20

Eve Gabereau[1]

Eve Gabereau is a film entrepreneur based in London, who has worked in distribution, production, event cinema, festivals, new media, the public sector and journalism. Unlike many of the subjects profiled in these pages, she came from a media background, albeit a Canadian one. She even acted in a feature when she was a child (*Three Card Monte* in 1978). However, she did not have any pre-existing ties to the British film industry.

Her father emigrated to Canada in the 1960s as a tech researcher and developer of language software at Trent University, went on to be a soundman for a weekly television news programme mostly covering war stories around the world, then a computer programmer and eventually became a hotelier in the Eastern Townships of Quebec.

Gabereau would spend part of most summers in the French countryside but had no links to Britain, other than stopovers en route to Roissy-Charles de Gaulle and an educational tour of Europe with British students when she was fifteen. When she left school, she enrolled in McGill University to study for a Bachelor of Arts in politics and languages. Once she graduated, she set off to Japan and China to teach English as a foreign language. She ended up in Aizu-Wakamatsu, a small city in Fukushima Prefecture where she also worked at the town hall helping with cultural events. At the time, in 1993, the city was expanding, and a new cultural centre was built. A film festival was held here as part of the inaugural events programme. Gabereau helped out on this,

---

[1]The material in this chapter comes from the author's interview with Eve Gabereau in London during the summer of 2019.

Director Jim Jarmusch and the cast of vampire drama Only Lovers Left Alive *at its Cannes premiere in 2013. The film, released in the UK by Soda Pictures, was described by Eve Gabereau as 'fun, beautiful and timeless'. Photo: Ian Gavan/Getty Images.*

taking her first, tentative steps into what would soon become a career in the movie business. When she moved back to Canada, she started to work for the Vancouver Film Festival in brand partnerships, hospitality and international guest relations – with a focus on East Asian culture and cinema.

Gabereau was properly introduced to world cinema through the festival, its programmers and in particular the British critic Tony Rayns who was in charge of the 'Dragons & Tigers' section and invited such prominent guests as Takeshi 'Beat' Kitano and Hirokazu Koreeda from Japan, Bong Joon-ho from South Korea and Nonzee Nimibutr from Thailand to present their films. Rayns would become a mentor to her and later help her into the industry in the UK. She enrolled for a Masters in Communications and East Asian Studies at Simon Fraser University, a course requiring some formal study of film history. She was turning into a cinephile.

Gabereau's boyfriend, subsequently her husband, Craig Burnett, an aspiring art curator, was keen to move to London. It was the era of 'Cool Britannia' and of the 'Young British Artists' (YBAs) led by Damien Hirst and championed by wealthy collectors like Charles Saatchi. The British art world was buzzing. Gabereau and Burnett used to go on Saturday mornings to a magazine shop on Robson Street in Vancouver to drink coffee. Here, Burnett would read the latest issue of *Modern Painters*, the art magazine inspired by Victorian critic John Ruskin, which was set up and edited by the waspish and outspoken art critic and magazine editor Peter Fuller. Gabereau would read *Wallpaper**. 'He [Burnett] said I want to go to London and work at *Modern Painters*,' Gabereau remembers Burnett saying to her one Saturday morning. 'I said, OK.' He had a British passport and she a French one, so there were few barriers to moving – other than money and employment. The pound was at a high against the Canadian dollar, but none of this was a deterrent. Opportunity and adventure were a great lure.

They arrived in September 1998, and stayed with Burnett's aunt and uncle in Tufnell Park for the first six weeks. Over the course of the next year, Gabereau did a post-graduate year at the University of London's School of Oriental and African Studies (SOAS) and worked part-time at the London Film Festival (under Adrian Wootton and Sandra Hebron), Edinburgh Film Festival (under Lizzie Francke) and Alliance Atlantis (rebranded Momentum, now eOne), while Burnett took odd jobs and angled for work at *Modern Painters* – which he eventually landed. They were living in student accommodation in a Nash building overlooking Regent's Park.

One of Gabereau's fellow students at SOAS was Ali Kayley, a young film programmer who knew Dan Glaister, the arts editor at the *Guardian*, in charge of commissioning features and interviews on film. 'She [Kayley] said, "Dan needs more women writers. You're going to start writing for the *Guardian*",' Gabereau remembers the sequence of events which led her briefly into film journalism. 'I barely knew what distribution was,' Gabereau acknowledges, 'but I could see parallels between it and festivals.' She continued to freelance at the *Guardian* and was offered a full-time job there as 'web journalist for film and books' which, after great deliberation, she passed on.

Instead, Gabereau took a position for a dot.com company and began to travel regularly to Silicon Valley, as well as Paris and Zurich where her employers also had offices. 'Working in tech during a burgeoning time seemed exciting. I'd get my stock options, make my millions and then go back to film,' is how she envisaged it all unfolding. In the event, the bubble burst and she decided that didn't like the work much anyway. 'It wasn't fulfilling me. It was fun but it didn't feel like it was taking me where I wanted to go.'

Somehow, in spite of the demands of her job, Gabereau was still programming films for the Edinburgh Film Festival and later for the Cambridge Film Festival, run by exhibitor and City Screen founder Tony Jones. She was doing occasional reviews for the film section of *Time Out* and was making sure that the contacts in UK film and journalism she had so carefully cultivated didn't go stale.

When Gabereau was programming for the Edinburgh Film Festival and needed to secure some films from the distribution arm of the ICA (Institute of Contemporary Arts), she was dealing with a young executive, Edward Fletcher, who had managed a cinema in Cambridge. 'He said "who is this American [he thought she was American] demanding films (for example, the Japanese *Ring* trilogy)?" We just got along. We found we had similar interests in film,' she says of her future business partner.

At the Cannes Film Festival in 2002, Gabereau saw the French-Chinese film *Balzac and the Little Chinese Seamstress*, about the experiences of two middle-class Chinese boys in the wake of the Cultural Revolution, when members of the bourgeoisie were sent to remote villages for re-education and older professionals (academics, journalists and the like) were forced to take menial jobs. She thought this was just the type of film she'd like to distribute. Shortly afterwards, she and Fletcher decided to set up a company together. They bought the film and released it the following year.

But they were getting ahead of themselves, as they did not even have a company name yet. They brainstormed but couldn't agree on anything appropriate. Gabereau invited Fletcher to her house (by then she was living in a loft in Old Street that was owned by a banker friend who rented it to her at a low price because he wanted to support the arts) and told him he wasn't leaving until they thought of something that worked. They ransacked books, thought through their favourite movies and looked for inspiration around them. Eventually, they started leafing through a volume called *Colour and Meaning*. Fletcher read out colour names. Gabereau wrote them down. One, she thought, was 'solar orange'. She liked that but thought it was a bit too 'dot.com'. She thought, though, that 'Soda' might fly. It had fizz; it worked in different languages and, in Japanese, it means 'that's it' or 'that's right'. It also had an association with going to the cinema. The name stuck. At last, the company had an identity. Design agency All City Media created their logo and collaborated on their first theatrical campaign, which included a brand partnership with Shanghai Tang and Selfridges.

Between them, Gabereau and Fletcher raised enough money to set up a small office and buy the *Balzac* film Gabereau so admired. She didn't know any sales agents but went to visit TFI, the French company representing *Balzac*, in Toronto. Half-French herself, she persuaded them to sell it to her. It helped that no other British distributor had yet come in for the film.

In its first year, Soda looked to release between six and eight films. It was acquiring foreign-language arthouse fare – and successfully finding an audience for it. Films like *Balzac* and Pablo Trapero's police drama *El Bonarense* (2000) did reasonable business. *Balzac*, Gabereau remembers, made around £150,000 at the UK box office on three prints and a limited release. They went on to license it to the BBC and started to have enough income to reinvest in other films and grow the business.

The process of releasing an independent film was deceptively straightforward. You would organize a press screening at Soho Screening Rooms (then Mr Young's); you would book ads in the *Guardian* and *Time Out*. If the *Guardian*'s critic gave the film five stars, it would hold its screens in the West End. The 'window' – the gap between when a film is released in cinemas and when it appears on DVD or TV – was daunting. There would be a six-month gap between the theatrical and DVD releases – and then it would take at least a year for a film to make its way to television. However, the films had a longer life in the cinemas than they would during the later online and digital era. This was a risky business but, Gabereau remembers, it 'felt viable'. 'We were young and didn't think so much about the consequences. If it didn't work, we would move on to the next thing and if it did, we would keep building,' she says.

Physical distribution, the business Soda was in, meant … physical distribution. Gabereau and Fletcher would often carry the 35 mm film in tins from one London venue to another. They used couriers to transport the movies further afield. Sometimes, a reel would go missing. That would spark a furious hunt. Where had it been seen last? Fletcher was particularly good at tracking them down.

Tony Jones at leading arthouse cinema circuit City Screen supported Soda from the outset, giving Gabereau and Fletcher access to his venues and providing their films with fair runs. At this stage, Jones programmed many leading arthouse sites including the Curzon Soho in London and ensured Soda's films were shown on their screens.

This was a relatively vibrant time for independent distribution in the UK. Optimum Releasing, set up by youngsters Will Clarke and Danny Perkins in 1999, had already had successes with films like Mexican drama *Amores Perros* (2001) and Japanese animated feature *Spirited Away* (2001). Redbus, set up by Simon Franks and Zygi Kamasa in 1997 and taken over by German company Helkon in 2001, had just had a big hit with Gurinder Chadha's *Bend It Like Beckham* (2002). Hamish McAlpine's Tartan Films, Artificial Eye run by Pam and Andy Engel and Robert Beeson, and Metrodome were among other indie distributors doing decent business in the marketplace.

At the point that Soda was founded, distributors were moving away from VHS and embracing DVD instead as the home-release format of choice. VHS may have been in its death throes but DVD was extraordinarily lucrative. At its launch, Soda did a deal with Optimum who agreed to release DVDs on the new company's behalf. Eventually, Soda ended this relationship and partnered with World Cinema, the video distribution business owned by Artificial Eye and Tartan, and later released its DVDs through Elevation Sales, the company bought by Optimum and Lionsgate in 2007.

Soda's business strategy was to target talented directors at the start of their careers, acquire their early films and hopefully grow with them. For example, they released *C.R.A.Z.Y.* (2005), the fourth feature from young Canadian director Jean-Marc Vallée, which was his international breakthrough. Not long after, Vallée was called by Martin Scorsese's office and asked to direct *Young Victoria* (2009). He went on to make Oscar winner *Dallas Buyers Club* (2013) and hit TV series *Big Little Lies* (2017).

'Put films on the internet' was one of the bullet points in the company's original business plan. After all, Gabereau came from the dot.com world. 'We sort of shelved that. We should have stuck with it,' she later noted of what seemed like a missed opportunity.

Early in the company's history, Gabereau told her business partner she had 'an extra project in development'. She was pregnant with her first child. Not that she let that get in the way of her work. She took her newborn son Lucas, then only eight weeks old, to Cannes with her. 'We felt like we needed to be there.'

Soda soon began to grow. Gabereau and Fletcher hired more staff, moved offices from the shoebox which they started in (in Rupert Court in London's Chinatown) to more spacious premises in Covent Garden (in a building overlooking Bow Street Magistrates Court) and then, in 2008, to Shoreditch.

In this period, women were relatively strongly represented in senior positions at UK distributors. Liz Wrenn had run Alliance; Romaine Hart had been at the helm of Mainline Releasing; Pam Engel had been at the helm of Artificial Eye; executives like Laura De Casto at Tartan and Jane Giles at the ICA were key buyers for independent cinema; Maj-Britt Kirchner left WB in the late 1990s to be MD of Pathé's UK distribution company (formerly Guild), where she had a big hit with *Chicken Run* in 2000. It was the year of *Ratcatcher*, directed by Lynne Ramsay and distributed by Pathé.

Over the years, the two Soda principals developed relationships with all the main international sales agents. They ventured into the library business, setting up a 'Vintage Soda' arm through which to re-release films like *Hotel du Nord*, *Signs and Wonders* and *Afterlife*. The company's growth was helped by the EU's Creative Europe MEDIA support programme and by the UK Film Council's P&A (Prints & Advertising) Fund. The UK Film Council, the lead public agency for film in the UK, could be prescriptive but its support was welcome. It was something her industry colleagues working for distribution companies outside the UK could only have dreamed about. 'It was a luxury that there was a National Lottery-backed public fund supporting independent arthouse film for no other reason other than to contribute to cultural vibrancy and plurality of choice. Not a lot of other countries have that. In English-speaking countries, the US and Canada, people are quite astounded. It seems quite straightforward that there is a fund to support English-speaking films but to support non-national films just for the sake of diversity is quite something.'

There was ferocious competition for titles from rival distributors, among them the flamboyant McAlpine, owner of Tartan Films, who behaved for a few years like a rich kid in a sweet shop, buying almost everything available from Asian extreme horror to Ingmar Bergman titles to the work of maverick directors like Gaspar Noé and Larry Clark. 'They were very reckless but also super-confident,' Gabereau remembers of a company which eventually collapsed in spectacular fashion, leaving sizeable debts.

The obvious downside to Tartan's disappearance was that the suppliers – the labs, the trailer cutters, the printers and all the other unseen functionaries who enable a film to be released – weren't paid. They became 'super-anxious' and lost confidence in their clients. Tartan's collapse was followed a few years later by that of another independent, Revolver, which also left behind great debts. Then, the DVD market began to soften and home entertainment retailers were being squeezed. Releasing patterns changed as the new 'digital disruptors' led by Netflix emerged as major forces; they continue to change the ways in which films are consumed. All of a sudden, the distribution business didn't seem as straightforward as it had in the earlier days of Soda, but there also seemed to be so many new ways to take it.

Around this time, two major events happened in her life: Gabereau had her second child and nine months later was involved in an accident that landed her in hospital for an extended period with serious injuries and with a long road to recovery ahead. Head of Distribution Kate Gerova (who later moved on to Curzon) took on much of Gabereau's work. She put her boss's conscience at ease, so that she could concentrate on getting better.

Gabereau made a slow and gradual return to work. Her sabbatical had allowed her to think differently about the company, how it operated and what she was looking for from the business. Gabereau remembers that she and Fletcher 'didn't have exit plans' when they launched Soda Pictures. That is something investors always ask about the moment they start talking about supporting a company. They want to know how the principals will handle their departure, whether they are looking to sell their company on or merge with a rival. Such thoughts didn't occur to Gabereau and Fletcher in the first instance. They were self-sufficient and happy to be independent. However, as the years passed, Gabereau felt increasingly 'stunted' at what Soda could do. The company had enough money to operate but not enough to grow. It released plenty of films that did well enough – Fatih Akin's *Head-On* (2004), Guy Maddin's *The Saddest Music in the World* (2003), Lenny Abrahamson's *Garage* (2007) and Shimmy Marcus's *Soulboy* (2010) – but never had that one runaway hit like a *Fahrenheit 9/11* (2004), released by Optimum, or a *Bend It Like Beckham* (2002), released by Redbus, which could transform its position. Gabereau and Fletcher realized they needed an influx of cash or the risk was that Soda would never evolve.

Gabereau established a 'Soda Film Fund', an investment consortium which raised $3 million for a slate of films for the company to buy and release. This enabled them to acquire bigger titles like *Norwegian Wood* (2010), *Meek's Cut Off* (2010), *Habemas Papam* (2011), *Barbara* (2012), *Wadjda* (2012) and *Only Lovers Left Alive* (2013), all films which screened at major festivals and which Soda's rivals were vying to buy.

A few years later, thanks to her Canadian connections, Gabereau was able to bring aboard the Canadian outfit Thunderbird Entertainment Group, which owned Vancouver-based Atomic Cartoons, Great Pacific and scripted television production company Thunderbird. This was a company which specialized in high-end reality TV but wanted to expand. They liked what Soda was doing and were ready to take it over. Gabereau liked the idea of being part of a wider, more international group, having professional support from a parent company and being able to buy bigger films.

In 2014 at the Toronto International Film Festival, Soda announced its merger with Thunderbird and its movement towards distributing in North America, as well as continuing in the UK and Ireland. The company acquired such films as *The Riot Club* (2014), directed by Lone Scherfig, *Disorder* (2015), by Alice Winocour, and John Maclean's *Slow West* (2015), starring Michael Fassbender. Soda now commanded more market power and was able to secure the rights to *Paterson* (2016) by Jim Jarmusch and starring Adam Driver before its Cannes world premiere and to German comedy (and festival sensation) *Toni Erdmann* (2016). There had been fierce competition for both titles.

The films were successful commercially and critically. They went on to sell to Amazon Prime in its early days of subscription VOD in the UK. Other notable pick-ups from this period include the Oscar-nominated stop-motion animation *My Life as a Courgette* (2016) and Terence Davies's *A Quiet Passion* (2016), starring Cynthia Nixon as reclusive nineteenth-century New England poet Emily Dickinson.

For the first three years of the partnership, Soda Pictures continued to trade under its own name. But in 2017, the company closed down. A new entity emerged in its place, Thunderbird Releasing. These changes timed with Gabereau's departure after fifteen years.

During her time under the Thunderbird umbrella, Gabereau executive produced *I Am Not a Witch* (2017), alongside lead producer Emily Morgan. Just after she left the company that year, the film premiered in Directors' Fortnight at the Cannes Film Festival and went on to win awards and to be chosen as the UK entry for the Academy Awards. Gabereau and Morgan managed the UK distribution deal with Curzon themselves, with the support of their sales agent, the BFI and Film4.

'When we brought Adam Driver over for *Paterson*, I remember approving a first-class ticket for him and his assistant when I was outside London and my trains had been cancelled. I was stuck in Brighton, sitting on the dirt ground eating a curry out of a van and approving junket costs,' Gabereau recalls, providing a surreal image of herself dealing with the talent towards the end of her tenure at Thunderbird/Soda. The pay-off was having Driver in town to promote the film and to sit together backstage at Picturehouse Central talking about acting and politics, including the possibility that Trump could actually become president. This was 4 November 2016 – election day was four days later.

Gabereau thought she would take a career break, rethink her position in the industry and consider what else she might do. But she did not stay idle for long. After a summer in Canada, she returned to London and launched Modern Films as a vehicle through which to release a film she had retained from Thunderbird – *Manifesto* starring Cate Blanchett in thirteen different roles.

Modern Films would quickly grow into a female-led, social issues-driven film distribution, production and event company. Gabereau launched *Manifesto* the day after the Harvey Weinstein scandal broke, adding to the film's topicality. 'With Modern, I call it a bit of an accidental company. I didn't really mean to set it up. I was going to take some time out and work out what I was going to do next but I had taken *Manifesto* with me because I had acquired it through Thunderbird, Gabereau recalls. She wasn't sure that Thunderbird would have had the conviction to release the film successfully.

Blanchett got behind *Manifesto*. Even so, the economics and challenges in handling art-based films were different from those for more mainstream films. Gabereau arranged a partnership with Tate Modern, organized an event release and showed huge tenacity in ensuring it reached the UK public. It helped too that by then she had an identity in the art world, on her own and through her husband. Burnett had established himself as a curator and writer and had worked at the Tate as a Curator of Interpretation and as a Director at White Cube, collaborating with such artists as Sam Taylor-Johnson (then Taylor-Wood), Carroll Dunham (father of Lena) and Christian Marclay.

From early on in her time at Soda, Gabereau had been exploring the overlap between art and film. She had co-created a new division within the company: Soda Film + Art (SoFA), which released works that, as its press release proclaimed, 'fell within the nexus of film and art'. Soda struggled to find a model that worked for this division. Collectors who supported the artists didn't want to buy £20 DVDs of the work – they wanted £100,000 limited edition DCPs 'in a bespoke box'. These collectors didn't necessarily want the work to be widely released. For them, exclusivity and ownership mattered more.

However, Gabereau could see the immense interest in the film sector shown by the art establishment – and the fascination that filmmakers had with that establishment. Big names like Steve McQueen and Sam Taylor-Johnson have moved between fine art and cinema. At Modern, Gabereau continues to handle work which straddles the two worlds. For example, one of the company's 2019 releases was Florian Henckel von Donnersmarck's Oscar-nominated *Never Look Away* (2018), inspired by the life and work of the East German artist Gerhard Richter, and of his family's experiences in the Nazi and Cold War eras.

As a producer, Gabereau has been able to raise financing for production from collectors who follow the work of particular artists. 'Film financing is so different from art collecting that the whole negotiation process almost goes into reverse,' she points out. Collectors 'don't do contracts', instead trusting in handshake deals. That doesn't work when public film funders are also supporting the film. These collectors looked askance when they were asked to pay an advance. 'They'd say, oh no, we don't pay until delivery.' Gabereau would patiently point out to them that the film then couldn't be made. She would try to reassure them saying, 'Don't worry, there's a recoupment schedule. You'll get paid back.' This would confuse the collectors even more. 'They'd say, oh no, we don't want to be paid back. We just want to have our (special) edition to donate to a museum.'

Gabereau realized that these collectors needed to be treated with kid gloves but they were interested in supporting the work. She also saw the advantage in the growing field of event releasing. Rather than releasing a film over a period of time, it is often better to make a big event of it where everybody can watch it at once.

On event releases, Gabereau looks to strike partnerships with organizations like the National Gallery or the Tate or the Royal Opera House or the British Library. If there are films that are relevant to them, they will get behind the event releases. With their reputations and huge mailing lists, they can ensure a level of awareness that a conventional cinema marketing campaign would struggle to match.

Gabereau is currently one of the few women running a UK distribution company. (Kezia Williams, Managing Director of Entertainment One, is another.) Throughout her career, she has successfully released films which wouldn't have reached British audiences without her to champion them. 'Our remit is female directors, female-driven stories and focusing on social issues. In the end, it is [still] about good ideas, good writing and good content,' she says.

Distributors, she notes, rarely get the credit. 'As a distributor, it's a weird thing. You're the person who services the production and audiences. If a film works, it is because it is great. If it doesn't, it is because you didn't do a good enough job. It's hard to win . . . but it's a great ride!'

21

Andy Whittaker[1]

Founding your own company is really hard and not everybody is cut out to do it, in addition to being good at it. What I learnt is two things. A founder is an artist, responsible for a creative vision and purpose. The other key quality is determination. In business, especially film distribution, you are going to hit a lot of obstacles, so you need the ability to solve problems, and not be demoralized. (Andy Whittaker, 2019)

Andy Whittaker likes to cite a famous quote by Albert Camus, 'one must imagine Sisyphus happy', when he is describing the qualities needed to survive in a ruthless business like UK film distribution. The quote is used in one of the films that his company, Dogwoof, released early in its existence, Raman Bahrani's *Man Push Cart* (2005). This was a drama about a once successful Pakistani musician who earns a living by selling coffee and doughnuts from a cart he pushes around on the streets of New York. This man was a contemporary equivalent to Sisyphus, the king of the city of Corinth, condemned for his pride to push a gigantic rock up a hill – and then to find it rolling back down to the bottom every time he neared the top. Distribution entails the same endless repetition. In his darker moments, Whittaker felt that each new film Dogwoof released was like Sisyphus' rock. He was in a world in which you were always on the verge of success but, somehow, it remained tantalizingly out of reach. The trick was to maintain an entrepreneurial spirit and a 'can do', determined approach, whatever the setbacks.

---

[1]Unless specified otherwise, the material in this chapter comes from the author's interviews with Andy Whittaker in London during the summer of 2019.

Andy Whittaker. Photo: Courtesy of Andy Whittaker.

When Whittaker (born in 1967) was growing up on a small dairy farm in Cheshire, the morning routine was punishing. He would rise at 6 a.m. to milk the cows and would then have to walk five miles down country lanes to Betley Junior School in nearby Nantwich. By the time he was twelve, he was driving the family tractor. The farm had around fifty cattle and was supplying the Co-op (by coincidence, later to be Whittaker's backers when he set up a film distribution company). It wasn't an especially idyllic childhood. In spite of EU subsidies, money was tight. Whittaker's parents were working so hard that they didn't have much time to mollycoddle him.

Life improved a little when he was eight and he was given a bike. That meant he could ride to school. Later, when he won a place at grammar school, he would use the bike to get to the nearest bus stop, two miles away, leave it hidden in the hedge and hope it was still there when the bus dropped him back off again. The idea then that he would one day run a film company would have seemed absurd. He didn't know anybody in the film business and didn't pay much attention to movies. However, when his parents were too busy to look after him, he would watch television. The alternative was to play on his own in the farmyard – but that was risky given the dangerous equipment.

'After I was fed, they [his parents] would be busy working and setting up for the next day,' Whittaker remembers how, from a very early age, he would find himself in front of such grown-up fare as Granada's *World in Action*, John Pilger documentaries and foreign-language films that would be shown on the BBC, '*The Bicycle Thieves* and things like that'. He was also watching the TV shows presented by broadcaster and music impresario Tony Wilson, the maverick part-owner and manager of Factory Records. His TV viewing was providing him with an alternative 'education' about a world beyond the family dairy farm. His parents would also occasionally take him to the cinema in Crewe where he would watch *Star Wars* (1977) and *Raiders of the Lost Ark* (1981). As he grew older, he soon started going to the cinema (which he describes as 'the glue of the local community') on his own or to meet friends.

Whittaker's specialization as a film distributor has been in documentary and he credits films he saw in his childhood and adolescence, ranging from Ken Loach's *Kes* (1969) to Karel Reisz's *Saturday Night and Sunday Morning* (1960) with fostering his passion for hard-edged, realist stories.

At grammar school in Newcastle-under-Lyme, Whittaker was on free school dinners. He was a scholarship boy among fellow students who tended to be from much more affluent backgrounds. The school was around an hour away by bus – plus the two miles' journey by bike to reach the bus stop. One upside to such a long journey was that his parents no longer demanded he milk the cows before he set off. One downside was that, in winter, the sun would have set by the time the bus dropped him off and he would have to cycle home in the dark.

Whittaker dropped out from school at the age of sixteen because he 'wanted to earn some money and get out' from his stifling rural background. He landed an apprenticeship at the GEC–Marconi Company in Kidsgrove in Staffordshire. This was the mid-1980s. Whittaker was learning about electronics, computer-aided design and hi-tech. He was taught how to build circuit boards and worked on early mainframe computers. 'I think I've done OK [in my career] but around that same time, you had the Bill Gates of the world, working in their garages with similar access . . . but I took a different path.'

Manchester was a thriving cultural hub. This was the era of Factory Records, New Order and legendary nightclub The Haçienda. Rave culture was in its early days. Independent music labels were springing up. Whittaker would buy hand-pressed, limited edition vinyl records from bands like Magazine and the Buzzcocks. 'That was a huge change in my mindset. You'd be hearing this music and buying these records,' Whittaker says of when he first realized it was possible to produce and release music independently without relying on faceless big corporations.

If the 1980s was a fertile decade for indie music, it was also a time of widespread unemployment and industrial strife. Traditional manufacturing industries in the Midlands and the North West were wiped out. Whittaker saw the results of 'Thatcherism' at first hand as Prime Minister Margaret Thatcher's Conservative government acted to privatize companies previously under public ownership. Marconi itself was caught in the crossfire. The factory where Whittaker was working was closed down overnight. With his redundancy money and computer expertise behind him, he decided to go to university, and was accepted at Keele where he studied Artificial Intelligence and Automatic Identification. Whittaker went on to do a Masters, which included his thesis at Cambridge University under Dr Mike Lynch, the software entrepreneur who later co-founded Autonomy, Britain's largest software company. 'Mike Lynch was certainly an early inspiration for [setting myself] ambitious goals, and making things happen,' he says of the academic turned entrepreneur.

As well as developing AI software, Lynch and his team were developing software for music producers, among them British R&B group Soul II Soul. At this stage, Whittaker still had no notion of working in the film industry. His ambitions didn't stretch beyond building robots and playing with computers. However, he was fascinated by strategy and by the challenge of predicting how businesses were likely to evolve. 'Rather than the next three months, it's the next three years or even the next ten years,' he explains his interest in long-term planning, something also influenced by his farming background. 'It's less important to be able to solve predefined problems quickly than to be able to come up with surprising new ideas. Many good concepts appear crazy at first. If they were obviously good, someone would already be doing them.'

Whittaker's next significant job was as a management consultant at Ernst & Young (EY) in London, one of the so-called 'Big Four' British accountancy firms. It was the 1990s and he was advising big blue-chip companies on 'clicks and mortar' internet strategy. He also did a year at the United Nations, advising the UN on e-commerce during the Kofi Annan administration.

The movie business still seemed a long way away. He didn't think about film as a career because, as he puts it, 'apart from Granada TV', there were no available jobs in film and media – and no pathway into the industry unless you moved to London. If you did move to London, you had to survive – so Whittaker took the job with the big accountancy firm, as part of their new dot.com strategy team. Then he moved sideways into banking after being headhunted by Japanese investment bank Nomura. As the dot.com boom began in earnest, there was a rush among financiers to support new internet start-ups, and Whittaker was assembling the business cases.

At Nomura, Whittaker honed his financial skills. He worked with private equity expert Guy Hands, later to launch Terra Firma (which bought EMI in an ill-fated deal and also became owner of Odeon Cinemas). They were part of a bid to buy the London Dome, built for the millennium celebrations and now rebranded the O2 Arena.

Then came the internet crash. 'The valuations of internet companies went from blue sky to near zero overnight,' Whittaker remembers a collapse which had a Sisyphean feel about it. He took a 'golden parachute' in the form of a generous pay-off from his employers and went off to re-think his career, and what he really wanted to do. By chance, his sister, who had been working in the US, lent him a house in Oak Park, Chicago, free of charge for a year. Whittaker came up with two ideas for new businesses. One was online poker. The other was film production and film finance. In the end, he opted for the second and set up his then production company Dogwoof in 2003. The name came from a remark made by French writer André Gide to Truman Capote when Capote was complaining about receiving a negative review. 'The dogs bark but the caravan moves on,' Gide told Capote, quoting an old Arab proverb. 'It should have been Dogs Bark but Dogwoof was a fun version of that.'

Chicago seemed a sensible base. 'People in the film business would talk to you and take meetings,' he says, adding that if he had been in New York or Los Angeles, he would have struggled to open doors. The Chicago International Film Festival gave Whittaker an opportunity for making connections. He met *The Silence of the Lambs* director Jonathan Demme, who was at the festival with his documentary *The Agronomist* (2003). Whittaker blithely approached Demme and other equally prominent figures. 'At the Chicago Film Festival, people talk to you. If you did that in Sundance . . .' his voice tails off as he contemplates the social embarrassment he might have faced.

Fresh from Chicago, Whittaker also flew over to the MIFED, the film market held in the gigantic exhibition halls in Milan. He was exploring opportunities for raising gap finance for an Asia Argento and Winona Ryder project *The Heart Is Deceitful* (2004), and for acquiring films for distribution.

Whittaker quickly realized that films he saw and enjoyed, for example Japanese love story *Josee, the Tiger and the Fish* (2003), were showing at markets and festivals but then disappearing. No foreign distributors wanted to take a chance on them. The same went for many other 'amazing foreign-language films'. A British exhibitor, Mark Cosgrove, gave him some familiar advice about starting a new distribution company. 'Unless you have a million pounds, don't even think about it. If you have a million pounds, you start the company and then, when you lose it, you go and raise money.' Even so, he saw an opportunity. Whittaker realized that making films himself (his original intention) made little sense if he couldn't ensure that the films were seen by audiences. He had also done his sums. He could acquire the UK rights to a film for $10,000 but would have to spend many times that much as its producer. He therefore tweaked his business plans and pivoted Dogwoof towards distribution.

Distribution, though, had its own hazards. Whittaker analysed the likely costs for releasing *Josee, the Tiger and the Fish* (2003) on four or five screens in the UK and came back with some daunting figures:

BBFC Certification 1,000
Prints 5,000
Posters 40,00
Trailer 4,000
PR 10,000
Advertising 5,000
Shipping 1,000
Fly Postering 1,000
Misc 500

Design 1,000

Screenings 1,000

Equipment Hire 500

Office Costs n/a

Post Production & Editing n/a

Music Rights n/a

Professional Fees n/a

Subtitle Fees n/a

TOTAL COSTS 34,000 plus 10% contingency

He shared these figures with the film's Japanese sales agent Asmik Ace, along with ideas for marketing it and for finding a suitable festival at which to launch it in the UK. One suggestion was to fly out a few select journalists (*Guardian, Marie Claire, Time Out, Empire*) to Japan to meet the filmmakers. 'This seems initially expensive but would be a novel way of promoting the film, and good reviews from these publications would be a huge benefit,' he told the Japanese. However, with no sale to TV in place, it was impossible to see how *Josee* could turn a profit. Plans for the UK release were quietly shelved.

At the Cannes Film Festival in 2004, Whittaker was with his friend, property developer and music entrepreneur Lisa Voice, at the ultra-luxurious Hotel du Cap in Antibes, attending the *Vanity Fair* party. Fellow guests included Quentin Tarantino, Bruce Willis, Jerry Bruckheimer and Uma Thurman among others. With typical naivety, Whittaker spoke to several of these guests, asking Tarantino why so many films seemed to be left on the shelf, without proper distribution, and soliciting advice from Bruckheimer about how to set up a film company.

'I cringe when I think of the questions I asked Jerry Bruckheimer,' the Dogwoof boss remembers of his conversations with the powerhouse producer of *Pearl Harbor* (2001) and *Pirates of the Caribbean* (2003). Whittaker asked him why independent movies struggled in the marketplace. 'Well, they're little films. Try to do big films,' Bruckheimer replied. 'I've tried to do big films but my bank won't give me the money,' Whittaker replied. The conversation went round in circles. Whittaker struck more of a chord with Tarantino who listened to his plans for setting up the new company and said, 'Go and do it'.

The following morning, Whittaker met script editor Anna Godas (a Spaniard based in Barcelona) at breakfast. He brought her into Dogwoof as his business partner. At this point, Whittaker sold his house in London and invested all the money into his company. He may have been a newcomer with no track record whatsoever but the sales agents were still keen to meet him. The original vision for the business was for a mix of world cinema drama and documentary with a social impact angle.

Soon, with Godas's help, Dogwoof acquired its first feature, Sergio Castellitto's *Don't Move* (2004) starring Penelope Cruz. 'When you're a start-up that depends on deals with big companies to exist, it often feels like they're trying to ignore you out of existence. But when Anna [Godas] starts calling you, you may as well do what she asks, because she is not accepting a no,' Whittaker says of the tenacity of Godas in driving through Dogwoof's early acquisitions.

With his background in internet start-ups, Whittaker saw a chance for exploiting online rights – an area which the industry then had barely even begun to monetize. When he licensed a film, he took 'all' rights – and that included internet rights too. 'The world of start-ups is so unpredictable that you need to be able to modify your dreams on the fly. The best metaphor I've found for the combination of determination and flexibility you need is rugby fly-half. Fly-halves are determined to advance forward, but at any given moment may need to go sideways or even backwards to get there. I always think of 'Heads up play', which I would later read about in former CIA official Philip Mudd's *The Head Game*,' Whittaker says of the need from the outset to think on his feet.

Early in Dogwoof's existence, Whittaker approached telecom company Tiscali about putting films on their service. Their response was: 'Yes, that would be great.' He broached the subject with the films' producers and they responded that they didn't know anything about online releasing but that if this was another potential revenue stream, why not explore it? 'How much are they offering? A million dollars?' the producers would ask. 'No, a few hundred,' Whittaker would tell them. They'd shrug and say go ahead anyway on the basis that a little money was better than nothing.

Working with a well-known, A-list star like Penelope Cruz on *Don't Move* alerted Whittaker to challenges which few independent distributors could deal with. Dogwoof had to pay a fortune for 35 mm prints and also for a charity premiere in Leicester Square, which Cruz attended. The outlay was enormous. This prompted Whittaker to think about releasing digitally only, as it was key that Dogwoof was seen as a creative disruptor and innovator. At this time the landscape was a mix of 35 mm and digital. This didn't help the distributors at all. It effectively doubled the costs as the distributors needed to supply both formats to cinemas.

One ground-breaking early Dogwoof release was James Erskine's low-budget, London-set thriller *EMR* (2004). Whittaker and Godas released this 'day and date', putting it out in cinemas and on home entertainment at exactly the same time, Although some hailed their boldness and suggested that this might be a releasing model for the future, it wasn't a strategy exhibitors liked at all. Dogwoof weren't observing the traditional theatrical 'window', the period of around four months where new films were available to see only in cinemas. The experiment was a limited success. No major chains would book the film but independent venues programmed it.

Dogwoof enjoyed much more success with a subsequent release, Danish director Nikolaj Arcel's political thriller *The King's Game* (2004), one of the most popular films in Scandinavia that year. The film also helped launch the UK Film Council's new 'Digital Screen Network', the pioneering scheme to release films digitally rather than on 35 mm film.

At this point, Dogwoof was evolving as an adventurous but relatively traditional distributor, handling independent British and foreign-language arthouse fare. However, its profile and business model changed dramatically when it acquired *Black Gold* (2006), a feature documentary about ethical coffee farming in Africa. 'Of course we will do this. We loved the film, and it was also available for free,' Whittaker remembers of a project for which Dogwoof didn't have to pay any upfront fee.

The film's directors, Marc J. Francis and Nick Francis, were ingenious and relentless users of social media during its release campaign. 'It was the first time where we did a model with a lot of in-kind partnerships attached and extremely strong filmmaker support. We released the film and it did very well,' Godas later noted.[2] This was regarded as a 'low-cost, low-effort' release but Whittaker saw an opportunity. Instead of spending £50,000 or more on advertising and press opportunities for big-name actors, they were spending £10,000 or less. The indefatigable Francis brothers were 'like a machine', doing interview after interview. Awareness around the documentary grew.

Dogwoof later followed up on the success of *Black Gold* with *Burma VJ* (2008), a Danish documentary about the protests against the military regime in Burma, and Franny Armstrong's eco-themed documentary *The Age of Stupid* (2009), a drama-documentary decrying climate change. Again, the filmmakers proselytized tirelessly on behalf of their own movie. Dogwoof supported Armstrong as she organized a 'green' premiere in Leicester Square. This had zero carbon emissions, a popcorn machine fuelled by pedal power, solar panels to charge up the generators and fashion designer/punk visionary Vivienne Westwood turning up on a bicycle. 'That was six figures at the box office with very little money actually spent.' Whittaker quickly noticed the way the social campaigning boosted audience numbers.

The company had occasionally picked up dramatic features, for example Bahrani's *Man Push Cart* (2005) and Lajos Koltai's holocaust drama *Fateless* (2005). However, from *Black Gold*, *The End of the Line*, *The Age of Stupid* and *Burma VJ* onward, Dogwoof began to focus almost exclusively on documentary. Ethics and profitability went hand in hand. By this time, his 'piggy bank' was running very low. As his savings vanished, Whittaker couldn't afford to pay big prices for new features anyway.

In 2006, Whittaker had hired Oli Harbottle, who went to head up distribution and acquisitions. Harbottle had been working at the perennially cash-strapped, London-based independent festival Raindance, and so was used to tight budgets. Like Godas and Whittaker, he had no previous experience in film distribution. This, though, was seen as an asset rather than a hindrance. After his time working in the dot.com start-up world, Whittaker had decided that, 'If you are inventing the future, you don't want people from the old world'.

---

[2]Anna Godas, quoted in *Screen Daily*, 19 December 2014. https://www.screendaily.com/features/andy-whittaker-and-anna-godas-dogwoof/5081256.article.

In this period, a handful of foreign-language films, generally from big-name directors like Pedro Almodóvar and Lars von Trier, would do decent business at the UK box office but most other independent, non-English-language titles would struggle. Dogwoof couldn't get access to the Almodóvar films. By pioneering a documentary-oriented strategy the company had a near free run. No one else was in the market for these films. In the UK, at least, documentary was still seen as a form best suited to television, not cinema.

In 2007, Dogwoof joined the UK trade body Film Distributors' Association, followed in 2015 by another British documentary specialist, Dartmouth Films; both remain active members today.

The Co-op, then one of the UK's longest-established and leading supermarkets, agreed to back Dogwoof through its 'ethics group' as part of its campaign to support ethical new companies. The Co-op (which years before had bought the milk from Whittaker's parents' dairy farm) paid the marketing costs for Dogwoof's films on such subjects as *Dirty Oil* (2009) and *The Vanishing of the Bees* (2009). These films did only modest business at the box office but with the Co-op support Dogwoof could afford to release them theatrically and would generally eventually make healthy profits through home entertainment. On their film about overfishing, *The End of the Line* (2009), they were part of an advertising campaign featuring naked celebrities (Dame Judi Dench, Richard E. Grant, Greta Scacchi) holding dead fish to draw attention to it. The campaign was covered by all the UK tabloids – and Dogwoof didn't have to pay much if anything for it.

Dogwoof was releasing films digitally before most of its rivals. Cinemas who had invested in digital projectors were therefore minded to take their titles on the grounds that there wasn't much else to show. After rocky beginnings, the company quickly became profitable. Margins may have been small but so were costs. 'That model of investing half a million and hoping for a million in box office [after] TV and DVD, we never got to work,' Whittaker says of the company's early misadventures with fictional features. 'Suddenly, we are about low cost, digital, PR, word of mouth and events – and it is all profits. When we have a hit, it is all money.' As an ex-Nomura banker, Whittaker was very different from the stereotype of the bearded, liberal do-gooder, making documentaries to save the world. He could talk in financial jargon. This gave him a credibility others in the documentary world lacked.

An added advantage was that documentary enjoyed a spectacular renaissance. Instead of occasional documentary hits, films like Michael Moore's *Bowling for Columbine* (2002) or *The March of the Penguins* (2005), competing with dramatic features at the box office, a steady stream of new titles found significant audiences. Thanks to the availability of affordable digital cameras and new sources of funding (for example, from eBay magnate Jeff Skoll's Participant), many more documentaries were being made – and the general quality rose. Filmmakers aspiring to see their films in cinemas looked to Dogwoof to release them. No longer did they have to rein in their ambition and pitch their projects to TV. 'We are the crazy people doing documentary in cinema. Nobody else is doing that anywhere in the world.'

Whittaker had met Ted Sarandos, the Chief Content Officer at VOD giant Netflix, when the company was still releasing films on DVD. Netflix was quick to acquire documentaries for its platform, licensing Dogwoof titles which had done only very paltry business at the UK box office, for example *Revenge of the Electric Car* (2011), and then finding very big audiences for them on its platform. Dogwoof also licensed films to Amazon – and helped Amazon to sell their documentaries internationally.

Since then there has been an expansive global growth of nonfiction programming, including all the new streaming platforms, creating an insatiable global demand for intelligent films. Key films in this period included the release of *Blackfish* (2013), a heart-rending, hugely popular documentary about a captive killer whale which raised Dogwoof's profile, *The Spirit of '45* (2013) directed by Ken Loach, *Cartel Land* (2015) and *The Act of Killing* (2012), which won a BAFTA for Best Documentary. In 2011 the company set up its own international sales agency which picks up rights to films and then licenses them worldwide, and this has opened up new markets.

In recent years, UK film distributors have consistently invested around £200 million each year to buy media advertising supporting their releases, according to Nielsen data. But this is far from the full picture in today's world where 'owned' and 'earned' media can exert a huge influence on the public's awareness of, and engagement with, a new film, in addition to the longer-established (still heavily used) 'paid-for' media outlets such as press, outdoor, radio and TV.

Whittaker, Godas and Harbottle remain the senior management team at Dogwoof today. In 2018/19, Dogwoof had two of its biggest hits, *Three Identical Strangers* (2018), which made £572,000 at the UK box office, and Jimmy Chin and Elizabeth Chai Vasarhelyi's *Free Solo* (2018), which depicts climber Alex Honnold's ascent of the sheer El Capitan rock face in California's Yosemite National Park, and which took £2 million.

It would be trite to suggest Whittaker's childhood experiences on a remote Cheshire dairy farm provided him with a grounding for the film business. He cites the influence of Mancunian broadcaster and music pioneer Tony Wilson, who used to say: 'The world is billions of years old. We are on this planet for 50 to 100 years – so just do things. Don't let barriers get in your way.' Whittaker shares Wilson's risk-taking entrepreneurialism and his impatience to test out new business models, however far fetched they may initially appear.

Dogwoof is now an international company with its own sales arm and a growing interest in production. As the company has blossomed, so has the documentary genre. 'Audiences are embracing documentary, not just the blockbusters. Documentary as a form will continue to develop, as filmmakers get more ambitious and have the budgets to back their vision,' Whittaker declares as he contemplates the future. 'It's an exciting time, and it's certain that audiences now see documentary as movies, not just films. And this opens up new opportunities. The streamers are transforming the film distribution business. At the same time, documentary budgets are now regularly in the multi-million dollar range, and in the USA are regularly generating over $10 million box office. This is truly a golden era for documentary!'

22

Maxine Leonard[1]

From Grimbsy to Hollywood, British publicist Maxine Leonard has been on an unlikely and upward career journey that now sees her running a marketing and publicity company in Los Angeles. She has worked on some of the most prestigious US independent films of recent times, among them Martin Scorsese's *The Gangs of New York* (2002), Steven Soderbergh's Oscar winner *Traffic* (2000) and Jean-Marc Vallée's *Dallas Buyers Club* (2011). A svelte and ebullient figure, Leonard is at pains to point out that being a Hollywood publicist isn't as exotic a profession as outsiders might imagine. She describes her job as 'more exhilarating than stressful . . . but still stressful'.

Leonard has had her share of bizarre experiences with clients at film festivals or on sets. She stood alongside Leonardo DiCaprio and escaped with him when a mob of rampaging, autograph-hungry fans knocked over restaurant tables and charged after him following a screening of a documentary he had produced. She got up very early to watch actors race naked across Regent's Park in London at dawn for a gross-out *National Lampoon* comedy she was publicizing. She was there in Cannes when a giant model of US shock jock Howard Stern was inflated a few yards from the beach to publicize Stern's 1997 feature *Private Parts* – and then shrivelled up after being punctured not long afterwards.

Nonetheless, she points out that most of the job is plain hard work. 'You soon learn to understand that PR and marketing are not glamorous. You might

[1]Unless specified otherwise, the material in this chapter comes from the author's interviews with Maxine Leonard in London during the summer of 2019.

Maxine Leonard. Photo: Jenna Bailey, Killer Imaging.

be in this glamorous world but you are literally sitting at a computer for most of the day, organizing people, answering emails and answering phones. It's not that you're on set or at premieres and parties all the time,' Leonard warns any newcomers looking to follow in her footsteps. (She adds, though, that you will be on sets or at premieres and parties for at least some of the time.)

Leonard was born in Cleethorpes, a seaside resort just outside Grimsby in north-east Lincolnshire. She was brought up in Grimsby and admits that she was mortified when Sacha Baron Cohen made his comedy *Grimsby* (2016), portraying most of the locals as gormless, hard-drinking football thugs. 'Not that I've ever hidden that I was brought up in Grimsby but it wouldn't be something I would necessarily advertise,' Leonard observes. 'It has seen better days. In its heyday, it was a very successful fishing town and during that time I think was great but then, as time went on, it just became bleaker.'

Leonard's parents divorced when she was very young and she was brought up by her mother, who had a full-time job as a secretary/clerk. Her grandmother, a larger-than-life figure who dressed in flowing red capes and had a wicked sense of humour, was a major influence on her life – and a well-known figure in the town. Her grandfather, who died in his fifties, was a successful Grimsby fish merchant. They were members of the Conservative Party in Grimsby and were 'quite well to do'.

As a schoolgirl, Leonard had been shy and self-conscious. She wasn't especially interested in cinema but remembers being enraptured by *Bedknobs and Broomsticks* (1971), which stirred a love that exists to this day. She would also troop off to the Odeon in Grimsby for the Saturday morning kids' screenings every week.

The local Grimsby secondary school, Wintringham, which Leonard attended, had a strong academic record. It retained the high scholastic standards from its previous existence as a selective grammar school but nobody would pretend it provided a grounding for a career in the movies. Teachers were conscientious but, Leonard remembers, generally uninspiring. They taught by rote and certainly didn't encourage any of their pupils to think that, one day, they might live and work in Hollywood. Nonetheless, Leonard passed her A levels (in English, geography and economics) and was accepted to study law at Nottingham University.

'I remember at five years old announcing to my grandmother that I was going to be a lawyer. I was not even sure what that meant at that time. I always just thought, "I am going to be a career girl." What I absolutely knew is that I didn't want to do what my mum did.' By the time she was eighteen, Leonard had lost any hankering to be a lawyer but felt a law degree would give her more career opportunities than one in history or English. She thrived at university, studying hard, socializing relentlessly, going to all her lectures and to plenty of parties, and 'got more personality' in the process.

When she graduated in the late 1980s, Leonard decided to travel the world rather than study immediately to become a solicitor or barrister. In the US, she worked in a seaside town as a waitress at The Egg and I in the morning and at the International House of Pancakes in the evening, and soon began picking up a small fortune in tips. 'You just get paid a lot of money when you are an English girl. At the time, I had blonde, curly hair. You just get loads of tips if you smile, be nice and serve them [the customers]. I actually saved up a lot of money.' Leonard even had a third job, helping a local garage with its accounts.

'I was in Hyannis Port. I just basically rocked up, went to the restaurant [where one of the jobs was pre-arranged], stayed on the couch with this really wonderful Irish girl who was doing pretty much the same thing I was doing. The next day, I looked in the local paper, got a bike so I could get around, looked at the accommodation and got myself shared accommodation with seven American college girls who all had these rather startling blue eyes,' Leonard remembers. Only later did she discover her new flatmates were wearing coloured contact lenses.

Leonard had a visa that allowed her to work for a set amount of months. Between jobs, she travelled. There was a brief return to Britain (where she had her graduation photos re-done after the original ones failed to come out). She bought a one-way ticket to Australia and carried on her life of hard work and eye-opening adventure. She was a singing hostess in a nightclub in Melbourne, and she was hired as a cook on a prawn trawler in Townsville, Queensland. ('I was swimming in the sea with one of the sailors on the side of the boat with a gun just in case a shark came.') She picked oranges and pickled onions.

It was all a long way removed from the film industry but Leonard was showing the resilience and acquiring the social skills that would later help her in the world of movie marketing and publicity. After six months in Australia, she 'trotted' her way to East Timor and gradually worked her way through south-east Asia. She worked in a bar in Hong Kong and took a second job there, teaching kids how to speak English. Leonard also ventured to Taiwan, the Philippines and South Korea. She bought herself a one-way ticket home to Britain from Delhi and planned to get to India by hitchhiking through China. 'But one day I woke up in a cold sweat and said to myself, Maxine, if you hitchhike through China, you may never be seen alive again. It doesn't seem like a good idea. This was the 1980s after all and there were not many hitchhikers in China.'

Leonard returned home to England where she soon landed a graduate job with the NatWest bank in London. She was put in corporate finance, in the aerospace division, looking after companies like Rolls-Royce, British Aerospace and McDonnell Douglas and working on defence contracts. The clients would show her the latest range of armaments they were going to be making that year. It wasn't appealing work. Leonard soon felt miserable and began to plot how she could get away.

She started to apply for jobs in entertainment but was invariably rebuffed. One of Leonard's interviews was with Guy East (an important financier, sales agent and producer whose credits ranged from *Dances with Wolves* and *Sliding Doors* to *Terminator 3* and *The Wedding Planner*). He asked if she liked films. Leonard replied that she loved cinema – that she 'laughed and cried and jumped and screamed' and became very emotionally involved with movies when she watched them. East told her bluntly, 'Well, this job will ruin that', but he didn't hire her anyway.

After a year of applications, Leonard finally landed a job as a fundraiser at Shakespeare's Globe, which was being rebuilt on London's South Bank over 350 years after its demolition – a project that had been under way for many years and that was driven by the passion of the inspirational but irascible American actor-director Sam Wanamaker (portrayed on screen by Nicholas Hammond in Quentin Tarantino's 2019 film *Once Upon a Time ... in Hollywood*). Two weeks after Leonard started, the head of fundraising left to take up a job at another charity. 'Sam Wanamaker called me into his office and said, "You seem quite smart. You should become the head of fundraising."'

Leonard was completely unqualified for such a position. However, she had already realized that the administration of the Globe project was 'a bit Keystone Cops'. If she didn't take the job, it would go to somebody 'who has no more clue than I do'. She accepted but told her new bosses they needed to send her on a course so that she could learn at least the basics of what the job entailed.

Over a period of four years, £21 million was raised to complete the reconstruction. Wanamaker himself died in 1993. Leonard had worked alongside the maverick American for around two years. She remembers him with a mixture of affection and exasperation. He was 'an incredible man' but could be a 'bit of a bully', a 'tyrant' and a 'polarizing' figure but the project would never have been completed if he had not had the 'tenacity' to stay with it for so many years. 'I learned a lot from Sam.' Wanamaker and Leonard would have disagreements when neither felt they should apologize. On one occasion, she went into his office after one of these disagreements and stood there without saying anything. He told her that he took her presence as proof that she wanted to apologize and they both then carried on as if the incident hadn't happened.

Along with the fundraising, Leonard became involved in PR for the Globe. She and her colleagues would stage special fundraising events 'over two sticks of wood in the mud because we had broken ground'. They would find ever more original ways to tap potential sponsors for money.

Once the main target had been reached, Leonard decided it was time to move on. The theatre was going to open. She was exhausted and keen to re-charge. There was a Shakespeare's Globe office in LA. This meant that she could get a visitor visa. 'I couldn't work but I could go there and visit and stay for quite a long time.' She had American friends and was keen to spend a few weeks in California. She stayed on, living off her savings, and began to cast around for jobs. It was the mid-1990s; Bill Clinton was US president and Los Angeles presented a world of great possibilities.

Under the Immigration Act, foreign nationals could secure what were called 'national interest waivers' if they could prove that they had exceptional abilities which would benefit the US economy. To her surprise, Leonard discovered that her mix of fundraising and legal skills qualified her and gave her the chance to get a green card. Her petition was accepted within seven days. She could therefore work legally in the US. The next step was to find a suitable job. She knew four or five people in LA and asked them all for advice and contacts. Using her fundraising skills, Leonard quickly widened her circle of acquaintances. One new contact, 'a friend of a friend', Leslie Schwartz, was a Hollywood publicist.

Schwartz quickly set to work introducing Leonard to Hollywood-based PR execs, among them Michael Dalling, a former British journalist who had co-founded publicity company DDA with Dennis Davidson and was now working independently in the US. Another introduction was to Dalling's colleague Nikki Parker, again British and who had recently set up her own fledgling movie PR company, Denmead. They met for coffee. At the time, Leonard had taken a stopgap job working for a focus group company, writing reports on consumers' preferences for fast food and boxer shorts. Parker was running Denmead as a boutique operation in the San Fernando Valley. She needed help and offered Leonard a job. Leonard dived in and soon discovered she was a natural in the world of Hollywood marketing and publicity. 'Those were great days working with Nikki, who I just love and adore. I learned so much from her and I look back on those days with incredible fondness.'

Denmead's clients included Rysher Entertainment, the independent film and TV company behind features like Morgan Freeman thriller *Kiss the Girls* (1997) and Don Roos's *The Opposite of Sex* (1997); Lionsgate, formed in 1997 and later to go on to make the *Hunger Games* trilogy; Initial Entertainment (the company set up by independent British financier/producer Graham King); and a string of German companies, looking to break into Hollywood, among them the fast-expanding Helkon Media.

The job entailed placing stories about clients with the film trade press, primarily rival magazines *Variety* and *The Hollywood Reporter* and their European counterpart *Screen International*, and helping the clients negotiate their way through the all-important film markets like Cannes, the American Film Market (AFM) in Santa Monica and Mifed in Milan. These were the places where producers, distributors and sales agents would announce their new projects, screen the completed ones and try to license them to or acquire them from the US and international distributors. Denmead looked after both the buyers and sellers.

The films that British cinema-goers might eventually see at their local multiplexes had often come through this clearing house. Denmead's artfully created press releases announcing the casting or financing had helped usher the films into existence. It was relentless, fast-paced work in a side of the industry that many of the general public didn't even know existed. 'The first big confab I went to was the AFM. I just loved it: negotiating placement of these stories with the journalists, trying to sell the stories to them, dealing with the clients . . . you just understood very quickly how the whole industry worked,' Leonard says of the horse-trading, stunts and hucksterism that went hand in hand with film PR and marketing. There were no cell phones. The internet was in its infancy. Leonard would have to hoof her way around the markets, delivering press releases by hand or faxing them. She struck up a rapport with most of the trade journalists, who were ultra-competitive with one another but generally polite to her. At moments of stress, Leonard would always remind herself that she was far happier doing film PR than she had been working at the bank.

Denmead had several clients at early stages of their careers but who would develop into major Hollywood players, among them Graham King, the British executive soon to become one of Martin Scorsese's most important collaborators, Joe Drake, who went on to launch the *Hunger Games* franchise, and Nick Meyer, who became President of Paramount Vantage and oversaw the production of Oscar winners *There Will Be Blood* and *No Country for Old Men*.

Every May, Denmead headed to the Cannes Film Festival. This was a key event for clients looking to buy, sell and finance movies. In those early days, Leonard was determined to attend every Cannes event and party she could. 'It was all so exciting and I wanted to see it all,' she said. She would even get herself a scooter so she could move around the seaside town as quickly as possible. Sometimes, she would stay up all night at the various events or just chatting to friends at the Petit Majestic, arrive back at her apartment and realize she would only have time to shower and change before she was due back at her desk. Her main focus at the company was on the corporate side but Denmead was also organizing junket interviews with the world's press for its clients.

This could be a harsh business and it attracted its share of shady characters who didn't always act honestly or honourably. Leonard was startled by the behaviour of one of the agents who was repping a high-profile actor who then denied any knowledge of the actor's involvement in a project announced at Cannes when it started to get negative press. 'I thought that is how they do it!' Leonard notes of the agent's duplicitous behaviour but cites it was 'a great learning moment about how Hollywood works'. The agent had 'plausible deniability'. Like a politician trying to get out of a hole, he simply changed the facts so they fitted the story about his client he now wanted to tell.

Regularly delighted by most of the films they got to work on, sometimes Leonard and Parker would experience that sinking feeling when they watched their clients' films for the first time. They knew all the energy and deal-making ingenuity which had gone into financing these movies but sadly occasionally they just didn't work. 'I remember one occasion watching a test screening of a new film and it really just wasn't very good. I leaned over to her [Parker] and said, "Are our expenses fully paid up?"'

Denmead was expanding, picking up more business and doing well enough to survive even when one major company might hit the reefs. Some of its clients were enjoying a prolonged run of success. Graham King's Initial Entertainment was growing very fast. It had a modest success with Peter Berg's dark comedy *Very Bad Things* (1998), distributed by PolyGram Filmed Entertainment, and was able to secure German investment from Splendid Medien and a multi-million-dollar credit line from Chase Manhattan Bank. Unlike many of his rivals in Hollywood, King wasn't just pursuing that big box-office success in the US. He realized that he could make even more substantial profits by selling his films overseas. Today, the international markets, outside the US, often generate as much as 70 per cent of a film's global box office.

When Martin Scorsese was looking for investment to help with his epic, long-gestating period gangster film *Gangs of New York* (2002), Graham King was perfectly positioned to help. The film had a massive budget of $100 million. King provided $60 million in return for the international rights. In effect, he was taking a punt, gambling that he would sell off these rights for more than he paid. Miramax had the North American rights and agreed to cover the 'overages' (the costs if Scorsese went over budget). *Gangs of New York* ended up grossing $194 million at the global box office, a relatively modest number given its cost and its cast (which included Leonardo DiCaprio, Daniel Day-Lewis and Cameron Diaz). The film, though, was very lucrative indeed for King. With Leonard and co. drafting and disseminating his press releases, and proselytizing on his behalf, he pre-sold *Gangs of New York* for multi-million-dollar amounts to distributors all over the world. In the UK it was released in January 2003 by the leading independent company Entertainment Film Distributors, who steered it to a box-office haul of more than £10 million, a rare achievement for an 18-certificate film.

'He [King] was just one of the best deal makers I have ever come across,' Leonard says of the British executive. At the same time he was investing a fortune (and gambling his company) on Scorsese's film, he was also backing Steven Soderbergh's *Traffic* (2000). Leonard and Nikki Parker saw it at an early screening but this time they were elated. They could sense immediately *Traffic* would be a commercial success and was likely even to be in the running for Oscars.

After the success of *Gangs of New York*, King decided to back Scorsese's next film, his epic Howard Hughes biopic *The Aviator* (2004). This time round, Miramax's Harvey Weinstein wanted the roles reversed. He'd put up the $60 million against foreign rights and leave King to invest in the domestic rights and pay for the overages. Again, the deal worked to King's advantage. He was on set of *The Aviator* every day. It didn't go over budget and he didn't have to pump in any extra money.

Having *Gangs of New York* and *The Aviator* available in the open marketplace was hugely exciting for the international distributors. Generally, such high-profile movies would have been controlled at every step of the way by the Hollywood studios. *The Lord of the Rings* films were financed in a similar way to *Gangs*. These were boom times for the indie film world. Money was flowing in. Distributors were paying and making fortunes. New German film companies were launching themselves on the Neuer Markt of the Frankfurt stock exchange, raising millions and then looking to invest it in Hollywood productions. Leonard had an inside view as some of them became very successful. With the Neuer Markt money behind it, Denmead's client Helkon Media quickly became one of the most important German production and distribution companies. Helkon flourished until its co-founder Werner

Koenig died in an avalanche in the Alps in 2000 while looking for locations for a new film.

Leonard had become a film lover, delighted to be working on some of the best independent films then being made but she was also pragmatic.

> But I never lost sight of the fact that people are buying and selling movies and need to make money. There is a place for all films, even the B movies and the not very good action flicks. There was an audience for them ... I never judged very harshly. It doesn't have to be an Oscar-winning or Palme d'Or-winning movie for it to be a good movie of its kind in its marketplace. There is a place for all of them.

As a good publicist, Leonard would know how to position and 'sell' a movie regardless of her own attitude towards it. From reading the script, knowing the cast, the director and the producer, she could work out the elements worth foregrounding.

In the early 2000s, Leonard left Denmead. She briefly worked as in-house publicist at indie sales and production company Myriad Pictures, a former client. She then took a job in-house with Graham King, joining him just in time for the release of Martin Scorsese's *The Departed* (2006), which won him an Oscar. At the time, King had a production deal with Warner Bros. before striking out on his own. Sony agreed to distribute some of the films he produced independently. There followed a run of high-profile films, among them Florian Henckel von Donnersmarck's *The Tourist* (2010), starring Angelina Jolie and Johnny Depp, *Edge of Darkness* (2010), starring Mel Gibson, and *London Boulevard* (2010), starring Colin Farrell and Keira Knightley. King went on to have several substantial hits, among them *Argo* (2012) and, later, *Bohemian Rhapsody* (2018).

Leonard and King decided to go their separate ways just before the release of Martin Scorsese's *Hugo* (2011), which won Oscars but reportedly went over budget. In 2011, she set up her own LA-based PR company, Maxine Leonard Marketing and Publicity. 'I thought, well, I am not going to work for a studio because there seems to be little security if there is a regime change. I didn't want to go back to an agency. I had done that already. So I jumped into another adventure – I wanted to be more in control of my own destiny,' she explains her rationale.

At her new company, Leonard started with just herself and an assistant. She quickly picked up clients, among them British producer Nigel Sinclair, for whom she handled publicity on films that included *The Beatles: Eight Days a Week* (2016) and Nicolas Chartier's Voltage Pictures, the outfit behind Oscar winner *The Hurt Locker* (2008). Leonard's first film for Voltage was *The Company You Keep* (2013), directed by Robert Redford, which launched at the Venice Film Festival.

At the time of writing, Leonard, the shy girl from Grimsby, has offices on Beverly Boulevard in a building once belonging to Liberace. She has ten full-time staff members alongside regular freelancers who help at markets and festivals. She now has clients in Asia and the UK as well as in the US. Maxine Leonard PR manages producers, writers and directors as well as representing independent companies to sales agents and film distributors worldwide.

While others become jaded and worn down after spending more than twenty years in the thick of the independent film industry, Leonard continues to thrive on her work. She takes crises and breakneck deadlines in her stride. On one film her company was handling *All the Money in the World* (2017), the director Ridley Scott replaced the lead actor Kevin Spacey (who had been caught up in a sex scandal) a matter of weeks before the film was due to be released. Replacing him as J. Paul Getty was Christopher Plummer. While Scott re-shot with Plummer, it was Leonard's job to keep the film's international distributors in the loop, tell them to discard the old posters, and to deal with all the journalists who had been on set when Spacey was still the star. It is reflective of Leonard's approach that rather than panic and complain, she found the experience exhilarating – a chance for everyone to show what they could do under extreme pressure. 'To see Ridley shoot, finish and deliver the film in a matter of weeks – it was a marvel. And to see how [distributors] Sony turned the materials around really fast was amazing,' she enthuses about a film she clearly enjoyed far more than some routine assignment where everything turned out just as expected.

23

Amma Asante[1]

When Amma Asante was growing up as a young black woman in south London, the idea that she would one day be a BAFTA-winning filmmaker with an MBE to her name didn't cross her mind.

Asante (born in 1969) lived in a street in Streatham where there was only one other black family in an otherwise all-white community. She, her parents and her siblings stuck out. The family endured consistent acts of racism. Lit matches would be posted through their letter box. Her father's car was regularly vandalized. Every so often, somebody would daub some offensive graffiti on their property. Her parents were one of the few families on the street who owned their home, something which inspired resentment among certain neighbours. It was normal for her father to put down trays beneath the letter box, on the inside part of the door, to stop the carpet catching fire. 'We were visible in that sense but we learned not to make ourselves any more visible than we needed to be.' In such an environment, filmmaking wasn't uppermost in the young Amma's mind. Her parents tried their hardest to downplay the risk but she couldn't help but be aware of the hostility towards them from some sections of the community.

Years later, even after she had achieved her first successes in the film and TV business, Asante still felt a little like an impostor. 'I feel like that is a luxury in many ways, to be in a position where you could imagine yourself as a film director,' Asante says. 'I already was a film director when I thought to myself maybe this was something I could do more than once.'

---

[1]Unless specified otherwise, the material in this chapter comes from the author's interviews with Amma Asante in London during the summer of 2019.

Amma Asante. Photo: © Joseph Sinclair.

Asante's earliest memories of cinema are of being taken to the cinema on Streatham High Road by her older brother, who is almost ten years older than she is. They would go to Disney films and other kids' movies together (*Bambi, Bedknobs and Broomsticks, Chitty Chitty Bang Bang*) on Saturday mornings. She would also watch old John Wayne westerns on Sunday afternoons, not out of conscious choice but because this is what was on the TV and was what her brother liked.

'My parents came from Ghana and they weren't really aware of the stranger in the room, so to speak – the idea of the television being an outside voice,'

Asante recalls. When her parents had been growing up themselves, they would come home from school and go outside and play. They didn't have television. Partly as a result of this, they didn't pay too much attention to what Amma watched. She has vivid recollections of seeing John Schlesinger's *Midnight Cowboy* (1969), a drama about the unlikely friendship between a male prostitute and a disabled con artist, when still a young kid. She didn't fully understand it and was disturbed by it but could still respond to some of its themes. She would also watch documentaries, for example hard-hitting films shown on ITV's *World in Action*.

This was the 1970s. Amma was the youngest in a family of five. Her mother would be in the kitchen, cooking. Her brother and sister would be doing homework. Her father wouldn't be home from work and Amma's attention would be caught by whatever happened to be showing. 'I learned about the society I was being raised in and I learned about conflict in various parts of the world through the documentaries that were on.' Forty years later, she still credits these documentaries with influencing her outlook on the world and her choice of subject matter in her movies, in which she has always dealt with exploitation, injustice, racism and sexism.

When she was in her teenage years, she would go to James Bond films with her friends and their parents. Her parents tended to be too busy for cinema trips. 'They worked really, really hard,' Amma remembers. Her father was an accountant. Her mother ('she loved to be an entrepreneur – she was really sharp') ran a hair and cosmetics business. During the recession of the 1980s, Asante's mother successfully transformed her shop into a delicatessen, importing perishable foods from Ghana on a twice-weekly basis.

Asante's parents were always looking for ways to keep her stimulated. When she was nine or ten, one of her best friends enrolled in a tap-dancing class in Streatham. 'I copied everything she did,' Amma remembers. 'She was at tap class and so I went to tap class with her.' The youngster's negative experience at the dance class was to have a huge influence on the way her career eventually developed. Amma was marginalized at the dance school. Most of the other kids were white. The defining moment came when her mother took time off from her business, which was based in Shepherd's Bush, to come home to Streatham to watch her daughter perform.

'I had begged my mother to come and see me in the show. She had shut the shop early to come all the way down to Streatham, where we lived, to see the show.' The mother sat patiently waiting for her daughter's appearance – but it never came. Amma was only seen on stage for a few moments during the finale. On the way home, Amma asked her mother if she had enjoyed the performance. 'She said, "Yes, but, sweetheart, you weren't really in it. I came all this way to see you but you weren't in the show."' Asante explained that she had been chosen to perform one routine to the song 'Blue Eyes', but that the dance teacher had told her at the last minute that she couldn't perform it because she didn't have blue eyes.

Asante's parents were incensed by the decision which seemed to them to be cruel and racially motivated. 'My father had noted that I was creative and needed a creative outlet,' Asante recalls. The parents were determined to find somewhere for her where the teachers wouldn't discriminate against her because of the colour of her eyes. They enrolled her in the Barbara Speake Stage School in west London. This was a fee-paying independent school which taught academic subjects as well as dance and drama. The school also acted as an agent for its pupils. Through the school, Asante landed her first significant acting role, in the hugely popular children's BBC TV drama *Grange Hill*.

'I think that, as a relatively shy child, stage school is quite a culture shock,' Asante says of her first impressions of the school. She was ten years old when she arrived. It was a huge change. 'Having all my life gone to school in south London, I was suddenly going to school in west London.' The other kids were boisterous and self-confident. After all, they were performers. Early on, she didn't want to be there. Gradually, though, she started to fit in. The kids were from different backgrounds and religions. The ages of the other pupils ranged from five to sixteen. 'When you are at school with five-year-olds, you have to learn empathy and responsibility,' Asante observes of the younger children she was studying alongside. 'What I was also really aware of was that it [the school] was expensive. I felt the sense of my parents having to work very, very hard, far harder than they had been, in order to be able to afford to send me there.'

This was early 1980s London. There were still hints of racism and snobbery but the school was 'a thousand times better' than the tap-dancing establishment where she had been prevented from going on stage because of the colour of her eyes. Her contemporaries included several other figures who would carve out significant careers, among them Naomi Campbell, soon to emerge as one of the most important British supermodels of the era, Kwame Kwei-Armah, the actor, playwright and director who, in 2019, was running the Young Vic, and actress and singer Michelle Gayle. Asante credits the school with allowing its pupils to find their creative voice, whether they decided to write, sing, dance or act.

Thanks to the school, Asante was soon earning money – and paying for her own school fees. There was a strong camaraderie among the pupils. Gayle, who was a little younger than Asante, had auditioned for the role in *Grange Hill* in which Asante was later cast. Rather than give in to jealousy or self-pity when she was passed over for the role, Gayle provided Asante with tips on what the casting directors were looking for. 'She told me what the process was, what they were looking for and really just gave me as much information as she could, as fast as she could.' Gayle briefed her so well that she was given the part after a single audition. Years later, Gayle (who did later get cast in *Grange Hill* too) was to sing at Asante's wedding.

As a teenager acting in *Grange Hill*, playing the sensible and mature Cheryl Webb from 1985 to 1987, Asante quickly began to pick up the craft of filmmaking. Before she appeared in *Grange Hill*, she had been a fan of the show anyway. 'I was one of those who, prior to being in the show, came home and actively switched the telly on to watch *Grange Hill*. Having watched it for many years, I had an understanding of where we had to get to in the process of filmmaking. The ultimate goal was to end up with an episode like the ones I had enjoyed watching.'

Asante compares the way she absorbed lessons about acting and filmmaking on the set of *Grange Hill* to the instinctive way a child learns languages. 'You don't necessarily know that you're learning but you're a sponge, taking in so much without understanding or really caring that you are learning. Before you know it, you are quite fluent in the language.' Years later, when Asante was beginning to write, produce and direct, she discovered that she already knew the jargon and many of the techniques of filmmaking. She knew what finding the light meant, she knew what a grip was and what a spark did. 'The language of telling visual stories can be quite alienating if it is not a world that you have been submerged in from a very young age.'

Some heavyweight talents were involved in *Grange Hill*, among them the series creator, Liverpudlian Phil Redmond, who was also behind such series as *Brookside* and *Hollyoaks*, and the series script editor Anthony Minghella, who was to become one of Britain's most important filmmakers and Chair of the British Film Institute (Asante had followed Minghella's career as he went from *Grange Hill* to working in theatre, directing TV dramas and then making big-budget movies like *The English Patient* (1996) and *Cold Mountain* (2003)). 'I think he was one of my first examples of somebody who navigated their way through the industry,' Asante says of the British director who, by the time he died in 2008, had established an international reputation. (See Chapter 17 on Anthony Minghella.)

The Stage School would take both the school fees and a cut as agent out of the money. Only a small amount of money trickled back down to her. Kids in the show who were under sixteen weren't paid directly anyway but she noticed that one or two of the older actors were 'driving very nice cars'.

Being a successful teenage TV actress was both rewarding and unsettling. Asante had no idea if her career would last beyond *Grange Hill*. She enjoyed herself on set but, back at home, 'it wasn't always fun'. When she came back to south London, people recognized her. Some of her contemporaries were jealous of her. She felt 'different' and a bit of an outsider. It didn't help that she hated acting, an irony considering the success she was enjoying. Asante loved watching the others in the cast perform. 'I was surrounded by very, very talented young actors who were just brilliant. My period in the show was around the period the show was tackling the heroin issue in the UK. The show was being used to communicate a message to young people of the devastation this drug could bring into your life.' Thanks to the anti-drugs storyline, Asante was part of the team from *Grange Hill* who travelled to Washington, DC to meet Nancy Reagan, who then was leading her own 'just say no' campaign against drug abuse.

Asante 'knew what good acting looked like,' as she puts it. She was also aware that she wasn't delivering it herself. She was strangely self-conscious in front of the cameras. When she looks back at some of the vintage episodes in which she appeared, her immediate reaction to her own performances is that she was 'as wooden as a tree trunk. For whatever reason, they [the producers] had me in the show. You'd have to ask them why.' What the young actress and aspiring writer did learn was 'the power of storytelling and my love for it.' She loved seeing the impact the show had on her friends and family, who weren't 'a community of actors or performers but a regular, ordinary south London community'.

By the time she left the series after two years in 1987, Asante knew she wanted to be a storyteller. She just didn't know how. 'Leaving *Grange Hill*, I wasn't only black and only female. I was also very, very young,' she remembers. Her colour, her gender and her age seemed like gigantic obstacles. She didn't know any other successful writers or filmmakers who were black, female and young. She felt completely lost. Asante was still only 'sixteen going on seventeen'. There wasn't any obvious route for her to go to college and then on to university. She didn't feel skilled in anything. She didn't have A levels (and wouldn't get any until she took exams in English literature at Chelsea and Westminster College in her late twenties in a break from writing her first TV series). Asante had an O level in art but that was about as far as her academic qualifications went.

Her mother, who had a ferocious work ethic and no time for self-pity, found her a secretarial college on Tottenham Court Road in central London. This was where Asante headed as part of a Youth Training Scheme (YTS) which would guarantee her some payment as she learned typing and shorthand. It was a bit of a come-down for the former *Grange Hill* star. Through the scheme, she was put on work placement at Heinemann Publishers.

Whatever her qualms about acting, Asante was comfortable enough as a presenter on a kids' TV show for The Children's Channel. Ron Smedley, one of the old producers at *Grange Hill*, had recommended her for the job. She co-hosted the show with Lee MacDonald, one of the other *Grange Hill* actors.

Asante had also been trying to get her typing speed up. At secretarial college she was taught to do this through copy typing, a process which she found increasingly frustrating. One day, rather than practising the typing by copying secondary material, she began to write whatever came into her head in a free-flowing stream of consciousness. She had read more scripts than she had books. It was therefore natural for her to write dialogue. The story she came up with was a sitcom heavily based on her family. 'I thought it might have something to it but at the same time I didn't have a clue who to send it to,' she remembers. Asante had contacts through *Grange Hill* but doubted very much that any of them would take her seriously as an aspiring author. She therefore came up with a pseudonym, which was her mother's maiden name. 'I decided to send it [the script] out to a few producers I knew and see what might happen but I didn't really expect anything.'

Sure enough, one of the producers 'bit'. Somehow, Sarah Stroud, an agent at literary agents Judy Daish Associates, saw the script too and offered immediately to represent the writer, even though she had no idea of her identity. Judy Daish Associates were the agents for Anthony Minghella, too. 'That overwhelmed me slightly. I thought, she can't really mean it because she's Anthony's agent.'

Chrysalis Entertainment expressed interest in producing the script. Others were also asking for meetings with the writer. Asante realized she was going to have to come out from behind her pseudonym. Twenty-one years old, Asante was still self-conscious about her youth. She hadn't managed to secure any work as a secretary but had been working for several months in the box office of a theatre. Eventually, she called Stroud and asked if the offer to represent her was genuine. Stroud quickly reassured her that it was.

Momentum built very quickly. Chrysalis presented the script to Channel 4 who were immediately enthusiastic and commissioned seven scripts. Then, the BBC came in with a four-script deal. From a standing start, Asante suddenly had contracts requiring her to deliver a lot of work for two different commissioners from two of the UK's main broadcasters. She gave up her day job and stayed home to write – and write.

The BBC provided her with a mentor, the experienced comedy writer, producer and script editor Paul Mayhew-Archer. He would give her practical advice about such matters as how to do rewrites without squeezing out the originality that made her scripts appealing in the first place. It helped, too, that she had done all those episodes of *Grange Hill*. She discovered that she already had an innate understanding of story structure. 'When you're turning around two scripts a month as a performer, with two weeks for each one, you're taking it in without realizing you are taking it in,' Asante says of the knowledge she had unconsciously developed. She repeats her point about 'learning a language without really realizing you are learning a language'.

Asante also learned about the harshness and arbitrary nature of the commissioning process. In the end, neither of the two dramas was made. New editors had come in to take over the departments and wanted to bring their own projects with them rather than inherit those of their predecessors. In the short term, Asante was disappointed. However, she also felt extremely lucky at being given the time to develop the projects, at being paid for her work and at having the opportunity to hone her skills in the process. 'At that point, I felt I had achieved just in getting the commissions really.' She also discovered that very little gets commissioned that others within the industry don't know about. Her two dramas might not have been made but now everybody at Channel 4 and the BBC was aware of her.

A little later, when the BBC had a slot for a low-budget soap, they turned towards Asante to come up with an idea. Writer, entrepreneur and restaurateur Vincent Osborne had submitted a loose idea to the BBC for what was to become the first black soap opera, *Brothers and Sisters*, on BBC2. This was set around a gospel church in the north of England. Asante was approached to flesh out the idea. She started writing in May. By September, the series was already filming. As the project got under way, Asante ended up taking on what became known a few years later on big US TV dramas as the showrunner role. She ran the production, wrote significant episodes and worked with other writers.

This was her first major narrative commission and she was effectively calling the shots. Even if she wasn't directing, she was doing everything she could to ensure that the project arrived on screen exactly as she wanted it. 'In my mind, I thought that was producing because I had, of course, seen female producers. What I didn't understand was what I wanted to do was actually called directing,' Asante remembers. It didn't help that she had so few role models. There had been one female director on *Grange Hill* but, other than that, all the filmmakers she had encountered at this stage were men.

Nor was Asante thinking in terms of feature films. 'I was absolutely television,' she says of this period of her career. By this point, she had become events officer on the committee at BAFTA. Quite apart from anything else, it enabled her to get out of the house. One of the downsides to being a professional writer, she discovered, was the solitude. She was gregarious and enjoyed meeting fellow professionals in the industry. One early event she oversaw was bringing Spike Lee over to London to accept a special BAFTA. She was a big admirer of Lee and of other black American directors like John Singleton, director of *Boyz n the Hood* (1991). By this point, she had also seen *Daughters of the Dust* from director Julie Dash, famous as the first feature film directed by an African-American woman that was given a proper theatrical release in US cinemas. She had also seen female British-Nigerian director Ngozi Onwurah's *Welcome to the Terror Dome* (1995). Again, though, Onwurah seemed to have achieved 'an unattainable position', not one that she felt she could easily reach herself. Instead, Asante envisaged a career in which she would script work and help usher it into existence through her production company, Tantrum Films. (The name was intended as 'a tongue-in-cheek way of putting the finger up at everybody that ever felt that if you were a woman in the industry, somehow you felt you had to be some kind of diva'. The logo for the company was a high heel.)

Asante's first feature, when she finally had the chance to make it, wasn't about black experience in the UK. Thanks to a friendship she had struck up with Welsh filmmaker and TV drama producer Peter Edwards, she ended up shooting a film in a deprived part of Cardiff instead. Asante had gone to an event celebrating the work of Welsh writers and directors. She started talking to Edwards (then head of drama at HTV). Six weeks later, Edwards contacted Asante and told her he wanted to work with her. *A Way of Life* sprang out of this encounter. After she had finished an early draft of the screenplay, Edwards told her he felt this 'was something that could be on around the country or perhaps that we could get film money for'. The story touched on teen pregnancy, poverty, racism and state indifference in a small community in Wales.

The story may have been Welsh but the writer-director felt its themes were universal. Certain aspects reminded her of the working-class Streatham she had grown up in. 'I felt at home there. I still do,' she says of South Wales. In her film, she was exploring the growth of an 'underclass', young British citizens who had fallen out of work and education and had next to no prospects. The Welsh embraced the young London filmmaker. She was never made to feel like an outsider and relished her trips to Wales while preparing the movie and the weeks she spent there shooting it. She talks of her relief at meeting Welsh filmmakers and writers and escaping the 'London-centric' world of British film and television. She was very aware that she wasn't Welsh herself but was determined that her project would mean something to Welsh audiences. She may have been from London but her crew and cast were Welsh.

By then, the UK Film Council, the new public body for film in the UK launched in 2000, had been in existence for three or four years. Asante herself had been offered a job as an executive at the new body. She didn't take it because she wanted to concentrate on her own work. However, even as she turned down the post, she mentioned that she had a project of her own that might be suitable for support. 'It was a very, very long-winded process. Needless to say, they turned it down in the first instance. I am not sure why,' Asante remembers of her initial attempts at securing UKFC backing for *A Way of Life*. Eventually, the Film Council financiers relented and decided to support the film after all.

Asante's directorial debut came at the suggestion of financier Paul Trijbits, then head of the New Cinema Fund at UK Film Council, who liked her screenplay for *A Way of Life* (2004), and had suggested she could direct it herself. Asante's initial reaction was that this was a very bad idea. She saw herself as a writer and hadn't even thought about amplifying her role. 'I didn't know anybody who looked like me or who was like me who was directing,' she remembers. 'I didn't know any black females who were directing. That's not to say they didn't exist – I just didn't know any. All the directors I knew were white and male.'

However, Trijbits's logic was compelling. He told her she knew her own characters far better than any other director. She took on the job and was 'very comfortable' doing it. In their meetings to discuss the film, Paul Trijbits recognized Asante's 'knack' for directing. He realized that she knew exactly how to take the characters she wrote on the page to fruition on the screen. 'He recognized very clearly that that was a writer-director, not a writer-producer.'

Asante remembers her first day on the set, directing the movie, as being 'terrifying. I thought I was completely mad.' She questioned 'why on earth I had said yes to this'. Impostor syndrome came in. 'But I couldn't even call it impostor syndrome because I hadn't even pretended I was capable of doing this.' As the writer-director would later discover, those feelings of anxiety never go away completely. In later years, even after winning her BAFTA and showing her films at festivals around the world, she would still feel a sense of panic at the start of a new project and start asking herself, 'Why the hell am I here? Why did I think I could do this?' She realized that this was part of the experience of filmmaking and that her creativity and insecurity were in some way intertwined. 'I am probably not alone in questioning my capabilities and then throwing out the doubts and getting on and doing it anyway.'

The UK Film Council had a reputation for interfering in the creative work of filmmakers whose movies they supported. *A Way of Life* had a budget of £1.3 million. 'The lower the budget of the film, the less there is an imperative to see a return on the investment,' Asante reflects on the reasons she was largely left alone to make the film on her own terms. She talks about the Film Council trying to give new talent its voice, at least on first films. 'Obviously, I've had other films financed by the Film Council and different films have required a different emphasis on notes,' the writer-director says of later experiences. 'Some have been very note heavy and some haven't. It has often depended on who the other partners are. I've done films which have had a much, much higher budget than my first film and the notes have been commensurate.' It's the nature of low-budget British filmmaking that, on any given feature, there will be several different financiers, all wanting a say in how the project evolves. If they don't all agree with each other or if they have questions for the director, lengthy negotiation may be required.

Asante saw welcome changes in the British film industry in the decade and a half after her debut feature. Many more 'people of colour' were being nominated for BAFTAs. (When she picked up her own award, the only other black female she knew of who had also won one was screenwriter and children's author Malorie Blackman.) It no longer seemed quite so outlandish to want to become a filmmaker. 'Young and talented names have picked up BAFTAs in the years since I won mine. But I think that only goes to show how terrible the problem was because we are still in a terrible place.' Asante remained diffident and self-conscious about her profession, She says it took until her third or fourth film before she would tell a cab driver asking her what she did that she was a film director.

Nor was Asante's progress through the industry especially smooth. It took a decade for her to follow up on *A Way of Life* with her second feature, *Belle*

(2013). 'Sophomore' films, as second movies are called in the US, remained very tough to get made. 'In 2005, we [in the UK] just weren't in any space to embrace female directors. The experience of having ten years between your first film and your second film as a female director was not unusual. I remember Gurinder Chadha talking about it,' Asante says of her fellow British filmmaker whose debut feature, *Bhaji on the Beach*, was made in 1993 but who then had to wait several years to direct another.

Asante attributes the hiatus in her career to a variety of factors: a recession, her private life (she fell in love and got married) and the conservatism of commissioners. As a black female director, she was part of the 0.4 per cent of filmmakers who had had films released in the cinema. 'As a woman, you can never rest on your laurels. There has never been a point where I've gone, "Phew, I can relax now",' Asante reflects. 'At the same time, it's important to acknowledge to myself that I have a body of work now and that puts me in a far better place than that first time when I was stepping on set and really had nothing to show for myself as to why a crew should follow my vision.'

Asante is aware that it is a huge privilege to have financiers and distributors spend millions in making and releasing your film. You don't expect it to come easy. 'It's tough whoever you are. [But] for those of us who come from marginalized backgrounds when it comes to the industry, it is even harder. In some ways, things have got better but in some ways they have remained the same.' That may sound like a downbeat conclusion but her own example has inspired others. She is the black female filmmaker from Streatham who won a BAFTA with her very first film, defying enormous odds in the process.

24

Julian Richards[1]

If European, Latin American or Asian distributors want to buy gory, blood-soaked new horror films at events like the Cannes or Berlin Film Festivals or the American Film Market, they will beat their way to the booth of small but respected British sales company Jinga Films. They'll find films with titles like *Infection, I Am Toxic, Sadistic Intentions, Echoes of Fear* and *Nazi Undead*. They will be dealing with Jinga's CEO and head of production Julian Richards and his Brazilian partner Rosana Couthino, experts who know the genre market inside out.

Richards is a stalwart of the British film sales scene. He is also a prolific filmmaker in his own right, famous for directing the very first Welsh horror movie. He is an example of someone who came into the industry because he loved cinema but then realized he needed to understand the business if he was going to be able to sustain a long-term career.

Richards was born in Newport, Gwent, a working-class steel town in South Wales. His father, William James Richards, ran his own business, DIY store Handiland, which prospered at a time when the region as a whole was entering a period of steep, post-industrial decline. At its peak, the Handiland empire extended to over twenty stores. Most were in Wales but some opened up in English cities as well. Richards's father was well enough off to take the family on foreign holidays to exotic destinations. The father had an 8 mm camera with which he filmed their holidays. He'd send the footage away to Kodak to

---

[1]Unless specified otherwise, the material in this chapter comes from the author's interviews with Julian Richards in London, November 2019.

Julian Richards. Photo: George Pimentel/WireImage/Getty Images.

be processed. Richards would watch him editing it on a Viewer, cutting and sellotaping the thin strips of footage into the order he wanted. 'It was actually through seeing him do that that I became aware of what filmmaking was,' Richards recalls.

Richards's uncle, Rex Richards (1934–89), was a celebrated figure in the community. He had played rugby once for Wales, as a prop in a match against France at Cardiff Arms Park in March 1956. Rex's nickname in the press was 'Tarzan'. He once received a 'cease and desist' letter from an American company, telling him he wasn't allowed to use the name of the Edgar Rice Burroughs hero. Rex, though, couldn't help what the media wrote about him. He was a strong and good-looking man whose appearances for his local team, Cross Keys, attracted not just rugby fans but lots of local women as well. Old friends later recalled 'streams of women flocking to the ground just to see Rex play on the hallowed ground of the Pandy,'[2] the park where the club hosted its home games.

News of a planned Hollywood remake of *Tarzan* filtered through to South Wales. Rex, whose rugby career hadn't gone as far as he had hoped, thought he might as well audition. He headed off to the US and flexed his torso for the Hollywood bosses. Out of the many hundreds vying for the loin cloth, he got through to the last five. In the end, the role of Tarzan stayed with Gordon Scott (who had played the ape man since 1955). Rex Richards had to content himself with the plum role of the King of Wongo in the celebrated B movie *The Wild Women of Wongo* (1958), which his nephew Julian proudly hails as 'one of the worst films ever made – they basically cast all the Tarzan rejects for that film'. He is also said to have appeared as an extra alongside Lon Chaney Jnr in the TV series *The Last of the Mohicans* (1957). Rex stayed in America, building a life for himself as an entertainer and aqua-diver. He worked with Esther Williams, the 'diving beauty' and 'Hollywood's mermaid' as she was called.

Back home in Wales, the Richards family was proud of Rex's achievements. Here was a man who had never been to drama school but had gone to America and built himself a career in the film business (or at least on its still glamorous periphery) on the basis of his looks and athleticism. He would come from the

---

[2]https://www.walesonline.co.uk/news/wales-news/incredible-story-wales-tarzan-2087204.

US to Newport every Christmas and regale his relatives with tales of what seemed to them to be a very exotic life.

Julian Richards, who was at the local comprehensive school, St Julian's, was beginning to watch movies on TV. One which made a particular impression on him was the original *King Kong* (1933), directed by Merian C. Cooper and Ernest B. Schoedsack. 'I remember being very amazed that King Kong was meant to be the bad guy, the monster, but actually he's not. I can remember feeling really emotional at the end of *King Kong*. There was something about the way the horror genre was dealing with outsiders. I was really engaged by the human side of the story.'

The youngster was also lapping up double bills of Universal horror movies from the 1930s (*Frankenstein*, *Dracula* and *The Wolfman*) shown on the BBC. He was keen, too, on the dinosaur movies with special effects by Ray Harryhausen, films like *Jason and the Argonauts* (1963) and *The Valley of Gwangi* (1969). 'It's the thrill ride, the rollercoaster. It's like you are going on a scary experience,' Richards tries to make sense of the youthful predilection for horror which has never left him. 'I was scared of the dark. I was scared of all kinds of things. There was no way I would put myself in any kind of danger at all. But through a horror film, I could do – and deal with that anxiety . . .'

Richards's parents would fall asleep and snore – so he would wake them up and send them to bed. That meant he would be left on the sofa on his own. The solitude would make the experience yet more frightening. He himself would sometimes fall asleep and wake up at one in the morning, in time for the end credits of the film he had been trying to watch. 'I missed many films that way.'

Richards was beginning to experiment with his father's super 8 mm camera. He would go out and make films with his friends at the weekend. He experimented with Ray Harryhausen-style stop motion, shooting a sequence with his Action Man doll and toy dinosaur but the camera wasn't customized for that style of filmmaking. His first completed movie, *The Curse of Cormac*, was made when he was thirteen years old. Richards was a subscriber to the *House of Hammer* magazine and borrowed the plot for the film from a comic-book story included in one of the editions. It took almost an entire year to complete the project, which was thirty minutes long. He edited it himself, did the post-production sound and added the music. 'It was such an effort to put it together but such a thrill to sit and watch it with an audience.'

The tyro director held a special screening at the school. It was well received. The local newspaper *South Wales Argus* ran a story on the film. His father (a regular advertiser) had tipped them off his son was an Orson Welles-like prodigy. The headmaster called him in. Richards anticipated he was going to be praised for his artistry and initiative. In fact, he was given a stern dressing-down because the *Argus* story headline had been 'Newport school boy makes devil worship film'. The headmaster was very perturbed at the idea of satanic goings-on in the classroom.

In spite of the telling-off, Richards continued with his weekend filmmaking. Throughout his adolescence, he went on to make a new 8 mm movie every year. Among the titles were *The Girl that Cried Wolf, Evil Inspirations* and *Gang Warfare*. His school friends, who played the leading roles, were enthusiastic but untrained and not especially talented. 'Most of them were terrible and I realized that the acting] was one of the weaknesses of the films I was making.' Richards responded by seeking out the best talent in the school drama class. 'But usually I then found they were way over the top,' he says of the cast members who'd shone in school plays but hadn't realized that a little Method-style minimalism worked best in front of camera. 'It was an education that what works for school theatre doesn't work for film. But I did find one or two people who were more naturalistic.'

The director's friends and family helped with the costumes, props and sandwich-making. Richards's films were lurid affairs. He'd either buy fake blood from the town's joke shop or mix it himself by blending tomato ketchup with other liquids and substances close to hand. When he needed a skeleton, he borrowed one from the life-drawing class at the local art college. (His older sister was enrolled there.) 'I left it lying in the hallways of my house. There was a lady who used to clean who looked through the letter box and saw this skeleton covered in blood. She screamed and didn't know what was going on.'

While Richards was a diehard horror fan, he also liked his martial arts films and was keen on films like *The Warriors, The Wanderers, Grease* and even *West Side Story*, coming-of-age stories with a gang element. Some of his own movies reflected this enthusiasm.

Still, growing up in South Wales, the young auteur didn't see any obvious route into the film business. This was a hobby, not a career. He was set on becoming a carpenter.

Eventually, though, Richards changed his mind. Film, he decided, really was his vocation. Seeing Steven Spielberg's *Jaws* (1975) at a packed screening convinced him of the fact. The young filmmaker had had his own encounter with a great white shark – or at least he thought he had – while on the family's most lavish family holiday, to Hawaii. He had been surfing for the first time when suddenly he saw a huge shadow on the sea bed. He paddled as fast as he could back to shore but the big, dark shadow followed him every inch of the way. It was only when he waded out of the water that he realized it was the shadow of his own surf board. 'But I could hear the music. I could imagine what was going to happen to me next. I think it was that moment where I just said, yeah, this is what I want to be. I want to be a filmmaker.'

Newport, it turned out, had its own film school, one which had been founded by John Grierson, the 'father' of British documentary in 1966. When he was around seventeen, he ventured down to investigate. He wasn't officially enrolled but hoped that by hanging around he could befriend some of the students and persuade them to help him borrow one of the school's Bolex cameras. Mark Milsome (later to become a very successful cameraman who worked on everything from *Four Weddings and a Funeral* (1994) to HBO's series *Game of Thrones*, and who died in Africa in 2017 when a stunt went wrong) was enrolled at the film school and took pity on Richards. With Milsome's help, Richards was able to use the school's equipment.

Richards applied to Bournemouth Film School but was turned down because his academic grades weren't good enough. He therefore took a year out and enrolled on the same art foundation course at Newport College of Art and Design through which his sister had once procured him a skeleton. He made a new film (*Evil Inspirations*), re-sat his A levels, got the grades he needed and re-applied to Bournemouth. This time, he was accepted. He studied there from 1985 to 1988. He had wanted to go to Bournemouth because of the practical dimension to the course. Other film schools had seemed to him to be too academic and too preoccupied with theory. Nonetheless, he struggled to conceal his dismay when the head of the school told the students at the beginning of the course: 'There are two things we don't do. We don't make horror films and we don't make films with car chases.' For Richards, that was like having his left leg and right leg amputated. He persevered, telling himself he could continue making his 8 mm horror films on the side, without the school finding out about it.

The school encouraged Richards to make more personal work, about his life's experience, and not to copy what he had seen on TV. That is how he came to direct his films *Pirates* and *Queen Sacrifice*, both autobiographical affairs about his experiences as a child and teenager growing up in South Wales. The former was a comedy drama about three 'very different guys – a bodybuilder, a punk and a college boy' – who get a summer job working in a DIY store very similar to Handiland. Richards describes it as a South Wales version of a brat-pack movie like *The Breakfast Club* (1985). It won the main prize at the Celtic Film Festival.

Bournemouth students used to go every year to a festival of student films in Munich. Richards was given the chance to see the best in student filmmaking from all over Western and Eastern Europe. The variety startled him. Work on show ranged from beautifully shot but deeply esoteric Polish movies to very commercial West German ones. He didn't feel that his own the work was inferior to what he was being shown.

Richards may have been accepted for one film school but he wanted to be at another. In this period in British film history, it was essential to have a union ticket, an ACTT card, to be allowed to work in the industry. Bournemouth didn't provide it but the National Film and Television School in Beaconsfield did. He decided he needed to be there. 'I started applying [to the NFTS] even during my first year at Bournemouth. I would get rejections but each year I would apply anyway. I think I had even applied before I started at Bournemouth. By the time I finished there, I had become very familiar to the National Film School.' Richards had applied four times and been rejected four times by the end of his Bournemouth course. He showed the NFTS admissions tutors his film *Pirates*. The tutors there were very impressed with his editing and were willing to offer him a place as an editor. However, he made it clear that he was only interested in directing. They therefore rejected him yet again.

Following the try, try and try again philosophy which has sustained him throughout his career, Richards reacted to the rejection by making yet another application. In the meantime, *Queen Sacrifice* (1988), a story about first love set against the backcloth of the British chess championships in Bournemouth, ended up winning the Best Fiction Film at the BP Expo – British Short Film Festival 1990. This gave the director extra ammunition for his assault on the NFTS. Eventually, after multiple rejections, he was accepted for the directing course at what is, by consensus, the most prestigious film school in Britain. The average age of a first-year NFTS student was twenty-six, but when Richards joined the course at twenty-two, he became one of the youngest students to be accepted.

Richards's near contemporaries at the school included figures like Michael Caton-Jones (director of *Scandal* (1990)), Danny Cannon (director of *The Young Americans* (1993)) and, in the animation department, future Oscar winner Nick Park.

The teaching was on the dogmatic side. 'Their whole agenda was to break you down. It was like, "You've already been to film school, you've learned how to make films but, now, what we want to do is for you to forget everything you've learned, start from zero and make films the National Film School way",' Richards remembers. The ethos here was one of British social realism. Students were taught that the best way to approach fiction was through documentary. During his second year at the school, Richards made a short called *Bad Company* (1992), a Welsh version of a *Boyz n the Hood*-style thriller about a young man in the valleys trying to avoid a life of crime. He was then headhunted by BBC Wales to direct part of a series called Wales Playhouse. The school reluctantly allowed him to take a sabbatical.

Richards was in demand in Wales for the simple reason that he was one of the few active Welsh filmmakers in this period. There were one or two other Welsh directors (Karl Francis, Marc Evans and Paul Turner among them) but it was a small pool. He was considered one of the young talents to watch. 'I realized it was good for me to play on my Welshness. I was making films about what I knew about – and what I knew about was growing up in Wales,' Richards recalls of this period when he was part of the so-called 'Cool Cymru' era in which Welsh artists, musicians and filmmakers with strong, distinctive voices were at last beginning to emerge. However, the young director's romance with his homeland was soon to turn a little sour. He was not a Welsh speaker. Much of the money available for filmmakers in Wales was targeted at Welsh-language cinema. 'I am Welsh but I am not that Welsh. I am very anglicized,' the director says of himself. 'Therefore, I started to feel like an outsider in Wales even though I was making significant short films [in Wales].'

Richards began to feel as if he was in no man's land. The Welsh wouldn't support him because he didn't make Welsh-language films. Across the border, the English public funders were much more interested in backing arthouse pictures than in his brand of genre cinema.

Not that he was deterred by the rejection. Richards had always been most inspired by what was happening in the US. That was where most of his cinematic heroes came from, directors like Spielberg and Martin Scorsese. He also saw that a new generation of indie US filmmakers were successfully starting careers in the 1990s without the crutch of public support, often by maxing out on their own or relatives' credit cards.

When he finally graduated from the National Film School, Richards therefore went straight to the US. His first stop was New York where he organized a screening of three of his films – *Pirates*, *Queen Sacrifice* and *Bad Company* – at Tribeca, in the recently opened film centre. He didn't have any contacts but simply rang up and asked how much it would cost to book a ninety-minute screening slot. Once a price was agreed, he wrote letters to all the production companies in the city, inviting them to the screening. His agents in London, Peters, Fraser and Dunlop, helped with a few other names. Richards was able to stay free of charge with Chris Westwood, a New York-based friend who was an author and whose young adult novel, *Calling All Monsters*, he was hoping to adapt. Nothing directly came from the New York screening although some of the biggest producers in the city attended the event.

After New York, Richards headed to LA. An old school friend was living there. 'I hadn't spoken to her for four or five years but I managed to get hold of her number and called her up.' She agreed to allow him to stay. He booked another screening, at the Pacific Design Center in West Hollywood. BAFTA LA was persuaded to share its list of members with him – and he invited every name he found on the list. Attendance was relatively spare but one person who did turn up was agent Michael Lewis, who took him on and quickly secured him a meeting with Spielberg's production company, Amblin Entertainment. Amblin then promptly optioned Westwood's novel and paid Richards and the author to write a screenplay. Had the film gone into production, Richards and Westwood would have split $500,000 between them. As it was, they were paid an option fee which amounted to £12,500 each followed by a further £27,500 to write the screenplay. Richards came back from his first trip to America with a deal with Spielberg and thousands of pounds in his bank account.

For a short while, getting ahead in the film business seemed very straightforward indeed. In 1992/93, Richards was on top of the world. He was convinced he would have a Hollywood career. As he waited for the big assignments to come, he kept going by directing episodes of TV soap opera *Brookside*, based in Liverpool. He was there during two of *Brookside*'s most far-out episodes – one featuring a lesbian kiss and one about a body buried under a patio. 'I did scenes around the body and the kiss but I didn't do the actual ones [episodes] but I did do the plague that came along and wiped out half the cast,' he remembers of his contribution to what was then one of Britain's most popular programmes. He also met one of the series' best-known writers, Jimmy McGovern, and realized through speaking to him and reading his work just how vital writers were.

The *Brookside* experience taught Richards how to work very quickly. He'd be shooting twenty minutes or more of footage a day. (At film school, he'd film five minutes of single-camera drama at most.) The producer would encourage him to film actors close together. He complained that such set-ups looked unnatural but the actors explained, '"We don't have time. If we spread out, you'll have to do singles [shots] of all of us but if we stand close enough, you can get us all in one shot."' Years later, Richards still draws on the experience. If he is directing a feature and is behind schedule, he knows that he can 'click into *Brookside* mode' and get the film back on track.

Richards had written a horror film, *Darklands*, during his time at the NFTS. At first, he simply couldn't get it funded in Britain. He tried in vain to interest US B movie producers like Roger Corman. Then, after 1994, National Lottery money became available for filmmaking. All of a sudden, financing was made available for filmmaking in Wales that wasn't linked to the Welsh language. It helped that he had met a producer, Paul Brooks, later to found independent distributor Metrodome, who was prepared to invest. *Darklands* (1997) was a horror film with a political angle. It was about an English-speaking Welshman sucked into a conspiracy of Welsh nationalists. It has its place in history as the first ever Welsh horror picture.

'There was a big part of Wales that didn't receive it very well. When it premiered at the Welsh Film Festival in Aberystwyth, I was accused of being racist to the Welsh. How can that be when I am Welsh,' the director says of a movie dubbed as the 'Welsh *Wicker Man*'. Whatever the response in Wales, the controversial film picked up awards at plenty of European fantasy festivals. Roger Corman tried to buy the US rights but Brooks, to Richards's frustration, turned down all the offers.

It was at this point that Richards's career stalled. Brooks sold Metrodome. Victor Films, the sales agent for *Darklands*, went bust. The film ended up in limbo. The director expected he'd be able to make a second feature quickly enough. Instead, this young filmmaker, who had already done a deal with Spielberg, ended up on the dole. His brand of genre filmmaking was deeply out of fashion. No one wanted to support him. Richards spent three years writing and developing projects while claiming benefits.

Eventually, through his agent, Richards was introduced to a writer called Simon Lubert who had a script for a thriller called *Silent Cry* (2002). Maverick British production company Little Wing (many of whose principals were later sent to prison for tax fraud) agreed to finance the film at a budget of £3 million – but only on the condition the film started shooting within six weeks. They needed it finished by the end of the tax year so their investors could get their write-offs. They deferred a large part of the budget – but claimed a tax break on the money that had been deferred.

Richards did his best, racing into pre-production. A cast, including Emily Woof and Douglas Henshall, was quickly assembled. The film was finished on time but proved a tough sale. Little Wing, the producer/financier, and Park Entertainment, the sales agent, fell out and the film was left, just as *Darklands* had been a few years before, in 'a black hole'. It wasn't properly distributed. Its UK premiere was to come on Channel 5.

By now, the Welsh director had seen enough of the inner workings of the industry to realize he couldn't rely on his partners to get his films into circulation. He had observed how the marketing and releasing of his films had been badly bungled. That is why, eventually, he moved into sales as well as directing himself. He had a script for a new project, *The Last Horror Movie* (2003), and ended up using his £60,000 fee from *Silent Cry* to get it funded. He shot it guerrilla style. This was the era of Lars von Trier, Dogme filmmaking, the advent of digital cameras and *The Blair Witch Project* (1999). He found a seasoned old sales agent, Bill Gavin, who agreed to sell it (that's to say, license it to professional film distributors for release in the territories they handled). His girlfriend Rosanna Coutinho joined as an assistant, working free of charge in return for learning how to sell films. True to form, Gavin's company went bust. Richards therefore took on the work himself, forming Jinga Films with Coutinho. 'It was my money. I needed to get it back,' he describes his initial motivation. 'I never really intended to become a sales agent but we had to in order to get ourselves out of trouble on *Last Horror Movie*.' It also has its place in history as the first British-found footage film and after its theatrical release in the UK and US, it is one of only a handful of British films of the period to recoup its production cost. That was in 2005.

Richards now lunged into the sales arena himself. He began to acquire rights to other people's projects while still directing and selling his own movies. He had begun as a kid making films in breaks from school. Now, he was directing them in breaks from attending film markets. He had exactly the same control over his work as when he was telling his school friends what to do. Thanks to his knack for distribution, he was also making money from his business. He had turned into what the Italians call a one-man orchestra: he directed, produced, sold and sometimes even distributed his own work including *Summer Scars* (2007), *Shiver* (2011), *Daddy's Girl* (2018), *Reborn* (2018) and *Deathcember* (2019). 'They say you should never spend your own money on your film but my belief is that if you're not going to put any money in, why should you expect anyone else to?' he argues.

Richards may not be a household name (yet) but he is a very well-known and influential figure in the close-knit world of genre production and distribution. 'I am kind of unique as a sales agent in the sense that I have a pretty solid filmmaking background. I come at it from a very different angle to how a lot of people in the sales world come at it. I think the distributors very quickly identified that. They saw that here was somebody who really truly knew the genre – knew what was good, knew what was bad and was able to select and curate. Likewise, as a director, my knowledge of sales and distribution also informs my creative decision-making. I like to think of myself as a Universal Soldier,' he laughs.

Jinga was also prepared to push boundaries. Some of the films Richards has represented have created interest and controversy all over the world. Srdjan Spasojevic's ultra-extreme thriller *A Serbian Film* was removed from Frightfest in London after Westminster Council ruled it couldn't be shown in its uncut form and the film provoked fainting fits among distributors in Cannes. Such notoriety was as good as free advertising.

Anyone writing a history of contemporary horror in Britain and beyond will have to refer to films on Jinga's slate – some directed by Richards himself and some directed by others. The company's name comes from a Brazilian term meaning balance, rhythm and stability – and that is what Richards has achieved in his multi-faceted and already lengthy career in the British film industry which has seen him direct, produce and license films. It's no surprise to learn one of his future plans is to distribute them too. He is an example of a self-made British director who has thrived in often adverse circumstances by the simple art of doing everything himself.

25

Tim Webber[1]

Over the last thirty years, the UK has witnessed surging growth in its visual effects industry. The country had had its share of special effects and production design wizards before, in the silent era and during the glory days of Korda and Rank. Artists like 'Poppa' Day (see Chapter 11) and Charles Staffell had achieved astonishing effects with trick photography and painted backdrops; Stanley Kubrick's collaborators did brilliant work while shooting *2001: A Space Odyssey* (1968) at Shepperton Studios while Ken Adam's sets for both Kubrick and James Bond movies were justly celebrated. However, by the 1980s, UK production was in the doldrums. In spite of the excellence of individual craftsmen, it would have been very fanciful then to claim that there was anything like a VFX industry.

It was in this period that a young Oxford University physics graduate, Tim Webber, took his first, very tentative, steps into the industry. The notion that he would, within a couple of decades, be associated with Oscar-winning films and some of the most successful franchises in cinema history would then have seemed wildly improbable both to him and to those he worked with.

To visit Webber's company Framestore (where in 2020 he was chief creative officer) in its enormous Chancery Lane offices in London was to be reminded of how far the British VFX industry has come. A gleaming multi-storey building, all steel and glass, with hundreds of employees, it looks like the

---

[1]Unless specified otherwise, the material in this chapter comes from the author's interview with Tim Webber in London, December 2019.

Tim Webber. Photo: © Framestore.

premises you would expect to find in Silicon Valley, not in the heart of the City of London.

Webber was Welsh born but left the Principality when he was nine months old. He grew up in the home counties, in Buckinghamshire. The family also spent three years in Paris. 'My dad worked for IBM which people at the time said stood for "I've been moved",' Webber jokes of his very peripatetic childhood during which his father was shunted from one IBM office to another. 'I don't really think I grew up anywhere in particular. Sometimes I feel a bit rootless in that way.' Years later, Webber was to become famous for his work with computers but he says none of his skills came from his father, who was a salesman and manager, not an engineer or designer.

At an early age, Webber, born in 1964, was sent off to boarding school. Film played only a modest part in his upbringing. 'I am not your traditional visual effects geek like a lot of people in this industry,' Webber says. He grew up liking movies but mostly watched them on TV as his parents rarely took him to the cinema. His earliest passion was for the Bond movies. 'I always like the first half of a James Bond film. I like the intrigue, the travel, the chases. I like the creeping around rather than, as the movies go on, they become more [about] gunfights and then they end up with a big battle at the end and lots of big explosions.' Watching 007, his interest would begin to wane the longer the films lasted. Nor, at first, was he aware of, or interested in, the trompe l'oeil effects used in the action sequences. 'I can't remember when it happened but I do remember a moment in my life when I suddenly realized it was all an artifice and there were tricks – camera tricks, editing tricks and all of that. It did come to me as quite a … shock.' In some ways, spotting the joins was a relief. Webber had occasionally noticed back-projection scenes which didn't look right. He had thought that, perhaps, films really were made in some exotic place he didn't know where the backgrounds really did look as if they were artificial.

Webber went to Marlborough College in Wiltshire. Founded in 1843 for the sons of the clergy, this was one of Britain's top public schools but, beyond the occasional actor with a double-barrelled name like Wilfrid Hyde-White or James Robertson Justice, it hadn't provided many notable figures in British film history.

As a teenager, Webber showed a natural facility for maths. He was also interested in art. He talks about an inspirational art teacher, Robin Child. 'I learned about all sorts of things [from him]. Not just art but how to look at things, which has been really useful I suppose, and to see them for what they really are rather than what you imagine them to be.' Leaving school, Webber faced a 'toss-up between art school and physics'. He chose the latter on the grounds that everybody told him it would be much more useful for his career. (Not that at that stage he had any idea what career this might be.)

When Webber went to Oxford University, he spent more time in the arts school than he did in the physics lab. ('But not a huge amount in either,' he confides.) He also became a regular film-goer. However, his enthusiasm was more for the subtle, character-driven dramas of French auteur Eric Rohmer than for effects-driven sci-fi or action films. His passion for cinema was growing but he still had no thoughts about a career in movies. 'I would have wanted to get into the film industry but I just didn't think it was something I could do in a way.'

At Oxford, Webber made a short film. This was a very arty affair, shot on 8 mm and without sound. 'Its themes? Teenage angst I would say. It was a mood piece about being a student, really. It was about a girl going through life. It was quite expressionistic. There wasn't dialogue or a fixed story.' Webber did the cinematography himself and he edited the film too. He screened it to friends, who quite liked it. 'It went down well for something that was so ... nothingy.' The young physics undergraduate also helped out on a bigger 16mm film being shot by another student whose family had film industry connections. This had dialogue and a full crew. 'Even having done all of that, I didn't join the filmmaking society properly. I wish I had. I didn't think I would get into the film industry because I didn't think I could. None of my friends, none of my family's friends, no one I knew was in the film industry.'

It was clear, though, that Webber wasn't much interested in physics. He scrambled through his degree, doing very little work. He had a natural ability for understanding numbers ('maths, physics, logical thinking,' as he puts it) which had enabled him to excel in his A levels and which carried him through Oxford.

After finishing his studies, Webber was on the lookout for a career which would enable him to combine his logical thinking with his love of art. That was why he paid so much attention to the then burgeoning field of pop videos in which the British excelled. Thanks to MTV, launched in 1981, there was huge demand for films of songs. MTV, which was a twenty-four-hour rolling service, launched with only 250 music videos to play but had an insatiable demand for more. All sorts of zany, surreal short films were being made with artists from David Bowie to Madness by a new generation of filmmakers who were young, defiant, entrepreneurial and with a punk ethos. They didn't need to go to film school or beg for funding from Rank and EMI. They did it themselves and created their own market. 'It was the heyday of pop videos, when they were having their golden age and people were doing new and inventive things,' Webber says of this period in the mid-1980s. 'I thought this was a way of combining the visual filmmaking aesthetic I enjoyed but then using technology in ways to be inventive.'

Webber wrote off to all the pop promo companies he could find addresses for. One, Framestore, agreed to hire him after he sat through two 'really long, gruelling' interviews. 'I had my short film, my portfolio of art and photography, I had all of that, and my degree from Oxford,' he remembers what he showed his prospective employers. Back then, Framestore wasn't the huge global company that it is today. It had ten or so employees and its work, other than on pop videos, was in TV commercials. William Sargent and Sharon Reed had founded the company in 1986 along with three others. They had raised £120,000 – 'far more money than we could afford to pay back' as they later told the *Independent*.[2] Neither was from a technical background but they had energy, optimism and were ready to invest in state-of-the-art equipment.

Webber had come through his two lengthy interviews – one on the creative side of the work and the other on the technical – and, at the end of it all, his job turned out to be as a runner who made the coffee. In other words, when he started at the company in 1987 (having left university the year before), he was right at the bottom. Filmmaker Steve Barron, whose eclectic credits range from *Teenage Mutant Ninja Turtles* (1990) to *Mike Bassett: England Manager* (2001), was closely associated with the company. He was a legendary figure in the pop promo world who shot videos for, among others, The Jam, Human League, Adam and the Ants and Michael Jackson. Webber went into his office and remembers being staggered by the tableful of MTV awards he had won.

At the time that Webber joined, Framestore had spent a huge amount of money buying a machine called a 'Harry'. Made by Quantel, this was the very first digital manipulation tool for moving images. It was a huge, ungainly object which took up most of the office. 'It was the size of a large, large fridge and it was incredibly slow, unbelievably slow,' Webber remembers of this ground-breaking piece of hardware. 'It was thousands of times slower than your mobile phone nowadays and it was challenging to get anything out of it.'

For all its drawbacks, Harry was still a workable instrument. The company used it on pop promos and adverts. Webber had graduated from being a runner and was working as what would later be described as a 'compositor'. ('Back then, we just called it a Harry operator.') He was involved in such sleight of hand as a car commercial in which the vehicle was covered in butterflies and another one in which a boy walked from an old BMW to a new one and grew into a man in a matter of seconds. This was labour-intensive work. The butterflies had to be cut out of cardboard. (Today they would be generated by computer.) There were hours of colour correction to try to make it seem like the car and the butterfly were both filmed in the same light. 'Then you would

[2]*Independent*, 4 October 2000.

try to move an image of the butterfly to make it look like it was a reflection in the car. Everything you did, you had to do in isolation. You couldn't put the butterfly over the car and then change the colour till it looked right.'

There was no one to tell Webber how to master Harry. He taught himself how to use the machine. He proved to be a quick learner. Soon he was improvising, 'plugging other bits of kit' into the Harry and, in effect, evolving a new screen language. In hindsight, it was a perfect apprenticeship for someone who would later be one of the pioneers of digital visual effects. 'We were breaking new ground all the time,' Webber remembers.

Framestore was charging its clients small fortunes in hourly rates for any projects involving Harry. This meant Webber and his colleagues were under continual time pressure. The clients wanted value for money and wouldn't tolerate any slacking or delays. 'If you'd go to the loo, they would tut at you,' Webber remembers of the advertising agencies on whose behalf he was using Harry. Peter Greenaway, the British director of *The Draughtsman's Contract* (1982) and *A Zed and Two Noughts* (1985), came into Framestore to investigate if he might be able to use Harry but soon discovered that the machine wasn't yet well suited to cinema. 'Back then, it was impossible to use those techniques on feature films because you needed a much higher resolution than the computers could cope with.'

The big change in Webber's fortunes came when he worked as a visual effects supervisor on the US miniseries *Gulliver's Travels* (1996), which was made through Hallmark, directed by Charles Sturridge (famous for his work on Granada's 1981 adaptation of *Brideshead Revisited*) and produced by Duncan Kenworthy (then still riding very high after *Four Weddings and a Funeral* (1994)). TV didn't need the same high resolution as film – and so Webber could use Harry's successor, a new, faster piece of Quantel hardware named, not very imaginatively, 'Henry'. 'We had rarely done anything long-form before. We had only done short-form because the equipment couldn't really cope with anything longer than sixty seconds.'

Framestore provided 450 shots for *Gulliver's Travels*, which was shot at Shepperton Studios. 'That was one of those things you pull off through naivety, not realizing how difficult it was going to be to do it. You drop yourself in it and you have to make it happen.' The series went down well.

Webber was beginning to see the emergence of a community of VFX specialists. The company's biggest rival in the field of adverts and pop promos was MPC. The Mill was also vying for business, as was CFC, which Framestore merged with. However, at this stage, these companies weren't working in film. Shortly after *Gulliver*, Framestore became one of the first to take the leap. As Framestore prospered, other companies also competed for film business, among them Double Negative and the UK offshoot of US company Cinesite. There were several reasons for the sudden growth, the prime among them being that the equipment was getting significantly better. By then, CFC had developed 'the first decent' digital scanning device which could take a piece of film, scan it in high resolution and still keep the quality.

Meanwhile, the VFX specialists were developing an appetite for working on long-form dramatic content rather than three-minute pop promos and even shorter commercials. 'Working on something that people are choosing to watch rather than being made to watch' is how Webber draws the obvious distinction between films and commercials. Movies were more fun and more creatively fulfilling.

Filmmakers themselves weren't sure what to make of the VFX newcomers. Directors and producers were often loath to engage with them in any meaningful creative way.

> Some people would just come to you too late. We were seen as an industry in those days as 'post production', as the people you took it to at the end [of the process] to do the clever things. It took a while for everybody to realize we had to be involved from the script stage and certainly in the planning and the shooting and all of that.

Webber remembers the disdain and hostility he sometimes encountered. 'It is still not 100 per cent there. When we were on set, we were always seen as these irritating people to begin with.'

Webber went on to work again with Sturridge on *Fairytale: A True Story* (1997), a period drama set in England towards the end of the First World War about two young girls who claim to have photographed fairies in their back garden. He describes this as a 'challenging and satisfying' production. Sturridge consulted fully with the VFX artists, knowing that their work would be crucial to the success of the film. Other filmmakers weren't so collegiate. They would come at the end of shooting to Framestore and say, 'We want you to do this'. Webber and co. would often have to tell them they couldn't help 'because you haven't shot it properly. You should have talked to us beforehand.'

VFX remains hugely competitive. Margins are small and several companies went bust even as London cemented its reputation as the centre of the industry. The one advantage that the city had over other rivals, including LA, was that the leading four or five companies were all based in Soho, within short walking distance from one another. (In LA, the companies are dotted across town in different locations, an hour's drive or more from one another.) The British companies were 'collaborative and competitive' at the same time. 'We benefited from each other's presence and also from [the thought that] we've got to do better than them.'

When the *Harry Potter* films started shooting in 2000, rival VFX companies would work alongside one another to ensure features were completed in time for their release dates. The fact that this was a cycle of movies enabled the companies to plan for the long term.

> It was the steadiness and knowing there was going to be a film every so often, made by the same people, that enabled the industry to have something solid to grow on . . . that was the spine of the growth of the industry because it went on for ten years or whatever. It was the same team. Everybody got to know each other and how to make it work.

Thanks to the UK government's tax incentives and soft money schemes, the UK became an increasingly attractive destination for runaway Hollywood production.

Framestore was given a small amount of work on the first *Harry Potter*, *Harry Potter and the Philosopher's Stone* (2001), but its involvement grew on most of the subsequent films. Webber himself worked on *Harry Potter and the Goblet of Fire* (2005) but was also slightly involved in *Harry Potter and the Prisoner of Azkaban* (2004), directed by Mexican Alfonso Cuarón, with whom he was later to collaborate on *Gravity* (2013).

Not every project was a success. The UK's VFX community came together to work on the film version of Philip Pullman's *His Dark Materials*, the trilogy of fantasy novels aimed at young adult readers. Everyone hoped this would turn into another franchise to rival *Harry Potter* or *Lord of the Rings* (also made through New Line). In the event, after the first film, *The Golden Compass* (2007), the series was abandoned mid-stream. The religious right had protested against Pullman's perceived atheistic beliefs, reviews were mixed and box office underwhelming. The work done by Framestore and others won BAFTAs and Oscars but box office was slow and there was no long-lasting legacy. 'I don't think the source material is as well suited to a one-off movie as it is to a TV series. It is too dense to be able to squeeze into a single [feature],' Webber suggests. (A BBC/HBO television version of Pullman's novels for which Framestore served as creative collaborator and VFX provider, whose first season aired in 2019, has been markedly more successful.)

One of the issues in VFX is that 'old stuff' quickly begins to look dated as equipment and technology evolve. For all their ingenuity, the old pop videos made using Harry and Henry are archaic to contemporary eyes. Even the early *Harry Potter* films seem old fashioned. 'Between each *Harry Potter*, things [technologically] would move on significantly,' Webber talks of the rapid pace of change.

VFX, however, has always been as much about artistry as about technology. 'When it became digital, there were a lot of digital artists who weren't necessarily artists working on it [but] after a few years, some of those old skills started to come back. Most of those people who painted things didn't want to touch a digital paintbrush and the digital people didn't necessarily understand those [older] skills. They thought they could do it their own way,' Webber explains the tensions between traditional crafts people and a new generation of computer experts. Now, there is an entente between them. Producers recognize that most effects-driven movies need artistry as well as digital expertise. Webber himself is highly unusual, straddling both worlds. He is the Oxbridge physicist who is also a skilled draughtsman.

Even as the company prospered, Webber wasn't thinking about the long term. He just enjoyed doing work, film by film, which enabled him to use both his technical knowledge and his artistic ability. The only long-term goal he had was to direct his own material. As an early recruit, who had joined the company when there were ten people at Framestore (as opposed to the 2,500 working at the company in 2019), he was considered one of the founding fathers and soon became a shareholder and partner. 'I joined when it was about two years old. A few years later, it was bought by Megalomedia, the investment company set up by Maurice Saatchi, and then a few years after that [in 2000], we bought it out from Megalomedia,' Webber explains.

Framestore continued to do commercials but its film arm grew. Now, as a visual effects supervisor, Webber, the former runner, is treated as one of the key creative figures on any movie on which he works. Directors talk to him months before shooting begins.

On Cuarón's *Gravity*, for example, Webber's involvement began before the script was even completed. He talks about an early meeting with the Mexican director, with whom he had also worked on sci-fi thriller *Children of Men* (2006). For that film, set in a near future in which women have become infertile, there is a four-minute single, continuous shot in which one mother finally manages to give birth. Webber supervised the sequence.

Webber wasn't supposed to have much involvement in *Children of Men*. A colleague had been assigned to the production but there were early problems on set. When Cuarón voiced his frustrations, his Framestore colleague was nowhere to be found. 'I had to step into the fray, answer questions and find solutions,' Webber remembers. 'Afterwards I had to do the job.'

Cuarón is a very congenial and collaborative filmmaker, held in the highest esteem by crews. He is also a perfectionist. Webber was undaunted by this encounter. If anything, the director rose in his estimation because he cared so much. Webber shared his dedication.

When *Gravity* was still an idea, Cuarón came into Framestore's offices to talk through the storyline of the film, which was about a female astronaut stuck in space. 'We just sat on the sofa for forty minutes. He hadn't written the script yet – he had this concept of the story in his head. I just remember sitting there, glued. It was fascinating. I remember coming out short of breath from that, just from him talking about it.'

From his earliest days in the business, Webber had used technology and artistry in tandem to achieve the effects he wanted. He wasn't just a technician who knew how to operate complicated machines. He was a storyteller. For *Gravity*, he did extensive research. This included both looking at previous space movies ('apart from *2001*, there is not a lot that would be considered successful now') and a short, stomach-churning voyage on a European Space Agency vessel nicknamed 'a vomit comet'. This is an aeroplane on which astronauts train and are subjected to zero-gravity testing. The plane flies up in the air and then goes into free fall as the pilot cuts the engine. 'As it is falling down, you are weightless inside it for about fifteen seconds.' Webber managed to endure the journey without throwing up but the stunt woman who was flying with him wasn't so lucky with the motion sickness. 'She was amazing. However sick she was, she was desperately soldiering through. I was filming her so I could show Alfonso.'

Ultimately, Cuarón wasn't able to shoot on the 'vomit comet' as he had originally hoped but Webber's experiences helped him to depict weightlessness in the studio in a convincing fashion. It helped that Webber had an Oxford University degree in physics. He understood how astronauts would move in space and was able to give very detailed instructions to the animators. 'Giving things weight is in their blood. We had to train that out of them. Part of that was that I gave them [the animators] lectures on the physics of space. I drew them pictures and explained why people float in space. It's not just zero gravity. It's also that there is no air resistance so nothing slows down.'

On big productions, the VFX technicians have to work punishing hours. The films will already have firm release dates, scheduled long in advance, and Webber and his colleagues will be under intense pressure to ensure the movie gets finished in time. They're the one part of the process in which no extra time will be given. 'The shoot can get delayed, the edit gets delayed, everything gets delayed – but the end date doesn't get delayed.'

A VFX supervisor will be working during pre-production, during production itself and during post-production. There is therefore never a break. 'These days, eighteen months is a short project. *Gravity* was three years, absolutely full on.' The one consolation with *Gravity* was that it was shot in London (at Shepperton) and the rest of the work was done in Framestore's offices in Soho. That at least meant Webber could go home occasionally. He is full of praise for actress Sandra Bullock, who played the stranded astronaut and who was always ready to clamber into whatever strange contraption Framework's VFX team came up with for her. 'She was incredibly physically adept. When she was floating around inside the space station, her ability to get the moves right and perform as if she was in zero gravity was excellent whilst at the same time, she was giving a great emotional performance. It made a massive difference to what we had to do.'

It's a measure of the importance VFX now has that filmmakers like Cuarón and Christopher Nolan (with whom Webber worked on *The Dark Knight* (2008)) are so dependent on them. Nolan's method is to make his film as 'real' as possible. ('If he could avoid using visual effects, he would.') Webber fully endorses his approach, trying to make all the effects seem 'photoreal'. Audiences can generally tell when something 'has been made in the computer'. When they spot the artifice, the suspension of disbelief can easily be lost and the film, unless it is a sci fi or Marvel superhero film celebrating its own effects, will seem markedly less powerful as a result.

The VFX sector isn't unionized. It's a labour-intensive business and Webber says the leading companies have to be careful not to exploit their workforce. 'At Framestore, we put a lot of work in trying to manage it but it's very hard. The studios have a lot of power and if we can't deliver what they want when they want, they will just go somewhere else.'

This is one of the paradoxes about the VFX industry. Prior to the global coronavirus outbreak, the sector had been booming but that doesn't mean the work has become easier or that companies like Framestore (which has offices in Montreal, LA, New York, Chicago and Mumbai as well as in London) can set their own terms. Nonetheless, Webber has witnessed extraordinary growth in a sector which scarcely existed when he first came into the business. He has played his part in the evolution of film language in that period. From sticking cut-out butterflies on cars for commercials in the 1980s to transporting Sandra Bullock to outer space for *Gravity*, he has achieved extraordinary feats with whatever technology has been available to him. He directed the second unit on *Paddington* (2014) and helped to create the bear. The kid who grew up watching James Bond films worked on the main titles sequences for such Bond films as *GoldenEye* (1995) and *Tomorrow Never Dies* (1997). More recently, he worked on the credits and a part of the main VFX for the twenty-fifth Bond film, *No Time to Die* (2020). Other projects in 2019 and 2020 included *Paddington 3*, the latest film about everybody's favourite bear from Peru, and *Wicked*, an adaptation of the musical featuring the green-skinned wicked witch from *The Wizard of Oz*. He is also now looking to make his own features. (He has several projects in development.)

As chief creative officer, Webber is involved in developing new talent. The company now has its own dedicated training team, who run workshops, seminars and top-up sessions on everything from the latest tech and software to dinosaur anatomy, improv and sculpting.

'I started when there wasn't really an industry. I've grown up with the industry and I've had to learn my way – and there haven't been people to learn from,' Webber reflects on how he had to school himself. Newcomers don't face the same challenges he once did. Whether you are an animator or a computer scientist, you will find mentors at Framestore. The pathway has become much more straightforward. There are now many more areas of specialization. What hasn't changed, though, is the commitment required – and the need to meet those terrifyingly tight deadlines inevitably demanded by the clients.

Conclusion[1]

'People recognize your passion, your enthusiasm and your commitment,' Film London chief executive Adrian Wootton pinpoints the qualities needed to build a career in the British film industry.

In this business, whether you are dealing with executives or filmmakers, that is the only thing that is going to get you by because they will smell a rat if they believe you haven't watched their movies or don't care about their movies. If you're not interested in them, they are not going to be interested in you. If they sense you have that passion, that enthusiasm, that commitment, you have done your homework, you do love their movies and are interested in their work, you are likely to get along . . .

'It was always that I want the best for my cinemas and I want the best for the films in general. I just pushed myself along really,' Clare Binns, Managing Director of leading independent arthouse cinema chain Picturehouse (also speaking in 2020) reflected on a journey which saw her become one of the most influential executives in independent British cinema.

At the age of sixteen, Adrian Wootton's life had come to a crossroads. He was faced with a choice. Either he was going to pass his O levels and A levels and then go to university to read English (which was his ambition) or he was going to work on a building site in the East Midlands with his father, something he had already done in the summers, and become a full-time plasterer. In the end,

---

[1]Unless specified otherwise, the material in this chapter comes from interviews done with Adrian Wootton and Clare Binns by the author in London, January 2020.

he passed his exams and was accepted by the University of East Anglia in 1980. By chance, at that very time, UEA, under its professors Charles Barr, Thomas Elsaesser and Don Ranvaud, had set up its first undergraduate film programme. Wootton immediately signed up for the course, taught as a 'minor' subject in the English and American studies department.

Equally important for Wootton's future career was the fact that Norwich had an independent arthouse cinema, Cinema City. He began to haunt this venue, seeing every film he could and writing about movies for the university newspaper. He met and interviewed filmmakers who visited the cinema and later became manager of the venue. 'Two things were happening. I was learning about the business of running cinemas but I was also making contacts with exhibitors, distributors and filmmakers,' Wootton recalls. 'My network started to expand.'

Eventually, after working in Bradford and Nottingham and launching the Shots in the Dark: Crime, Mystery and Thriller Film Festival, Wootton headed to London. He ran the BFI Southbank and then moved to Film London, where he still was in 2020 and had by then won an OBE for his services to the industry. He wasn't just chief executive of Film London but ran the British Film Commission. When coronavirus struck the UK in early 2020, he spearheaded attempts to keep the industry going in the face of the pandemic. He had worked his way to the heart of the British film establishment without having money or connections behind him.

'It was very much organic,' Wootton, like many others profiled in this book, observed of the way his career evolved. When he had arrived at UEA in 1980, he had expected he might forge a career in academia or perhaps land a job in journalism. Instead, he followed where the opportunities led. 'There was absolutely no game plan. I just thought, 'I like running cinemas, I like running festivals. This is fun. I find this really creatively rewarding. I'd like to do more of it.'

Clare Binns was another prominent figure in the industry (in 2020, Managing Director of Picturehouse) whose film career began from a standing start. Binns grew up in Newcastle upon Tyne. As a kid, she had a cinema, the Jesmond Picture House, a few hundred yards from her front door. Binns visited whenever she could. She was dyslexic and regarded film as a medium from which she could learn just as effectively as from books. She saw nothing strange in going on her own. Her father, a businessman working for Guinness, had divorced her mother and had left home. She was living with her mother, who was a 'culture vulture' and took her to concerts and galleries but had no contacts in the film industry.

Aged eighteen, Binns headed to London in search of a job. She didn't have any qualifications. The work she found included cleaning (for an agency called Problem), as a railway worker for London Underground and a stint making cardboard boxes. One of her more unlikely jobs was as a cleaner and mother's help for celebrated psychiatrist R. D. Laing. Eventually, in 1979, to keep company with her husband-to-be, she took an evening job as an usher at the Ritzy Cinema in Brixton, which had only just opened. 'It was a one-screen cinema. There was rain coming in,' Binns remembers of the dilapidated, hand-to-mouth condition of the venue, which showed the same cult movies as the Everyman and the Scala. 'I just fell in love with it.' Like Wootton, she had no long-term strategy for getting to the top of the British film industry. She just followed where the scent took her. This was the early 1980s. 'I didn't see a career in any shape or form. How I saw it was more an opportunity to watch films.'

Binns was a 'female in a very male-dominated world' and suggests that she might have struggled to get anywhere if she had tried to map out a career for herself in a conventional way. She was ready to take opportunities as they came and didn't waste time agonizing over the injustices of a chauvinistic corporate culture. 'I just pushed myself along really,' she says with evident understatement of a journey which saw her become one of the most influential executives in independent British cinema.

Speaking in early 2020, both Binns and Wootton believed the industry was changing. The #MeToo movement, the #OscarsSoWhite campaign and the heightened consciousness about diversity were already shifting long-held attitudes. At the same time, careers could still be built from the lowest rungs. 'You can still do it by being an usher. I think you can still get in there. A lot of people in programming today have come from working on the cinema floor … you have to be prepared to work very, very hard. It's not nine to five. You have to be prepared to get your hands dirty,' says Binns.

Alison Owen (born in 1961) is one of the UK's most formidable producers with credits from *Elizabeth* (1998) to *Shaun of the Dead* (2004). That didn't seem a very likely career for her when she was at Mayfield Secondary School in Portsmouth in the late 1960s. At the time, the school library had various career books for girls. When she was ten years old, she read *Claire in Television*, which told the rousing story of a young woman who headed to London and made a successful career in the media. In the book, Claire was hired as a researcher at Bush House, spotted as a talented newcomer and ended up, glory of glories, as a newscaster.

'Whilst the careers programmes were well intentioned, I would say the pinnacle at Mayfield Comprehensive was going on a teacher training course. The idea of leaving town and going to London and working in television was not something that anyone would have conceived of, let alone encouraged,' Owen reminisced in a keynote speech she gave during an industry event at the 2019 London Film Festival. However, the book about Claire inspired her to take a punt on a career in film and television. 'That book, silly though it was, really did illustrate to me that you could do that.'[2]

Looking back on her career, Owen emphasized accommodation and childcare as underpinning her later success. Her university provided her with childcare facilities. When she moved to London, Camden Council gave her a flat as a single mother and the Social Services allowed her a hardship grant. Britain's education system and welfare kept her afloat, providing her with the chance to break into the industry. Eventually, she landed a job, in the film department at Virgin, the record company owned by Richard Branson which was then venturing into film, learning a little about distribution.

Owen heard from acquaintances about the National Film and Television School. The School didn't have any courses for producers but that was to her advantage. She was told that the writers and directors there were trying to make their student films but didn't have anybody to produce them. She was also informed 'if you simply went along to the bus stop at Notting Hill Gate where the film school bus pulled up every morning and got on it and offered your services as a producer, you would produce student movies'. This is exactly what happened. She climbed on the bus (actually a van).

---

[2]Alison Owen, keynote address, Film London Production Finance Market, 7 October 2019.

Many of the students on the National Film School bus on that first morning, figures like directors Beeban Kidron and Michael Caton-Jones and cinematographers like John Mathieson, went on to have substantial careers in the industry. Owen had met them at the very start of their careers, produced their student films and picked up on the 'practicalities' of making a film very quickly. Not long afterwards she produced her first film, *Hear My Song* (1991), a wry comic drama based on a story about a Liverpool nightclub owner trying to hire the services of the Irish tenor Josef Locke.

Owen, the single mother from Portsmouth who had arrived in London without any film industry contacts, soon became firmly established as one of the British industry's most dynamic young producers. The way Owen talked about her career, she made it sound remarkably straightforward. That was with the benefit of hindsight, though. Once you've arrived at your destination, you can tell, looking back, precisely how you found it, even if you had felt you were stumbling around in the dark at the time.

These snapshots, of Wootton, Binns and Owen, are typical stories of how careers are forged in the British film industry. From unpromising beginnings, these three, like most of the others written about in these pages, took advantage of the opportunities which opened up in front of them in often random fashion. Their pathways weren't straightforward but they were allowed to work out eventually where they wanted to go and how to get there.

What the stories collected here attest is that there is no 'typical' career in the British film industry. You don't walk into a job centre and say that you want to work in cinema. The trait which the characters profiled in these chapters all share is perseverance. A mixture of tenacity, curiosity and optimism has kept them going where others would have decided that there were other, far less daunting ways to make a living. Their example continues to inspire others.

Index